Indian Economy

Mahesh Verma

SRISHTI BOOK DISTRIBUTORS
NEW DELHI (INDIA)

ISBN : 978-81-89948-97-9

Published by:
SRISHTI BOOK DISTRIBUTORS
4378/4-B-202, 2nd Floor,
J.M.D. House, Ansari Road,
Daryaganj, New Delhi-110002
E-mail : srishtibookdistributors@yahoo.co.in
Ph. : 011-23284904

***Edition* : 2012**

Rs. 1050/-

Typeset by :
Shubh-Deep Laser Printer
Delhi-110002

Printed at
Shivani Art Press
Delhi-110032

PREFACE

The Indian money market is classified into the organised sector, comprising private, public and foreign owned commercial banks and cooperative banks, together known as *scheduled banks*, and the unorganised sector, which includes individual or family owned indigenous bankers or money lenders and non-banking financial companies. The unorganised sector and microcredit are still preferred over traditional banks in rural and sub-urban areas, especially for non-productive purposes, like ceremonies and short duration loans.

There are very few concerns in India that are ready to open an estore. Conversely however, there are quite a few software development companies in India that provide e-commerce solution and e-commerce software to people living outside India. Many Indian concerns are into offshore software development. They have clients from all over the world who come to them for software development in order to do business online, but it's very rare that one would find an Indian company venturing into ecommerce web site development; one trend that so far India has not taken from the west!

In the early 1990s, considerable progress was made in loosening government regulations, especially in the area of foreign trade. Many restrictions on private companies were lifted, and new areas were opened to private capital. However, India remains one of the world's most tightly regulated major economies. Many powerful vested interests, including private firms that have benefited from protectionism, labor unions, and much of the bureaucracy, oppose liberalization. There is also considerable concern that liberalization will reinforce class and regional economic disparities.

While compiling research material for this book, we surf many concerned websites, blogs for ensuring the authenticity of the matter and for checking facts and figures. All the resources have been acknowledged in bibliography section of this book. We are sincerely indebted to all these resources and librarians who provided books of various authors on this subject topic.

—Mahesh Verma

CONTENTS

Chapter–1

Introduction to Indian Economy

Economically, India is very large, as large number of people have to live economically. Indians have been trying to deal with the growing population by buying cars, increasing the speed limit, and removing crosswalks.

India economy, the third largest economy in the world, in terms of purchasing power, is going to touch new heights in coming years. As predicted by Goldman Sachs, the Global Investment Bank, by 2035 India would be the third largest economy of the world just after US and China. It will grow to 60% of size of the US economy. This booming economy of today has to pass through many phases before it can achieve the current milestone of 9% GDP.

The primary export of India is India ink, which is produced in massive quantities by the Indian held mega corporation **India Inc.** for worldwide export. This makes India one of the worlds most powerful countries — if Indians wanted, they could wipe all Monkeys off the face of the Earth.

Some profane minds that fancy eating beef have conjectured elsewhere that the reason behind this phenomenal explosion of the cow population in India is because of the fact that Indians do not eat cows. That's like saying that the reason behind the exponential growth of humans in India is because of the fact that cows do not eat humans.</ref>); or too busy taking calls from mindless, frustrated Americans; or too busy building the digital cow milking machine for future generations or too busy breathing in and out.

A large part of the Indian economy is dependent on Mumbai and Bollywood. Founded by Robin Hood, wherefrom eponymous clones like Hollywood, Lollywood, Tollywood, Sexywood and many others 'woods' originated, Tiger Woods, in the year 1976, slapped a law suit on the Indian Government for infringing upon his Intellectual Property Rights. Robert Frost has simultaneously contended that the names were actually inspired by his famous poem, *Stopping By Woods on a Snowy Evening*...when, in reality, they were inspired by the *morning wood* people (usually male people) experience after watching late-night midnight songs.

Although there are talks of changing the national language to Java, the *HRD Ministry of India* believes that C++ would be a better choice. Currently, talks (read riots) are occurring all over India to resolve this issue peacefully. It has also been suggested that India is more of a mindset or hologram than a real place. Which means that I never wrote this — you just imagined you read it. It also means that i never came here: you imagined I did. **That,** by the way, is also the Indian Economy's infamous "Hindu Rate of Great Indian Rope Trick" (the Chinese trick is worse - It's nothing more than a rip-off). India's main contributions to the economy are outsourcing and inventing 0.

The Economy of India is the ninth largest in the world by nominal GDP and the fourth largest by purchasing power parity (PPP). The country is one of the G-20 major economies and a member of BRICS. The country's per capita GDP (PPP) was $3,408 (IMF, 129th in the world) in 2010, making it a lower-middle income economy.

The independence-era Indian economy (before and a little after 1947) was inspired by the economy of the Soviet Union with socialist practices, large public sectors, high import duties and lesser private participation characterizing it, leading to massive inefficiencies and widespread corruption. However, later on India adopted free market principles and liberalized its economy to international trade under the guidance of Manmohan Singh, who then was the Finance Minister of India under the leadership ofP.V.Narasimha Rao the then Prime Minister. Following these strong economic reforms, the country's economic growth progressed at a rapid pace with very high rates of growth and large increases in the incomes of people.

India recorded the highest growth rates in the mid-2000s, and is one of the fastest-growing economies in the world. The growth was led primarily due to a huge increase in the size of the middle class consumer population, a large workforce comprising skilled and non-skilled workers, good education standards and considerable foreign investments. India is the seventeenth largest exporter and eleventh largest importer in the world. Economic growth rates are projected at around 7.5%-8% for the financial year 2011-2012.

Social democratic policies governed India for sometime after India's Independence from the British. The economy was then characterised by extensive regulation, protectionism, public ownership, pervasive corruption and slow growth. Since 1991, continuing economic liberalisation has moved the country towards amarket-based economy. A revival of economic reforms and better economic policy in first decade of the 21st century accelerated India's economic growth rate. In recent years, Indian cities have continued to liberalise business regulations. By 2008, India had established itself as the world's second-fastest growing major economy.

However, as a result of the financial crisis of 2007–2010, coupled with a poor monsoon, India's gross domestic product (GDP) growth rate significantly slowed to 6.7% in 2008–09, but subsequently recovered to 7.4% in 2009–10, while the fiscal deficit rose from 5.9% to a high 6.5% during the same period. India's current account deficit surged to 4.1% of GDP during Q2 FY11 against 3.2% the previous quarter. The unemployment rate for 2009–2010, according to the state Labour Bureau, was 9.4% nationwide. As of 2010, India's public debt stood at 71.84% of GDP which is highest amongBRIC nations.

India's large service industry accounts for 57.2% of the country's GDP while the industrial and agricultural sectors contribute 28.6% and 14.6% respectively. Agriculture is the predominant occupation in Rural India, accounting for about 52% of employment. The service sector makes up a further 34%, and industrial sector around 14%. However, statistics from a 2009–10 government survey, which used a smaller sample size than earlier surveys, suggested that the share of agriculture in employment had dropped to 45.5%.

Major industries include telecommunications, textiles, chemicals, food processing, steel, transportation equipment, cement, mining, petroleum, machinery, software and pharmaceuticals. The labour force totals 500 million workers. Major agricultural products include rice, wheat, oilseed, cotton, jute, tea, sugarcane, potatoes, cattle, water buffalo, sheep, goats, poultry and fish. In 2009–2010, India's top five trading partners are United Arab Emirates, China, United States, Saudi Arabia and Germany.

Previously a closed economy, India's trade and business sector has grown fast. India currently accounts for 1.5% of world trade as of 2007 according to the World Trade Statistics of the WTO in 2006, which valued India's total merchandise trade (counting exports and imports) at $294 billion and India's services trade at $143 billion. Thus, India's global economic engagement in 2006 covering both merchandise and services trade was of the order of $437 billion, up by a record 72% from a level of $253 billion in 2004. India's total trade in goods and services has reached a share of 43% of GDP in 2005–06, up from 16% in 1990–91. India's total merchandisee trade (counting exports and imports) stands at $ 606.7 billion and is currently the 9th largest in the world.

History of Indian Economy

Pre-colonial period (up to 1773)

The citizens of the Indus Valley civilisation, a permanent settlement that flourished between 2800 BC and 1800 BC, practiced agriculture, domesticated animals, used uniform weights and measures, made tools and weapons, and traded with other cities. Evidence of well-planned streets, a drainage system and water supply reveals their knowledge of urban planning, which included the world's first urbansanitation systems and the existence of a form of municipal government.

Maritime trade was carried out extensively between South India and southeast and West Asia from early times until around the fourteenth century AD. Both the Malabar andCoromandel Coasts were the sites of important trading centres from as early as the first century BC, used for import and export as well as transit points between theMediterranean region and southeast Asia. Over time, traders organised themselves into associations which received state patronage. However, state patronage for overseas trade came to an end by the thirteenth century AD, when it was largely taken over by the local Parsi, Jewish and Muslim communities, initially on the Malabar and subsequently on the Coromandel coast. Further north, the Saurashtra and Bengal coasts played an important role in maritime trade, and the Gangetic plains and the Indus valley housed several centres of river-borne commerce. Most overland trade was carried out via the Khyber Passconnecting the Punjab region with Afghanistan and onward to the Middle East and Central Asia. Although many kingdoms and rulers issued coins, barter was prevalent. Villages paid a portion of their agricultural produce as revenue to the rulers, while their craftsmen received a part of the crops at harvest time for their services.

Assessment of India's pre-colonial economy is mostly qualitative, owing to the lack of quantitative information. The Mughal economy functioned on an elaborate system of coined currency, land revenue and trade. Gold, silver and copper coins were issued by the royal mints which functioned on the basis of free coinage. The political stability and uniform revenue policy resulting from a centralised administration under the Mughals, coupled with a well-developed internal trade network, ensured that India, before the arrival of the British, was to a large extent economically unified, despite having a traditional agrarian economy characterised by a predominance of subsistence agriculture dependent on primitive technology. After the decline of the Mughals, western, central and parts of south and north India were integrated and administered by the Maratha Empire. After the loss at the Third Battle of Panipat, the Maratha Empire disintegrated into several confederate states, and the resulting political instability and armed conflict severely affected economic life in several parts of the country, although this was compensated for to some extent by localised prosperity in the new provincial kingdoms. By the end of the eighteenth century, the British East India Company entered the Indian political theatre and established its dominance over other European powers. This marked a determinative shift in India's trade, and a less powerful impact on the rest of the economy.

Colonial period (1773–1947)

Company rule in India brought a major change in the taxation and agricultural policies, which tended to promote commercialisation of agriculture with a focus on trade, resulting in decreased production of food crops, mass impoverishment and destitution of farmers, and in the short term, led to numerous famines. The economic policies of the British Raj caused a severe decline in the handicrafts andhandloom sectors, due to reduced demand and dipping employment. After the removal of international restrictions by the Charter of 1813, Indian trade expanded substantially and over the long term showed an upward trend. The result was a significant transfer of capital from India to England, which, due to the colonial policies of the British, led to a massive drain of revenue rather than any systematic effort at modernisation of the domestic economy. India's colonisation by the British created an institutional environment that, on paper, guaranteed property rightsamong the colonisers, encouraged free trade, and created a single currency with fixed exchange rates, standardised weights and measures and capital markets. It also established a well-developed system of railways and telegraphs, a civil service that aimed to be free from political interference, a common-law and an adversarial legal system. This coincided with major changes in the world economy – industrialisation, and significant growth in production and trade. However, at the end of colonial rule, India inherited an economy that was one of the poorest in the developing world, with industrial development stalled, agriculture unable to feed a rapidly growing population, a largely illiterate and unskilled labour force, and extremely inadequate infrastructure.

The 1872 census revealed that 91.3% of the population of the region constituting present-day India resided in villages, and urbanisation generally remained sluggish until the 1920s, due to the lack of industrialisation and absence of adequate transportation. Subsequently, the policy of discriminating protection (where certain important industries were given financial protection by the state), coupled with the Second World War, saw the development and dispersal of industries, encouraging rural-urban migration, and in particular the large port cities of Bombay, Calcutta and Madras grew rapidly. Despite this, only one-sixth of India's population lived in cities by 1951.

The impact of the British rule on India's economy is a controversial topic. Leaders of the Indian independence movement and left-wing people who opposed India's independence movementeconomic historians have blamed colonial rule for the dismal state of India's economy in its aftermath and argued that financial strength required for industrial development in Europe was derived from the wealth taken from colonies in Asia and Africa. At the same time, right-wing historians have countered that India's low economic performance was due to various sectors being in a state of growth and decline due to changes brought in by colonialism and a world that was moving towards industrialisation andeconomic integration.

Pre-liberalisation period (1947–1991)

Indian economic policy after independence was influenced by the colonial experience, which was seen by Indian leaders as exploitative, and by those leaders' exposure to democratic socialism as well as the progress achieved by the economy of the Soviet Union. Domestic policy tended towards protectionism, with a strong emphasis onimport substitution industrialisation, economic interventionism, a large public sector, business regulation, and central planning, while trade and foreign investment policies were relatively liberal. Five-Year Plans of Indiaresembled central planning in the Soviet Union. Steel, mining, machine tools, telecommunications, insurance, and power plants, among other industries, were effectively nationalised in the mid-1950s.

Jawaharlal Nehru, the first prime minister of India, along with the statistician Prasanta Chandra Mahalanobis, formulated and oversaw economic policy during the initial years of the country's existence. They expected favorable outcomes from their strategy, involving the rapid development ofheavy industry by both public and private sectors, and based on direct and indirect state intervention, rather than the more extreme Soviet-style central command system. The policy of concentrating simultaneously on capital- and technology-intensive heavy industry and subsidising manual, low-skillcottage industries was criticised by economist Milton Friedman, who thought it would waste capital and labour, and retard the development of small manufacturers. The rate of growth of the Indian economy in the first three decades after independence was derisively referred to as the Hindu rate of growth by economists, because of the unfavourable comparison with growth rates in other Asian countries.

Since 1965, the use of high-yielding varieties of seeds, increased fertilisers and improved irrigationfacilities collectively contributed to the Green Revolution in India, which improved the condition of agriculture by increasing crop productivity, improving crop patterns and strengthening forward and backward linkages between agriculture and industry. However, it has also been criticised as an unsustainable effort, resulting in the growth of capitalistic farming, ignoring institutional reforms and widening income disparities.

Post-liberalisation period (since 1991)

In the late 1970s, the government led byMorarji Desai eased restrictions on capacity expansion for incumbent companies, removed price controls, reduced corporate taxes and promoted the creation of small scale industries in large numbers. He also raised the income tax levels at one point to a maximum of 97.5%, a record in the world for non-communist economies. However, the subsequent government policy of Fabian socialism hampered the benefits of the economy, leading to high fiscal deficits and a worsening current account. The collapse of the Soviet Union, which was India's major trading partner, and the Gulf War, which caused a spike in oil prices, resulted in a major balance-of-payments crisis for India, which found itself facing the prospect of defaulting on its loans. India asked for a $1.8 billion bailout loan from the International Monetary Fund (IMF), which in return demanded reforms.

In response, Prime Minister Narasimha Rao, along with his finance minister Manmohan Singh, initiated the economic liberalisation of 1991. The reforms did away with the Licence Raj, reduced tariffs and interest rates and ended many public monopolies, allowing automatic approval of foreign direct investment in many sectors. Since then, the overall thrust of liberalisation has remained the same, although no government has tried to take on powerful lobbies such as trade unions and farmers, on contentious issues such as reforming labour laws and reducing agricultural subsidies. By the turn of the 20th century, India had progressed towards a free-market economy, with a substantial reduction in state control of the economy and increased financial liberalisation. This has been accompanied by increases in life expectancy, literacy rates and food security, although the beneficiaries have largely been urban residents.

While the credit rating of India was hit by its nuclear weapons tests in 1998, it has since been raised to investment level in 2003 by S&P and Moody's. In 2003, Goldman Sachs predicted that India's GDP in current prices would overtake France and Italy by 2020, Germany, UK and Russia by 2025 and Japan by 2035, making it the third largest economy of the world, behind the US and China. India is often seen by most economists as a rising economic superpower and is believed to play a major role in the global economy in the 21st century.

Industry and services in Indian Economy

Industry accounts for 28% of the GDP and employ 14% of the total workforce. In absolute terms, India is 12th in the world in terms of nominal factory output. The Indian industrial sector underwent significant changes as a result of the economic reforms of 1991, which removed import restrictions, brought in foreign competition, led to privatisation of certain public sector industries, liberalised the FDI regime, improved infrastructure and led to an expansion in the production of fast moving consumer goods. Post-liberalisation, the Indian private sector was faced with increasing domestic as well as foreign competition, including the threat of cheaper Chinese imports. It has since handled the change by squeezing costs, revamping management, and relying on cheap labour and new technology. However, this has also reduced employment generation even by smaller manufacturers who earlier relied on relatively labour-intensive processes.

Textile manufacturing is the second largest source of employment after agriculture and accounts for 20% of manufacturing output, providing employment to over 20 million people. As stated in late January, by the then Minister of Textiles, India, Shri Shankersinh Vaghela, the transformation of the textile industry from a degrading to rapidly developing industry, has become the biggest achievement of the central government. After freeing the industry in 2004–2005 from a number of limitations, primarily financial, the government gave the green light to the flow of massive investment – both domestic and foreign. During the period from 2004 to 2008, total investment amounted to 27 billion dollars. By 2012, still convinced of the government, this figure will reach 38 billion as expected; these investments in 2012 will create an additional sector of more than 17 million jobs. But demand for Indian textiles in world markets continues to fall. According to Union Minister for Commerce and Industries Kamal Nath, only during 2008–2009 fiscal year (which ends 31 March) textile and clothing industry will be forced to cut about 800 thousand new jobs – nearly half of the rate of two million, which will have to go all the export-oriented sectors of Indian economy to soften the impact of the global crisis. Ludhiana produces 90% of woollens in India and is known as the Manchester of India. Tirupur has gained universal recognition as the leading source of hosiery, knitted garments, casual wear and sportswear.

India is 13th in services output. The services sector provides employment to 23% of the work force and is growing quickly, with a growth rate of 7.5% in 1991–2000, up from 4.5% in 1951–80. It has the largest share in the GDP, accounting for 55% in 2007, up from 15% in 1950. Information technology and business process outsourcing are among the fastest growing sectors, having a cumulative growth rate of revenue 33.6% between 1997–98 and 2002–03 and contributing to 25% of the country's total exports in 2007–08. The growth in the IT sector is attributed to increased specialisation, and an availability of a large pool of low cost, highly skilled, educated and fluent English-speaking workers, on the supply side, matched on the demand side by increased demand from foreign consumers interested in India's service exports, or those looking to outsource their operations. The share of theIndian IT industry in the country's GDP increased from 4.8 % in 2005–06 to 7% in 2008. In 2009, seven Indian firms were listed among the top 15 technology outsourcing companies in the world.

Mining forms an important segment of the Indian economy, with the country producing 79 different minerals (excluding fuel and atomic resources) in 2009–10, including iron ore, manganese, mica, bauxite, chromite, limestone, asbestos, fluorite, gypsum, ochre, phosphorite and silica sand. Organised retail supermarkets accounts for 24% of the market as of 2008. Regulations prevent most foreign investment in retailing.

Moreover, over thirty regulations such as "signboard licences" and "anti-hoarding measures" may have to be complied before a store can open doors. There are taxes for moving goods from state to state, and even within states. Tourism in India is relatively undeveloped, but growing at double digits. Some hospitals woo medical tourism.

Agriculture in Indian Economy

India ranks second worldwide in farm output. Agriculture and allied sectors like forestry, logging and fishing accounted for 15.7% of the GDP in 2009–10, employed 52.1% of the total workforce, and despite a steady decline of its share in the GDP, is still the largest economic sector and a significant piece of the overall socio-economic development of India. Yields per unit area of all crops have grown since 1950, due to the special emphasis placed on agriculture in the five-year plans and steady improvements in irrigation, technology, application of modern agricultural practices and provision of agricultural credit and subsidies since the Green Revolution in India. However, international comparisons reveal the average yield in India is generally 30% to 50% of the highest average yield in the world. Indian states Uttar Pradesh, Punjab, Haryana, Madhya Pradesh, Andhra Pradesh, Bihar, West Bengal and Maharashtra are key agricultural contributing states of India.

India receives an average annual rainfall of 1,208 millimetres (47.6 in) and a total annual precipitation of 4000 billion cubic metres, with the total utilisable water resources, including surface and groundwater, amounting to 1123 billion cubic metres. 546,820 square kilometres (211,130 sq mi) of the land area, or about 39% of the total cultivated area, is irrigated. India's inland water resources including rivers, canals, ponds and lakes and marine resources comprising the east and west coasts of the Indian ocean and other gulfs and bays provide employment to nearly six million people in the fisheries sector. In 2008, India had the world's third largest fishing industry.

India is the largest producer in the world of milk, jute and pulses, and also has the world's second largest cattle population with 175 million animals in 2008. It is the second largest producer of rice, wheat, sugarcane, cotton and groundnuts, as well as the second largest fruit and vegetable producer, accounting for 10.9% and 8.6% of the world fruit and vegetable production respectively. India is also the second largest producer and the largest consumer of silk in the world, producing 77,000 million tons in 2005.

Banking and finance in Indian Economy

The Indian money market is classified into the organised sector, comprising private, public and foreign owned commercial banks and cooperative banks, together known as *scheduled banks*, and the unorganised sector, which includes individual or family owned indigenous bankers or money lendersand non-banking financial companies. The unorganised sector and microcredit are still preferred over traditional banks in rural and sub-urban areas, especially for non-productive purposes, like ceremonies and short duration loans.

Prime Minister Indira Gandhi nationalised 14 banks in 1969, followed by six others in 1980, and made it mandatory for banks to provide 40% of their net credit to priority sectors like agriculture, small-scale industry, retail trade, small businesses, etc. to ensure that the banks fulfill their social and developmental goals. Since then, the number of bank branches has increased from 8,260 in 1969 to 72,170 in 2007 and the population covered by a branch decreased from 63,800 to 15,000 during the same period. The total bank deposits increased from ₹5,910 crore (US$1.12 billion) in 1970–71 to 3,830,922 crore (US$727.88 billion) in 2008–09. Despite an increase of rural branches, from 1,860 or 22% of the total number of branches in 1969 to 30,590 or 42% in 2007, only 32,270 out of 500,000 villages are covered by a scheduled bank.

India's gross domestic saving in 2006–07 as a percentage of GDP stood at a high 32.7%. More than half of personal savings are invested in physical assets such as land, houses, cattle, and gold. The public sector banks hold over 75% of total assets of the banking industry, with the private and foreign banks holding 18.2% and 6.5% respectively. Since liberalisation, the government has approved significant banking reforms. While some of these relate to nationalised banks, like encouraging mergers, reducing government interference and increasing profitability and competitiveness, other reforms have opened up the banking and insurance sectors to private and foreign players.

Energy and power in Indian Economy

India's oil reserves meet 25% of the country's domestic oil demand. As of 2009, India's total proven oil reserves stood at 775 million metric tonnes while gas reserves stood at 1074 billion cubic metres. Oil and natural gas fields are located offshore at Mumbai High, Krishna Godavari Basin and the Cauvery Delta, and onshore mainly in the states of Assam,

Gujarat and Rajasthan. India is the fourth largest consumer of oil in the world and imported $82.1 billion worth of oil in the first three quarters of 2010, which had an adverse effect on its current account deficit. The petroleum industry in India mostly consists of public sector companies such as Oil and Natural Gas Corporation (ONGC), Hindustan Petroleum Corporation Limited (HPCL) and Indian Oil Corporation Limited (IOCL). There are some major private Indian companies in the oil sector such as Reliance Industries Limited(RIL) which operates the world's largest oil refining complex.

As of 2010, India had an installed power generation capacity of 164,835 megawatts (MW), of which thermal power contributed 64.6%, hydroelectricity 24.7%, other sources of renewable energy 7.7%, and nuclear power 2.9%. India meets most of its domestic energy demand through its 106 billion tonnes of coal reserves. India is also rich in certain renewable sources of energy with significant future potential such as solar, wind and biofuels (jatropha, sugarcane). India's huge thorium reserves – about 25% of world's reserves – are expected to fuel the country's ambitious nuclear energy programin the long-run. India's dwindling uranium reserves stagnated the growth of nuclear energy in the country for many years. However, the Indo-US nuclear deal has paved the way for India to import uranium from other countries.

Global trade Relations

Until the liberalisation of 1991, India was largely and intentionally isolated from the world markets, to protect its economy and to achieve self-reliance. Foreign trade was subject to import tariffs, export taxes and quantitative restrictions, while foreign direct investment (FDI) was restricted by upper-limit equity participation, restrictions on technology transfer, export obligations and government approvals; these approvals were needed for nearly 60% of new FDI in the industrial sector. The restrictions ensured that FDI averaged only around $200 million annually between 1985 and 1991; a large percentage of the capital flows consisted of foreign aid, commercial borrowing and deposits ofnon-resident Indians. India's exports were stagnant for the first 15 years after independence, due to general neglect of trade policy by the government of that period. Imports in the same period, due to industrialisation being nascent, consisted predominantly of machinery, raw materials and consumer goods.

Since liberalisation, the value of India's international trade has increased sharply, with the contribution of total trade in goods and services to the GDP rising from 16% in 1990–91 to 43% in 2005–06. India's major trading partners are the European Union, China, the United States and the United Arab Emirates. In 2006–07, major export commodities included engineering goods, petroleum products, chemicals and pharmaceuticals, gems and jewellery, textiles and garments, agricultural products, iron ore and other minerals. Major import commodities included crude oil and related products, machinery, electronic goods, gold and silver. In November 2010, exports increased 22.3% year-on-year to 85,063 crore (US$16.16 billion), while imports were up 7.5% at 125,133 crore (US$23.78 billion). Trade deficit for the same month dropped from 46,865 crore (US$8.9 billion) in 2009 to 40,070 crore (US$7.61 billion) in 2010.

India is a founding-member of General Agreement on Tariffs and Trade (GATT) since 1947 and its successor, the WTO. While participating actively in its general council meetings, India has been crucial in voicing the concerns of the developing world. For instance, India has continued its opposition to the inclusion of such matters as labour and environment issues and other non-tariff barriers to tradeinto the WTO policies.

Balance of Payments

Since independence, India's balance of payments on itscurrent account has been negative. Since economic liberalisation in the 1990s, precipitated by a balance of payment crisis, India's exports rose consistently, covering 80.3% of its imports in 2002–03, up from 66.2% in 1990–91. However, the global economic slump followed by a general deceleration in world trade saw the exports as a percentage of imports drop to 61.4% in 2008–09. India's growing oil import bill is seen as the main driver behind the large current account deficit, which rose to $118.7 billion, or 9.7% of GDP, in 2008–09. Between January and October 2010, India imported $82.1 billion worth of crude oil.

Due to the global late-2000s recession, both Indian exports and imports declined by 29.2% and 39.2% respectively in June 2009. The steep decline was because countries hit hardest by the global recession, such as United States and members of the European Union, account for more than 60% of Indian exports. However, since the decline in imports was much sharper compared to the decline in exports, India's trade deficit reduced to 25,250 crore (US$4.8 billion). As of June 2011, exports and imports have both registered impressive growth with monthly exports reaching $25.9 billion for the month of May 2011 and monthly imports reaching $40.9 billion for the same month. This represents a year on year growth of 56.9% for exports and 54.1% for imports.

India's reliance on external assistance and concessional debt has decreased since liberalisation of the economy, and the debt service ratio decreased from 35.3% in 1990–91 to 4.4% in 2008–09. In India, External Commercial Borrowings (ECBs), or commercial loans from non-resident lenders, are being permitted by the Government for providing an additional source of funds to Indian corporates. TheMinistry of Finance monitors and regulates them through ECB policy guidelines issued by the Reserve Bank of India under the Foreign Exchange Management Act of 1999. India's foreign exchange reserves have steadily risen from $5.8 billion in March 1991 to $283.5 billion in December 2009.

Foreign direct Investment

As the fourth-largest economy in the world in PPP terms, India is a preferred destination for FDI; India has strengths in telecommunication, information technology and other significant areas such as auto components, chemicals, apparels, pharmaceuticals, and jewellery. Despite a surge in foreign investments, rigid FDI policies were a significant hindrance. However, due to positive economic reforms aimed at deregulating the economy and stimulating foreign investment, India has positioned itself as one of the front-runners of the rapidly growing Asia-Pacific region. India has a large pool of skilled managerial and technical expertise. The size of the middle-class population stands at 300 million and represents a growing consumer market.

During 2000–10, the country attracted $178 billion as FDI. The inordinately high investment from Mauritius is due to routing of international funds through the country given significant tax advantages; double taxation is avoided due to a tax treaty between India and Mauritius, and Mauritius is a capital gains tax haven, effectively creating a zero-taxation FDI channel.

India's recently liberalised FDI policy (2005) allows up to a 100% FDI stake in ventures. Industrial policy reforms have substantially reduced industrial licensing requirements, removed restrictions on expansion and facilitated easy access to foreign technology and foreign direct investment FDI. The upward moving growth curve of the real-estate sector owes some credit to a booming economy and liberalised FDI regime. In March 2005, the government amended the rules to allow 100% FDI in the construction sector, including built-up infrastructure and construction development projects comprising housing, commercial premises, hospitals, educational institutions, recreational facilities, and city- and regional-level infrastructure. Despite a number of changes in the FDI policy to remove caps in most sectors, there still remains an unfinished agenda of permitting greater FDI in politically sensitive areas such as insurance and retailing. The total FDI equity inflow into India in 2008–09 stood at 122,919 crore (US$23.35 billion), a growth of 25% in rupee terms over the previous period. .

Currency

The Indian rupee is the only legal tender in India, and is also accepted as legal tender in the neighbouring Nepal and Bhutan, both of which peg their currency to that of the Indian rupee. The rupee is divided into 100 paise. The highest-denomination banknote is the 1,000 rupee note; the lowest-denomination coin in circulation is the 10 paise coin. However, with effect from 30 June 2011, 50 paise is the minimum coin accepted in the markets as all denominations below have ceased to be legal currency. India's monetary system is managed by the Reserve Bank of India (RBI), the country's central bank. Established on 1 April 1935 and nationalised in 1949, the RBI serves as the nation's monetary authority, regulator and supervisor of the monetary system, banker to the government, custodian of foreign exchange reserves, and as an issuer of currency. It is governed by a central board of directors, headed by a governor who is appointed by the Government of India.

The rupee was linked to the British pound from 1927–1946 and then the U.S. dollar till 1975 through afixed exchange rate. It was devalued in September 1975 and the system of fixed par rate was replaced with a basket of four major international currencies – the British pound, the U.S. dollar, the Japanese yen and the Deutsche mark. Since 2003, the rupee has been steadily appreciating against the U.S. dollar. In 2009, a rising rupee prompted the Government of India to purchase 200 tons of gold for $6.7 billion from the IMF.

Income and Consumption

India's gross national income per capita had experienced astonishing growth rates since 2002.India's Per Capita Income has tripled from $ 423 in 2002–03 to $ 1219 in 2010–11, averaging 14.4% growth over these eight years. It will further go up to $ 1440 during 2011–12 fiscal. Indian official estimates of the extent of poverty have been subject to debate, with concerns being raised about the methodology for the determination of the poverty line. As of 2005, according to World Bank statistics, 75.6% of the population lived on less than $2 a day (PPP), while 41.6% of the population was living below the new international poverty line of $1.25

(PPP) per day. However, data released in 2009 by the Government of India estimated that 37% of the population lived below the poverty line.

Housing is modest. According to *The Times of India*, a majority of Indians had a per capita space equivalent to or less than a 100 square feet (9.3 m^2) room for their basic living needs, and one-third of urban Indians lived in "homes too cramped to exceed even the minimum requirements of a prison cell in the US." The average is 103 sq ft (9.6 m^2) per person in rural areas and 117 sq ft (10.9 m^2) per person in urban areas.

Around half of Indian children are malnourished. The proportion of underweight children is nearly double that of Sub-Saharan Africa. However, India has not had any major faminessince Independence.

Since the early 1950s, successive governments have implemented various schemes to alleviate poverty, under central planning, that have met with partial success. All these programmes have relied upon the strategies of the *Food for work* programme and *National Rural Employment Programme*of the 1980s, which attempted to use the unemployed to generate productive assets and build rural infrastructure. In August 2005, the Parliament of India, in response to the perceived failure of economic growth to generate employment for the rural poor, passed the *Rural Employment Guarantee Bill* into law, guaranteeing 100 days of minimum wage employment to every rural household in all the districts of India. The Parliament of India also refused to accept Union Government's argument that it had taken adequate measures to reduce incidence of poverty in India.The question of whether economic reforms have reduced poverty has fuelled debates without generating clear-cut answers and has also increased political pressure against further economic reforms, especially those involving the downsizing of labour and cutting agricultural subsidies. Recent statistics in 2010 point out that the number of high income households has crossed lower income households.

Education

India has made huge progress in terms of increasing primary education attendance rate and expanding literacy to approximately three-fourth of the population. India's literacy rate had grown from 52.2% in 1991 to 74.04% in 2011. The right to education at elementary level has been made one of the fundamental rights under the eighty-sixth Amendment of 2002, and legislation has been enacted to further the objective of providing free education to all children. However, the literacy rate of 74% is still lower than the worldwide average and the country suffers from a high dropout rate. Further, there exists a severe disparity in literacy rates and educational opportunities between males and females, urban and rural areas, and among different social groups.

Employment

Agricultural and allied sectors accounted for about 52.1% of the total workforce in 2009–10. While agriculture has faced stagnation in growth, services have seen a steady growth. Of the total workforce, 7% is in the organised sector, two-thirds of which are in the public sector. The NSSO survey estimated that in 2004–05, 8.3% of the population was unemployed, an increase of 2.2% over 1993 levels, with unemployment uniformly higher in urban areas and among women. Growth of labour stagnated at around 2% for the decade between 1994–2005, about the same as that for the preceding decade. Avenues for employment generation have been identified in the IT and travel and tourism sectors, which have been experiencing high annual growth rates of above 9%.

Unemployment in India is characterised by chronic (disguised) unemployment. Government schemes that target eradication of both poverty and unemployment (which in recent decades has sent millions of poor and unskilled people into urban areas in search of livelihoods) attempt to solve the problem, by providing financial assistance for setting up businesses, skill honing, setting up public sector enterprises, reservations in governments, etc. The decline in organised employment due to the decreased role of the public sector after liberalisation has further underlined the need for focusing on better education and has also put political pressure on further reforms. India's labour regulations are heavy even by developing country standards and analysts have urged the government to abolish or modify them in order to make the environment more conducive for employment generation. The 11th five-year plan has also identified the need for a congenial environment to be created for employment generation, by reducing the number of permissions and other bureaucratic clearances required. Further, inequalities and inadequacies in the education system have been identified as an obstacle preventing the benefits of increased employment opportunities from reaching all sectors of society.

Child labour in India is a complex problem that is basically rooted in poverty, coupled with a failure of governmental policy, which has focused on subsidising higher rather than elementary education, as a result benefiting the privileged rather than the poorer sections of society. The Indian government is implementing the world's largest child labour elimination program, with primary education targeted for ~250 million. Numerous non-governmental and voluntary organisations are also involved. Special investigation cells have been set up in states to enforce existing laws banning the employment of children under 14 in hazardous industries. The allocation of the Government of India for the eradication of child labour was $21 million in 2007. Public campaigns, provision of meals in school and other incentives have proven successful in increasing attendance rates in schools in some states.

In 2009–10, remittances from Indian migrants overseas stood at 250,000 crore (US$47.5 billion), the highest in the world, but their share in FDI remained low at around 1%. India ranked 133rd on theEase of Doing Business Index 2010, behind countries such as China (89th), Pakistan (85th), and Nigeria (125th).

Infrastructure in Indian Economy

In the past, development of infrastructure was completely in the hands of the public sector and was plagued by slow progress, poor quality and inefficiency. India's low spending on power, construction, transportation, telecommunications and real estate, at $31 billion or 6% of GDP in 2002 had prevented India from sustaining higher growth rates. This has prompted the government to partially open up infrastructure to the private sector allowing foreign investment, and most public infrastructure, barring railways, is today constructed and maintained by private contractors, in exchange for tax and other concessions from the government.

Some 600 million Indians have no electricity at all. While 80% of Indian villages have at least an electricity line, just 44% of rural households have access to electricity. Some half of the electricity is stolen, compared with 3% in China. The stolen electricity amounts to 1.5% of GDP. Transmission and distribution losses amount to around 20%, as a result of an inefficient distribution system, handled mostly by cash-strapped state-run enterprises. Almost all of the electricity in India is produced by the public sector. Power outages are common, and many buy their own power generators to ensure electricity supply. As of 2006–07 the electricity production was at 652.2 billion kWh, with an installed capacity of 128400 MW. In 2007, electricity demand exceeded supply by 15%. However, reforms brought about by the Electricity Act of 2003 caused far-reaching policy changes, including mandating the separation of generation, transmission and distribution aspects of electricity, abolishing licencing requirements in generation and opening up the sector to private players, thereby paving the way for creating a competitive market-based electricity sector. Substantial improvements in water supply infrastructure, both in urban and rural areas, have taken place over the past decade, with the proportion of the population having access to safe drinking water rising from 66% in 1991 to 92% in 2001 in rural areas, and from 82% to 98% in urban areas. however, quality and availability of water supply remains a major problem even in urban India, with most cities getting water for only a few hours during the day.

India has the world's third largest road network, covering about 3.3 million kilometers and carrying 65% of freight and 80% of passenger traffic. Container traffic is growing at 15% a year. India has a national teledensity rate of 67.67% with 806.1 million telephone subscribers, two-thirds of them in urban areas, but Internet use is rare—there were only 10.29 million broadband lines in India in September 2010. However, this is growing and is expected to boom following the expansion of 3G andwimax services.

Economic disparities

A critical problem facing India's economy is the sharp and growing regional variations among India's different states and territories in terms of poverty, availability of infrastructure and socio-economic development. Six low-income states – Bihar, Chhattisgarh, Jharkhand, Madhya Pradesh, Orissa and Uttar Pradesh – are home to more than one third of India's population. Severe disparities exist among states in terms of income, literacy rates, life expectancy and living conditions.

The five-year plans, especially in the pre-liberalisation era, attempted to reduce regional disparities by encouraging industrial development in the interior regions and distributing industries across states, but the results have not been very encouraging since these measures in fact increased inefficiency and hampered effective industrial growth. After liberalisation, the more advanced states have been better placed to benefit from them, with well-developed infrastructure and an educated and skilled workforce, which attract the manufacturing and service sectors. The governments of backward regions are trying to reduce disparities by offering tax holidays and cheap land, and focusing more on sectors like tourism which, although being geographically and historically determined, can become a source of growth and develops faster than other sectors.

Taxation in India

Taxes in India are levied by the Central Government and theState Government. Some minor taxes are also levied by the local authorities such the Municipality or the Local Council.

The authority to levy a tax is derived from the Constitution of Indiawhich allocates the power to levy various taxes between the Centre and the State. An important restriction on this power is Article 265 of the Constitution which states that "*No tax shall be levied or collected except by the authority of law.*" Therefore each tax levied or collected has to be backed by an accompanying law, passed either by the Parliament or the State Legislature.

Effect of Corruption in Indian Economy

Corruption has been one of the pervasive problems affecting India. The economic reforms of 1991 reduced the red tape, bureaucracy and the *Licence Raj* that were largely blamed for the institutionalised corruption and inefficiency. Yet, a 2005 study by Transparency International (TI) found that more than half of those surveyed had firsthand experience of paying bribe or peddling influence to get a job done in a public office.

The Right to Information Act (2005) which requires government officials to furnish information requested by citizens or face punitive action, computerisation of services, and various central and state government acts that established vigilance commissions, have considerably reduced corruption and opened up avenues to redress grievances. The 2010 report by TI ranks India at 87th place and states that significant setbacks were made by India in reducing corruption.

The current government has concluded that most spending fails to reach its intended recipients. A large, cumbersome and overworked bureaucracy also contributes to administrative inefficiency. India's absence rates are one of the worst in the world; one study found that 25% of public sector teachers and 40% of public sector medical workers could not be found at the workplace.

The Indian economy continues to face the problem of anunderground economy with a 2006 estimate by the Swiss Banking Association suggesting that India topped the worldwide list for black money with almost $1,456 billion stashed in Swiss banks. This amounts to 13 times the country's total external debt.

Challenges before Indian economy:

Population explosion: This monster is eating up into the success of India. According to 2001 census of India, population of India in 2001 was 1,028,610,328, growing at a rate of 2.11% approx. Such a vast population puts lots of stress on economic infrastructure of the nation. Thus India has to control its burgeoning population.

Poverty: As per records of National Planning Commission, 36% of the Indian population was living Below Poverty Line in 1993-94. Though this figure has decreased in recent times but some major steps are needed to be taken to eliminate poverty from India.

Unemployment: The increasing population is pressing hard on economic resources as well as job opportunities. Indian government has started various schemes such as Jawahar Rozgar Yojna, and Self Employment Scheme for Educated Unemployed Youth (SEEUY). But these are proving to be a drop in an ocean.

Rural urban divide: It is said that India lies in villages, even today when there is lots of talk going about migration to cities, 70% of the Indian population still lives in villages. There is a very stark difference in pace of rural and urban growth. Unless there isn't a balanced development Indian economy cannot grow.

These challenges can be overcome by the sustained and planned economic reforms.

These include:

- Maintaining fiscal discipline
- Orientation of public expenditure towards sectors in which India is faring badly such as health and education.
- Introduction of reforms in labour laws to generate more employment opportunities for the growing population of India.
- Reorganization of agricultural sector, introduction of new technology, reducing agriculture's dependence on monsoon by developing means of irrigation.
- Introduction of financial reforms including privatization of some public sector banks.

Tourism in India

Every year, travellers set out on holidays and vacations, breathing new life into the economy of the places they visit. In India, the largest service industry is tourism. More than five million foreign visitors make their way to India annually to experience the rich culture of one of the economical giants of the world.

The impact of tourism on India's national gross domestic product is estimated at US$275.5 billion by 2018. In fact, the World Travel and Tourism Council declares India as a travel hotspot from now until 2018. People are not only drawn to India for cultural history, but they also travel for business, medical purposes, and sports such as the 2010 Commonwealth Games.

Medical tourism is on the rise in India. Travellers can receive high-quality treatments at a fraction of the prices they expect. Surgery costs average thirty percent lower than other well-known medical tourism destinations such as Thailand. Procedures people come to undergo include bone marrow transplants, cardiac surgery, orthopedic surgeries and liver transplants. India is best known for heart surgery. Access to leading medical technology at alluring rates is not the only place tourists spend their money on. Many people come seeking a taste of the unique culture and history India possesses.

India's 5,000 year old history promises to deliver an unmatched travel experience to tourists. The Taj Mahal is one of the most familiar sights of India. Millions of travellers visit the historical site each year. Other sites that draw people in include the Mahabodi Temple, skiing in Shimla, and the stunning Lotus Temple in Dehli.

India's Place in the Agricultural Landscape of the World

Both the World Bank and the CIA World Fact Book rank India's economy fourth worldwide. A country's gross domestic product is a good indicator of the standard of living within that country. Among India's economical make-up, agriculture plays an important role in the fabric of society.

With a population of 1,189,172, 186 and counting, one of the biggest challenges for the Indian agricultural industry is the population grows faster than farm production. The CIA World Fact Book lists India as the second most populated country in the world. Food items such as rice and wheat rise demand to keep up with the population boom. For many years, India has been an autarky, or self-sufficient economy. But since the 1990, it continues to develop an open-market policy. Agricultural output for India ranks second among the world economies.

Agricultural policy is focused on improving self efficiency of food production to combat hunger issues. India is among the world's highest producers of rice, cow milk, sugar cane, buffalo milk and wheat. The Sugarcane Breeding Institute of Coimbatore, India was established in 1912 to improve sugarcane production. It is one of the oldest crop research institutes worldwide. Indian stock of the sweet crop is used in 26 other countries across the globe.

The institution is now conducting a research project to help the about 35 million farmers who cultivate and rely on the crop. The project is focused on creating a website where information can be shared easily. It's main goals are to aid farmers and support sugarcane reasearch.

New Auto Plant in India

In an effort to increase the competition between BMW, Daimler and Audi, Jaquar Land Rover opened their first plant today in India. This plant is opened in Pune and will start to build Freelander 2 sport utility vehicles from the ground up from kits shipped to them from the Liverpool plant. This is great news for both India and for Jaquar Land Rover as it will open up new business in both. The company will be afforded the ability to put together more vehicles, quickly and at a decent price keeping the prices of the vehicles affordable in comparison to the competitors.

This will also bring great employment opportunity to the area of Pune and will give them a boost economically that they are much in need of. Taking this step is great for all involved on several levels and offers the company the chance to keep on producing the quality vehicles they have always built. These steps for the community will produce additional employment and will also cause an increase in other economic areas within the community. The future for the company and the area look bright with the prospect of turning out large numbers of vehicles. Barring an unexpected issues they are well on their way to creating a great income with the help of India. The next year will bring signs of the success or demise of this plan for the auto manufacturer and the area. Through great efforts they will do the best to create a new advantage to the competitors.

Investing in India Worth Looking At

It is no secret that India grows quickly each year. This country, with the second highest population globally, possesses a thriving world economy that is on the increase. As India expands in the world market, windows for foreign investment open wider to those who would step inside. Here is why you should look into investing in India.

In March of this year, investment icon Warren Buffett stated he was looking to invest in economic powerhouses like India. Asian Development Bank reports that the equity market in India ranks third in the world. With about US$600 billion in market capitalization, it sits right behind China and Japan as one of the major equity markets in the Asian region. India is expected to boost economic growth by at least nine percent annually within the next ten years. India's economy offers investors a variety of opportunities. India's service sector forms fifty percent of its economy. Other industries include pharmaceuticals, energy and consumer goods.

Domestic industry is on the rise in India. Last July, New Delhi opened a 3 billion dollar addition to the Indira Gandhi International Airport. Terminal 3 (T3) took 37 months to complete. Prime Minister Manmohan Singh, who dedicated the new terminal, stated its creation was a global benchmark for India. India's government has worked to strengthen its country's infrastructure.

The Bombay Stock Exchange is the fourth largest stock exchange in Asia. It's also the second oldest in the world, with a history dating back to the 18502 s. With a youthful demographic and a solid work ethic, the global economy will see more from India in years to come.

Industries and Investment in the Economy in India

The population of India is estimated at over 1 billion, and continues to grow every year. It has the third largest economy in Asia, and has plenty of industries that help push the growth. There have been reforms put into place over the last twenty years, which have helped the country to become more prominent in importing and exporting, and other forms of overseas business.

More than 10% of those employed work in industrial fields, and these include manufacturing and production of textiles. Thisindustry was part of the reform, which was altered by reducing costs of the factories in order to sell the materials at a lower cost and stay competitive with the materials produced in China and other nearby countries. Another sector of business in which India's economy has grown drastically over the years is process outsourcing for large companies which are often located in the United States. Since many residents of India are fluent in English, they are able to telecommute and answer calls for customer service, tech support, and other similar service industries. In fact, seven of the large firms located in India make up almost half of the top fifteen outsourcing companies across the globe. India also produces a good amount of agriculture, including logging, fishing, and forestry. Investment is increasing as banks become more stable and secure, which was also part of the economic reform.

India's growth rate is approximately 7% on average, and has greatly reduced the amount of poverty among its residents over the years. The main industries continue to grow, which has given more individuals the opportunity to have stable employment and provide for their families.

Issues and Trends in the Indian Economy

In the past 15-20 years, Inc a has seen some excellent growth and progression in its economic situa ion. Current affairs point to continued growth, and has been the second fastest rising large economy. However, there have been a few changes in the past few months that could lead to a dip and cause a struggle for those employed in this country.

It isn't too big of a surprise that importing/exporting and automobile sales have been on the decline, since the economy worldwide is struggling and many individuals are choosing to buy locally to support their economies. Inflation in India has increased more rapidly than it has in years past, making it more difficult for families to be able to afford groceries, clothing, and other necessities. The Prime Minister of India is trying to take matters into his own hands, especially after suffering backlash from scandal, corruption among the government agencies, and contentment with the current situation. Many residents of India are frustrated with their government, who seems unwilling to make the necessary reforms in an attempt to boost the economy. Such reforms have been seen in the United States, such as tax credits for homebuyers and those who were employed for the whole year, and helped increase the amount of money received on many tax returns. However, without sufficient funds to pay for such programs, it can be difficult to upswing an economy that is spiraling downward.

There is hope that the Indian economy is simply encountering a speed bump in its growth. Some predict that it will turn around, but only time can show what the future holds for those living and working in India.

Current Affairs – India

India's economy has gone through some ups and downs throughout the past few years, as it has grown to the third largest in Asia. There are beautiful buildings and hotels within its cities, appealing to tourists and visitors, as well as fancy car dealerships and high rise office buildings lining the streets. However, there is a great divide among the very rich and very poor in India, which makes it difficult to have a society that is on equal footing.

It is interesting to note the stark differences among those residing in India; in 2010, it was estimated that the economy grew more than 8%, but the investment rate dropped by over 30%. The restrictions on business make it very difficult to start a company; certain cities require as many as 37 licenses obtained over seven months in order to open a warehouse. Even once it has been properly built, it can be difficult for trucks and workers to get to the doors due to rough and crowded roads, limited water, and power outages. While on the other hand, businesspeople are hopeful that it will rise to be one of the strongest economies within the next twenty years.

Before this can happen, however, India will need to find some level ground among its residents. This may require assistance from the government, but the political scene has been writhe with scandal and corruption.

Once India is able to strengthen its monetary system, those who are returning to the country and investing in local businesses can help increase the stability of the economy. This might mean a very promising future for those residing in the beautiful country.

Land Value at a Great Place

Thanks to a difficult economy there are many changes made regarding the value of the properties across the world. This includes properties fully built and land value. While a short time ago the value ofproperty dropped extremely low making it difficult for sellers to get what they had invested in property, the value has started a steady increase. Purchasing land today is a great way to invest money since it is not at the same rate it was recently but appears to be on the rise. This means buyers will be increasing their property value after purchase fairly quickly. Clearly this changes based on the location of the property and the marketability of it in general.

Finding the right property for your situation can be a challenge given the many obstacles you might find regarding financing today. This having been said, there are some great options available all over the world that will easily have you purchasing your next property in no time at all at a rate that is well within your range. With some basic guidelines, understanding what you are looking for and knowing what your limitations are you can easily find property that at will easily increase in value. It is a great time to invest in new property regardless of your future goals for the property. There are great properties to be had with a little research and planning ahead. Having a plan before you get started is the key to a successful hunt for the right property with the right land value for your needs. You want to be sure the property increases in value as fast as possible.

India's Foreign Trade and Global Economic Policies

India is quickly emerging as a powerful trade partner in the global economy. What was once an undeveloped, closed-off economy is now becoming a massive economic force in Asia, rivaling all in the region.

The economy of India is twelfth largest in the world (in exchange rates, with a GDP of US $1.089 trillion) and the fourth largest in the world by purchasing power.

India has a population of 1,147,995,904, making it the second largest country in the world. In 2006, India's trade reached 24% of GDP, which is by no means excessive, but is a huge increase from the 6% it was in 1985. On a global scale, Indian trade represents 1% of the world's commerce.

India's Exports

In 2007, India's exports stood at $140.8 billion, making it the 26th-largest export economy in the world. The country's exports have grown steadily in the past few decades, ever since foreign direct investment (FDI) was allowed on a large scale, and most of the state-run industries were privatized. Most of these changes have occured since the economic reforms India implemented in 1991.

Below is a table illustrating the volume of exports India has seen between 2003 and 2008:

Total Exports: $140.8 billion (2007)

Year	Exports Rank	% Change	Date
2003	$44,500,000,000 32		2001 est.
2004	$57,240,000,000 31	28.63%	2003 est.
2005	$69,180,000,000 33	20.86%	2004 est.
2006	$76,230,000,000 33	10.19%	2005 est.
2007	$112,000,000,000 29	46.92%	2006 est.
2008	$140,800,000,000 26	25.71%	2007 est.

- Products exported by India include: Petroleum products
- Textile goods
- Gems and jewelry
- Engineering goods
- Chemicals
- Leather products

In addition to these goods and products, much of India's GDP is contributed to by the business process outsourcing (BPO) industry, call centres, and other service-based jobs from the US, Europe, and some of Asia.

India's Imports

- Machinery
- Vehicles, including aircraft
- Mineral fuels and lubricants

- Beverages and tobacco
- Chemical fertilizers
- Medical equipment
- Electronics and computer accessories

As the middle class of India becomes more affluent and wealthy, domestic consumption will continue to increase, as it has been doing in recent years. This will fuel more imports.

Interestingly, India banned all toy imports from China in February 2009. This was due to fears about safety issues of the Chinese toys and worries about the fate of domestic toy producers in India.

India Economy: Effects of the US Financial Crisis in India

New Delhi[...] It is often said that when the US sneezes the rest of the world catches a cold. This three-part series looks at how India, China, and Russia have been affected by the US financial crisis.

Before we get into detail about how much this US problem is spreading globally, we should understand the severity of it and the possible consequences in the US. How sick is the US?

Some have compared the situation in the US with the Great Depression of 1929, but this situation is far from a depression – in fact it's not even a recession. In the Great Depression there was no work and there was widespread poverty. People struggled through the winter with no heating and no food. We are not seeing such extensive suffering in the US.

In the US, August 2008 unemployment figures were at 6.1%, according to the US Bureau of Labor Statistics. In the Great Depression unemployment was higher than 25%. The Commerce Department reported that GDP growth was at 2.8%, hardly indicative of a recession, although this was revised down from the 3.3% figure it projected a month ago.

But one cannot ignore yesterday's 777 point drop in the Dow Jones Industrial Average after the $700 billion bailout plan failed to pass through Congress. These paper losses of more than a trillion dollars may be the sneeze that disrupts global markets.

Even before this controversial rescue plan was shot down, Indian markets took a dive of their own on Monday 29 September. The stock market sank to an 18-month low and the rupee a 5-year low. The stock market dropped 5.3% to 12,595.75.

According to Business Standard, vice president of Karvy Stockbroking Ambareesh Baliga, said, "We are advising our clients to stay away from trading till selling by Foreign Institutional Investors (FIIs) stops. Also, there is no support to the markets from any domestic institution.

While markets are below their fundamental levels, fear has gripped investors and there is panic selling."

Indian Economy Disparity in Wealth Distribution

Bill gates, the one name that is almost synonymous to Wealth and to Microsoft was till recently the richest man in the world, with assets worth 59 billion dollars! Declared the richest man in the world in the year 1995, he adorned this prestigious and coveted title for almost a decade. Some time back he was briefly overtaken by Mexican tycoon Carlos Slim, but Slim's stint at the top was short term and was again overtaken by Gates. Recently, the whole world was shocked when it was declared that Mukesh Ambani, the chairperson and managing director of Reliance Industries has become the richest man in the world with assets worth 63.2 billion USD. The magic run of the Indian share market was largely responsible for this somewhat unprecedented development.

It is quite expected and accepted when a person from the countries like the US or the UK adorn the crown of the richest man, but it is hard to believe that a man from a third world country that is counted among the poorest in the world would house the richest man in the world. India is a country that is plagued by much social malice like poverty, population, illiteracy, unemployment, superstitions, gender biasness, social stigmas etc. In this country that has a population of over a billion; around 22-23 crores of people are still living below the poverty line. Disparity in the distribution of wealth continues to be a big blow to the Indian economy. Many of them are not even earning 1 dollar a day. On one hand there are people who are not even earning a dollar per day, on the other hand Indian youth is counted among the highest spending youths in the world. On one hand mergers and acquisitions have been made worth millions, on the other hand the rate of poverty has almost remained static in the span of the last two decades. On one hand larger then life malls, luxury foreign car showrooms are opening, on the other hand the agricultural sector, the backbone of the Indian economy is yet to show profits and improvements. One would not know whether to be happy for India or sad at the superficiality of its development. The rich are growing richer and the poor are growing poorer, thanks to the highly unequal distribution of income in the Indian economy!

The question is whom to blame. Nobody is to be blamed solely yet everybody is responsible for the situation India is in today. The population, the government, the entrepreneurs, the system, or the constitution?

Everybody has a role to play. Venturing into this topic is like counting the stars in the sky. Vast and unending. The affluent society of the country is no doubt not apprehensive of spending, yet there are certain concepts that inspite of being very popular in the west and inspite of being quite upmarket are not that popular in India. Ecommerce is one such concept. There are people who buy stuff online. Infact there are many who are too short of time or energy to go hunting for stuffs. Thus they take the easy way out and buy things online. But there are very few concerns in India that are ready to open an estore. Conversely however, there are quite a few software development companies in India that provide ecommerce solution and ecommerce software to people living outside India. Many Indian concerns are into offshore software development. They have clients from all over the world who come to them for software development in order to do business online, but it's very rare that one would find an Indian company venturing into ecommerce web site development; one trend that so far India has not taken from the west!

CHAPTER-2

HISTORY OF INDIAN ECONOMY

Indus valley civilization, which flourished between 2800 BC and 1800 BC, had an advanced and flourishing economic system. The Indus valley people practiced agriculture, domesticated animals, made tools and weapons from copper, bronze and tin and even traded with some Middle East countries.

Agriculture was the main economic activity of the people in the Vedic age but with the second urbanization a number of urban centers grew in North India. This gave a major fillip to trade and commerce. The ancient Indians had trade contacts with far off lands like the Middle East, the Roman Empire and the South East Asia. Many Indian trading colonies were settled in other countries.

Most of the Indian population resided in villages and the economy of the villages was self-sustaining. Agriculture was the predominant occupation of the populace and satisfied a village's food necessities. It also provided raw materials for industries like textile, food processing and crafts. Besides farmers, other classes of people were barbers, carpenters, doctors, goldsmiths, weavers, etc. In towns and urban centers trade took place through coins but in villages barter was the main system of economic activities.

The system of castes and sub-castes ensured division of labor and functioned much like guilds, providing training to apprentices. The caste system restricted people from changing ones occupation and aspiring for an upper caste's lifestyle. Traditionally, there was joint family system and the members of a family pooled their resources to invest in business ventures.

Products like the muslin of Dhaka, calicos of Bengal, shawls of Kashmir, textiles and handicrafts, agricultural products like pepper, cinnamon, opium and indigo were exported to Europe, Middle East and South East Asia in return for gold and silver.

With the coming of Europeans in the 16th century trade and commerce was completely transformed. The Europeans concentrated mainly on spices, handicrafts, cotton clothes, indigo etc. Of all the European powers the British proved most strong and drove their competitors out of India. Slowly and gradually the British acquired political supremacy and hold over India and subverted the Indian economy according to their own needs. With the establishment of British rule in India the drain of wealth from India began. There was poor industrial infrastructure when the British left India.

After independence, India opted for planned economic development. The key concern was to develop thrust and heavy industries. With this there began rapid industrialization. Here, it is important to note that our economic policies were socially oriented and controlled by the state. India began to follow a mixed economy pattern. But in the late eighties and in the beginning of the 1990s, the Indian policy makers realized that state controlled economy was not able to produce desired results in almost 45 years. It was decided to pursue economic policy based on liberalization, privatization and globalization. In this era of liberalization, privatization and globalization, India has witnessed rapid growth in some sectors of economy, even though better results were expected when India began to follow the new economic policy.

The known Economic history of Indiabegins with the Indus Valley civilization. The Indus civilization's economy appears to have depended significantly on trade, which was facilitated by advances in transport. Around 600 BC, the Mahajanapadas minted punch-marked silver coins. The period was marked by intensive trade activity and urban development. By 300 B.C., the Maurya Empire united most of the Indian subcontinent. The political unity and military security allowed for a common economic system and enhanced trade and commerce, with increased agricultural productivity.

For the next 1500 years, India produced its classical civilizations such as the Rashtrakutas, Hoysalasand Western Gangas. During this period India is estimated to have had the largest economy of the ancient and medieval world between the 1st and 17th centuries AD, controlling between one third and one fourth of the world's wealth up to the time of the Marathas, from whence it rapidly declined during European rule.

India has followed central planning for most of its independent history, which have included extensive public ownership, regulation, red tape, and trade barriers. After the 1991 economic crisis, the central government launched economic liberalization. India has turned towards a more capitalistsystem and has emerged as one of the fastest growing large economies of the world.

Indus Valley civilization

The **Indus Valley Civilization (IVC)** was a Bronze Agecivilization (3300–1300 BCE; mature period 2600–1900 BCE) that was located in the northwestern region of the Indian subcontinent, consisting of what is now mainly modern-day Pakistan and northwest India. Flourishing around the Indus River basin, the civilization primarily centred along the Indus and the Punjab region, extending into the Ghaggar-Hakra River valley and the Ganges-Yamuna Doab. Geographically, the civilization was spread over an area of some 1,260,000 km², making it the largest ancient civilization in the world.

The Indus Valley is one of the world's earliest urban civilizations, along with its contemporaries, Mesopotamia and Ancient Egypt. At its peak, the Indus Civilization may have had a population of well over five million. Inhabitants of the ancient Indus river valley developed new techniques in metallurgy and handicraft (carneol products, seal carving) and produced copper, bronze, lead, and tin. The civilization is noted for its cities built of brick, roadside drainage system, and multistoried houses.

The mature phase of Indus Valley Civilization is known as the**Harappan Civilization**, as the first of its cities to be unearthed was located at Harappa, excavated in the 1920s in what was at the time the Punjab province of British India (now in Pakistan).

The Indus Valley civilization, the first known permanent and predominantly urban settlement that flourished between 2800 BC to 1800 BC boasted of an advanced and thriving economic system. Its citizens practiced agriculture, domesticated animals, made sharp tools and weapons from copper,bronze and tin and traded with other cities. Evidence of well laid streets, layouts, drainage system and water supply in the valley's major cities, Harappa, Lothal, Mohenjo-daro andRakhigarhi reveals their knowledge of urban planning. One of the theories about their end is that they eventually overused their resources, and slowly died out. Another theory is that invaders overran their civilization. RV 6.27.5: At Hariyupiyah (Harappa) he (Indrah) smote the vanguard of the Vrcivans, and the rear fled frightened."

Ancient and Medieval Characteristics

Though ancient India had a significant urban population, much of India's population resided in villages, whose economy was largely isolated and self-sustaining. Agriculture was the predominant occupation of the populace and satisfied a village's food requirements besides providing raw materials for hand based industries like textile, food processing and crafts. Besides farmers, other classes of people were barbers, carpenters, doctors (Ayurvedic practitioners), goldsmiths, weavers etc.

Religion

Religion, especially Hinduism, played an influential role in shaping economic activities. The Indian caste system castes and sub-castes functioned much like medieval European guilds, ensuring division of labour and provided for training of apprentices. The caste system restricted people from changing one's occupation and aspiring to an upper caste's lifestyle. Thus, a barber could not become a goldsmith and even a highly skilled carpenter could not aspire to the lifestyle or privileges enjoyed by a Kshatriya (person from a warrior class). This barrier to mobility on labour restricted economic prosperity to a few castes.

Pilgrimage towns like Allahabad, Benares, Nasik and Puri, mostly centred around rivers, developed into centres of trade and commerce. Religious functions, festivals and the practice of taking a pilgrimage resulted in a flourishing *pilgrimage economy*.

Family business

In the joint family system, members of a family pooled their resources to maintain the family and invest in business ventures. The system ensured younger members were trained and employed in the family business and the older and disabled persons would be supported by the family. The system, by preventing the agricultural land from being split ensured higher yield because of the benefits of scale. The system curbed members from taking initiative because of the support system and family or work.

Organizational entities

Along with the family-run business and individually owned business enterprises, ancient India possessed a number of other forms of engaging in business or collective activity, including the gana,pani, puga, vrata, sangha, nigama and sreni. Nigama, pani and sreni refer most often to economicorganizations of merchants, craftspeople and artisans, and perhaps even para-military entities. In particular, the sreni was a complex organizational entity that shares many similarities with moderncorporations, which were being used in India from around the 8th century BC until around the 10th century AD. The use of such entities in ancient India was widespread including virtually every kind of business, political and municipal activity.

The sreni was a separate legal entity which had the ability to hold property separately from its owners, construct its own rules for governing the behavior of its members, and for it to contract, sue and be sued in its own name. Some ancient sources such as *Laws of Manu* VIII and Chanakya's *Arthashastra*have rules for lawsuits between two or more sreni and some sources make reference to a government official (*Bhandagarika*) who worked as an arbitrator for disputes amongst sreni from at least the 6th century BC onwards. There were between 18 to 150 sreni at various times in ancient India covering both trading and craft activities. This level of specialization of occupations is indicative of a developed economy in which the sreni played a critical role. Some sreni could have over 1000 members as there were apparently no upper limits on the number of members.

The sreni had a considerable degree of centralised management. The headman of the sreni represented the interests of the sreni in the king's court and in many official business matters. The headman could also bind the sreni in contracts, set the conditions of work within the sreni, often received a higher salary, and was the administrative authority within the sreni. The headman was often selected via an election by the members of the sreni, who could also be removed from power by the general assembly. The headman often ran the enterprise with two to five executive officers, who were also elected by the assembly.

Coinage

Punch marked silver ingots, in circulation around the 5th century BC and the first metallic coins were minted around 6th century BC by the Mahajanapadas of the Gangetic plains were the earliest traces ofcoinage in India. While India's many kingdoms and rulers issued coins, barter was still widely prevalent. Villages paid a portion of their agricultural produce as revenue while its craftsmen received a stipend out of the crops at harvest time for their services. Each village, as an economic unit, was mostly self-sufficient.

GDP estimate

According to economic historian Angus Maddison in his book *Contours of the world economy, 1-2030 AD: essays in macro-economic history*, India had the world's largest economy during the years 1 AD and 1000 AD.

Maurya Empire

During the Maurya Empire (c. 321-185 BC), there were a number of important changes and developments to the Indian economy. It was the first time most of India was unified under one ruler. With an empire in place, the trade routes throughout India became more secure thereby reducing the risk associated with the transportation of goods. The empire spent considerabie resources building roads and maintaining them throughout India. The improved infrastructure combined with increased security, greater uniformity in measurements, and increasing usage of coins as currency enhanced trade. During this time, the *Arthasastra* ("science of the state") was written by the Chanakya, an adviser to Chandragupta Maurya. The Arthasastra is one of the most important ancient texts on economics, politics and administration. It was a treatise on how to maintain and expand power, obtain material gain, and administer an empire. It covers both theory and implementation and contains many clear and detailed rules regarding the governing of an empire. The exhaustive account of the economic ideas embedded in the Arthasastra has been given by Ratan Lal Basu in his famous work "Ancient Indian Economic Thought, Relevance For Today".

The economic situation in the Maurya Empire is comparable to the Roman Empire several centuries later, which both had extensive trade connections and both had organizations similar to corporations. While Rome had organizational entities which were largely used for public state-driven projects, Maurya India had numerous private commercial entities which existed purely for private commerce. This was due to the Mauryas having to contend with pre-existing sreni hence they were more concerned about keeping the support of these pre-existing private commercial entities. The Romans did not have such pre-existing entities to contend with; hence, they were able to prevent such entities from developing.

Mughal Empire

During the Mughal period (1526–1858) India went from the first to the second-largest economy in the world. The gross domestic product of

India in the 16th century was estimated at about 25.1% of the world economy.

An estimate of India's pre-colonial economy puts the annual revenue of Emperor Akbar's treasury in 1600 at £17.5 million (in contrast to the entire treasury of Great Britain two hundred years later in 1800, which totalled £16 million). The gross domestic product of Mughal India in 1600 was estimated at about 24.3% the world economy, the second largest in the world.

By this time the Mughal Empire had expanded to include almost 90 per cent of South Asia, and enforced a uniform customs and tax-administration system. In 1700 the exchequer of the Emperor Aurangzeb reported an annual revenue of more than £100 million.

Maratha Empire

In the 18th century, Mughals were replaced by the Maratha Empire in much of India, Maratha rule expanded to almost 2.8 million km². While the other small regional states who were mostly late Mughal tributary states such as the Nawabs in the north and the Nizam in south India remained. Tax administration system in India was collected by officers of the Maratha empire, however, the Mughal tax administration system was left largely intact.

By this time India again had the largest economy in the world, with a (27.3%) share of world GDP, followed by Manchu China and Western Europe. Nevertheless, a devastating famine broke out in the eastern coast in early 1770s killing 5 per cent of the national population.

British rule

After gaining the right to collect revenue in Bengal in 1765, the East India Company largely ceased importing gold and silver, which it had hitherto used to pay for goods shipped back to Britain. In addition, as under Mughal rule, land revenue collected in the Bengal Presidency helped finance the Company's wars in other part of India. Consequently, in the period 1760-1800, Bengal's money supply was greatly diminished; furthermore, the closing of some local mints and close supervision of the rest, the fixing of exchange rates, and the standardization of coinage, paradoxically, added to the economic downturn. During the period, 1780–1860, India changed from being an exporter of processed goods for which it received payment in bullion, to being an exporter of raw materials and a buyer of manufactured goods. More specifically, in the 1750s, mostly fine cotton and silk was exported from India to markets in Europe, Asia, and

Africa; by the second quarter of the 19th century, raw materials, which chiefly consisted of raw cotton, opium, and indigo, accounted for most of India's exports. Also, from the late 18th century British cotton mill industry began to lobby the government to both tax Indian imports and allow them access to markets in India. Starting in the 1830s, British textiles began to appear in—and soon to inundate—the Indian markets, with the value of the textile imports growing from £5.2 million 1850 to £18.4 million in 1896.

The British colonial rule created an institutional environment that did stabilise the law and order situation to a large extent. The British foreign policies however stifled the trade with rest of the world. They created a well-developed system of railways, telegraphs and a modern legal system. The infrastructure the British created was mainly geared towards the exploitation of resources ofin the world and totally stagnant, with industrial development stalled, agriculture unable to feed a rapidly accelerating population. They were subject to frequent famines, had one of the world's lowest life expectancies, suffered from pervasive malnutrition and were largely illiterate.

GDP estimates

An estimate by Angus Maddison argues that India's share of the world income went from 27.3% in 1700 . While Indian leaders during the Independence struggle and *left-nationalist* economic historianshave blamed the colonial rule for the dismal state of India's economy, a broader macroeconomic view of India during this period reveals that there were segments of both growth and decline, resulting from changes brought about by colonialism and a world that was moving towards industrialization andeconomic integration.

The fall of the Rupee

After its victory in the Franco-Prussian War(1870–71), Germany extracted a huge indemnity from France of £200,000,000, and then moved to join Britain on a gold standard for currency. France, the US and other industrializing countries followed Germany in adopting a gold standard throughout the 1870s. At the same time, countries, such as Japan, which did not have the necessary access to gold or those, such as India, which were subject to imperial policies that determined that they did not move to a gold standard, remained mostly on a silver standard. A huge divide between silver-based and gold-based economies resulted. The worst affected were economies with a silver standard that traded mainly with economies with a gold standard. With discovery of more and more silver reserves, those currencies based on gold continued to rise in value and those based on silver were declining due to demonetization of silver. For India which carried out most of its trade with gold based countries, especially Britain, the impact of this shift was profound. As the price of silver continued to fall, so too did the exchange value of the rupee, when measured against sterling.

The gold exchange standard (1870–1914)

Towards the end of the 19th century, some of the remaining silver standard countries began to peg their silver coin units to the gold standards of the United Kingdom or the USA. In 1898, British Indiapegged the silver rupee to the pound sterling at a fixed rate of 1s 4d, while in 1906, the Straits Settlements adopted a gold exchange standard against the pound sterling with the silver Straits dollar being fixed at 2s 4d.

At the turn of the century, the Philippines pegged the silver Peso/ dollar to the US dollar at 50 cents. A similar pegging at 50 cents occurred at around the same time with the silver Peso of Mexico and the silver Yen of Japan. When Siam adopted a gold exchange standard in 1908, this left only China and Hong Kong on the silver standard.

Adopting the gold standard many European nations changed the name of their currency from Rixdaler(Sweden and Danemark) or Gulden (Austria-Hungary) to Crown, since the former ones were traditionally associated with silver coins and the latter with gold coins.

Economy of India under Company rule

During this period, the East India Company began tax administration reforms in a fast expanding empire spread over 250 million acres (1,000,000 km^2), or 35 per cent of Indian domain. Indirect rule was also established on protectorates and buffer states. China was the world's largest economy followed by India and France. The Company treasury reported annual revenue of £111 million in circa 1800 . This needs to converted to Indian Rupees with the falling price of Rupee to assess the impact on Indian economy. Almost all of the Indian land revenues were diverted by the Company to help the British Crown defend herself in the Napoleonic Wars.

China was the world's largest economy followed by India and France. The gross domestic product of India in 1825 was estimated at about 50 per cent that of China. British cotton exports reach 3 per cent of the Indian market by 1825.(pdf) China was the world's largest economy followed by the UK and India. Industrial revolution in the UK catapulted the nation to the top league of Europe for the first time ever. During this period, British foreign and economic policies began treating India as an unequal partner for the first time. English replaced Persian as the official language of India. The gross domestic product of India in 1850 was estimated at about 40 per cent that of China. British cotton exports reach 30 per cent of the Indian market by 1850.

Ray (2009) raises three basic questions about the 19th-century cotton textile industry in Bengal: when did the industry begin to decay, what was the extent of its decay during the early 19th century, and what were the factors that led to this? Since there is no data on production, Ray uses the industry's market performance and its consumption of raw materials. Ray challenges the prevailing belief that the industry's permanent decline started in the late 18th century or the early 19th century. The decline actually started in the mid-1820s. The pace of its decline was, however, slow though steady at the beginning, but reached crisis point by 1860, when 563,000 workers lost their jobs. Ray estimates that the industry shrank by about 28% by 1850. However, it survived in the high-end and low-end domestic markets. Ray agrees that British discriminatory policies undoubtedly depressed the industry's export outlet, but suggests its decay is better explained by technological innovations in Britain. The Economy of India under Company rule describes the economy of those regions (contemporaneously British India) that fell under Company rule in India during the years 1756 to 1857.

Land revenue

In the remnant of the Mughal revenue system existing in pre-1765 Bengal, zamindars, or "land holders," collected revenue on behalf of the Mughal emperor, whose representative, or diwansupervised their activities. In this system, the assortment of rights associated with land were not possessed by a "land owner," but rather shared by the several parties with stake in the land, including the peasant cultivator, the *zamindar*, and the state. The *zamindar* served as an intermediary who procured economic rent from the cultivator, and after withholding a percentage for his own expenses, made available the rest, as revenue to the state. Under the Mughal system, the land itself belonged to the state and not to the *zamindar*, who could transfer only his right to collect rent. On being awarded the *diwani* or overlordship of Bengal following the Battle of Buxar in 1764, the East India Comı any found itself short of trained administrators, especially those famil ar with local custom and law; tax collection was consequently farmed out. This uncertain foray into land taxation by the Company, may have gravely worsened the impact of a famine that struck Bengal in 1769-70 in which between seven and ten million people—or between a quarter and third of the presidency's population—may have died. However, the company provided little relief either through reduced taxation or by relief efforts, and the economic and cultural impact of the famine was felt decades later, even becoming, a century later, the subject of Bankim Chandra Chatterjee's novel *Anandamath.*

In 1772, under Warren Hastings, the East India Company took over revenue collection directly in theBengal Presidency (then Bengal and Bihar), establishing a Board of Revenue with offices in Calcutta and Patna, and moving the existing Mughal revenue records from Murshidabad to Calcutta. In 1773, after Oudh ceded the tributary state of Benaras, the revenue collection system was extended to the territory with a Company Resident in charge. The following year—with a view to preventing corruption—Company *district collectors*, who were then responsible for revenue collection for an entire district, were replaced with provincial councils at Patna, Murshidabad and Calcutta and with Indian collectors working within each district. The title, "collector," reflected "the centrality of land revenue collection to government in India: it was the government's primary function and it moulded the institutions and patterns of administration."

The Company inherited a revenue collection system from the Mughals in which the heaviest proportion of the tax burden fell on the cultivators, with one-third of the production reserved for imperial entitlement; this pre-colonial system became the Company revenue policy's baseline. There was vast variation across India in the methods by which the revenues were collected; with this complication in mind, a Committee of Circuit toured the districts of expanded Bengal presidency in order to make a five-year settlement, consisting of five-yearly inspections and temporary tax farming. In their overall approach to revenue policy, Company officials were guided by two goals: preserving as much as possible the balance of rights and obligations that were traditionally claimed by the farmers who cultivated the land and the various intermediaries who collected tax on the state's behalf and who reserved a cut for themselves and identifying those sectors of the rural economy that would maximize both revenue and security. Although their first revenue settlement turned out to be essentially the same as the more informal previous Mughal one, the Company had created a foundation for the growth of both information and bureaucracy.

In 1793, the new Governor-General, Lord Cornwallis, promulgated the permanent settlement of land revenues in the presidency, the first socio-economic regulation in colonial India. It was named*permanent* because it fixed the land tax in perpetuity in return for landed property rights for zamindars; it simultaneously defined the nature of land ownership in the presidency and gave individuals and families separate property rights in occupied land. Since the revenue was fixed in perpetuity, it was fixed at a high level, which in Bengal amounted to £3 million at 1789-90 prices. According to one estimate, this was 20% higher than the revenue demand before 1757. Over the next century, partly as a result of land surveys, court rulings and property sales, the change was given practical dimension. An influence on the development of this revenue policy were economic theories which regarded agriculture as the engine of economic development and consequently stressed the fixing of revenue demands in order to encourage growth. The expectation behind the permanent settlement was that knowledge of a fixed government demand would encourage the zamindars to increase both their average outcrop and the land under cultivation, since they would be able to retain the profits from the increased output; in addition, it was envisaged that land would become a marketable form of property that could be purchased, sold or mortgaged. A feature of this economic rationale was the additional expectation that the zamindars, recognizing their own best interest, would not make unreasonable demands on the peasantry.

However, these expectations were not realized in practice and in many regions of Bengal, the peasants bore the brunt of the increased demand, there being little protection for their traditional rights in the new legislation. Forced labor of the peasants by the zamindars became more prevalent as cash crops were cultivated to meet the Company revenue demands. Although commercialized cultivation was not new to the region, it had now penetrated deeper into village society and made it more vulnerable to market forces. The zamindars themselves were often unable to meet the increased demands that the Company had placed on them; consequently, many defaulted, and by one estimate, up to one-third of their lands were auctioned during the first three decades following the permanent settlement. The new owners were often Brahmin and Kayastha employees of the Company who had a good grasp of the new system, and in many cases, had prospered under it.

Since the zamindars were never able to undertake costly improvements to the land envisaged under the Permanent Settlement, some of which required the removal of the existing farmers, they soon became rentiers who lived off the rent from their tenant farmers. In many areas, especially northern Bengal, they had to increasingly share the revenue with intermediate tenure holders, called *jotedars*, who supervised farming in the villages. Consequently, unlike the contemporaneous Enclosure movement in Britain, agriculture in Bengal remained the province of the subsistence farming of innumerable small paddy fields.

The zamindari system was one of two principal revenue settlements undertaken by the Company in India. In southern India, Thomas Munro, who would later become Governor of Madras, promoted the*ryotwari* system, in which the government settled land-revenue directly with the peasant farmers, or*ryots*. This was, in part, a consequence of the turmoil of the Anglo-Mysore Wars, which had prevented the emergence of a class of large landowners; in addition, Munro and others felt that *ryotwari*was closer to traditional practice in the region and ideologically more progressive, allowing the benefits of Company rule to reach the lowest levels of rural society. At the heart of the *ryotwari* system was a particular theory of economic rent—and based on David Ricardo's Law of Rent—promoted by utilitarianJames Mill who formulated the Indian revenue policy between 1819 and 1830. "He believed that the government was the ultimate lord of the soil and should not renounce its right to 'rent', *i.e.* the profit left over on richer soil when wages and other working expenses had been settled." Another keystone of the new system of temporary settlements was the classification of agricultural fields according to soil type and produce, with average rent rates fixed for the period of the settlement. According to Mill, taxation of land rent would promote efficient agriculture and simultaneously prevent the emergence of a "parasitic landlord class." Mill advocated *ryotwari* settlements which consisted of government measurement and assessment of each plot (valid for 20 or 30 years) and subsequent taxation which was dependent on the fertility of the soil. The taxed amount was nine-tenths of the "rent" in the early 19th century and gradually fell afterwards. However, in spite of the appeal of the *ryotwari*system's abstract principles, class hierarchies in southern Indian villages had not entirely disappeared—for example village headmen continued to hold sway—and peasant cultivators sometimes came to experience revenue demands they could not meet. In the 1850s, a scandal erupted when it was discovered that some Indian revenue agents of the Company were using torture to meet the Company's revenue demands.

Land revenue settlements constituted a major administrative activity of the various governments in India under Company rule. In all areas other than the Bengal Presidency, land settlement work involved a continually repetitive process of surveying and measuring plots, assessing their quality, and recording landed rights, and constituted a large proportion of the work of Indian Civil Service officers working for the government. After the Company lost its trading rights, it became the single most important source of government revenue, roughly half of overall revenue in the middle of the 19th century; even so, between the years 1814 and 1859, the government of India ran debts in 33 years. With expanded dominion, even during non-deficit years, there was just enough money to pay the salaries of a threadbare administration, a skeleton police force, and the army.

Trade

After gaining the right to collect revenue in Bengal in 1765, theEast India Company largely ceased importing gold and silver, which it had hitherto used to pay for goods shipped back to Britain. In addition, as under Mughal rule, land revenue collected in the Bengal Presidency helped finance the Company's wars in other part of India. Consequently, in the period 1760-1800, Bengal's money supply was greatly diminished; furthermore, the closing of some local mints and close supervision of the rest, the fixing of exchange rates, and the standardization of coinage, paradoxically, added to the economic downturn. During the period, 1780–1860, India changed from being an exporter of processed goods for which it received payment in bullion, to being an exporter of raw materials and a buyer of manufactured goods. More specifically, in the 1750s, mostly fine cotton and silk was exported from India to markets in Europe, Asia, and Africa; by the second quarter of the 19th century, raw materials, which chiefly consisted of raw cotton, opium, and indigo, accounted for most of India's exports. Also, from the late 18th century British cotton mill industry began to lobby the government to both tax Indian imports and allow them access to markets in India. Starting in the 1830s, British textiles began to appear in—and soon to inundate—the Indian markets, with the value of the textile imports growing from £5.2 million 1850 to £18.4 million in 1896. The American Civil War too would have a major impact on India's cotton economy: with the outbreak of the war, American cotton was no longer available to British manufacturers; consequently, demand for Indian cotton soared, and the prices soon quadrupled. This led many farmers in India to switch to cultivating cotton as a quick cash crop; however, with the end of the war in 1865, the demand plummeted again, creating another downturn in the agricultural economy.

At this time, the East India Company's trade with China began to grow as well. In the early 19th century demand for Chinese tea had greatly increased in Britain; since the money supply in India was restricted and the Company was indisposed to shipping bullion from Britain, it decided upon opium, which had a large underground market in China and which was grown in many parts of India, as the most profitable form of payment. However, since the Chinese authorities had banned the importation and consumption of opium, the Company engaged them in the First Opium War, and at its conclusion, under the Treaty of Nanjing, gained access to five Chinese ports, Guangzhou, Xiamen,Fuzhou, Shanghai, and Ningbo; in addition, Hong Kong was ceded to the British Crown. Towards the end of the second quarter of the 19th century, opium export constituted 40% of India's exports.

Another major, though erratic, export item was indigo dye, which was extracted from natural indigo, and which came to be grown in Bengal and northern Bihar. In late 17th and early 18th century Europe, blue apparel was favored as a fashion, and blue uniforms were common in the military; consequently, the demand for the dye was high. In 1788, the East India Company offered advances to ten British planters to grow indigo; however, since the new (landed) property rights defined in thePermanent Settlement, didn't allow them, as Europeans, to buy agricultural land, they had to in turn offer cash advances to local peasants, and sometimes coerce them, to grow the crop. The European demand for the dye, however, proved to be unstable, and both creditors and cultivators bore the risk of the market crashes in 1827 and 1847. The peasant discontent in Bengal eventually led to the *Indigo rebellion* in 1859-60 and to the end of indigo production there. In Bihar, however, indigo production continued well into the 20th century; the centre of indigo production there, Champarandistrict, became the staging ground, in 1917, for Mohandas Karamchand Gandhi's first experiment innon-violent resistance against the British Raj.

Economy of India under the British Raj

The formal dissolution of the declining Mughal Dynasty heralded a change in British treatment of Indian subjects. During the British Raj, massive railway projects were begun in earnest and government jobs and guaranteed pensions attracted a large number of upper caste Hindus into the civil service for the first time. British cotton exports reach 55 per cent of the Indian market by 1875. Industrial production as it developed in European factories was unknown in India until the 1850s when the first cotton mills were opened in Bombay, posing a challenge to the cottage-based home production system based on family labour.

The worldwide Great Depression of 1929 had a small direct impact on traditional India, with relatively little impact on the modern secondary sector. The government did little to alleviate distress, and was focused mostly on shipping gold to Britain. The worst consequences involved deflation, which increased the burden of the debt on villagers while lowering the cost of living. In terms of volume of total economic output, there was no decline between 1929 and 1934. Falling prices for jute (and also wheat) hurt larger growers. The worst hit sector was jute, based in Bengal, which was an important element in overseas trade; it had prospered in the 1920s but was hard hit in the 1930s. In terms of employment, there was some decline, while agriculture and small-scale industry also exhibited gains. The most successful new industry was sugar, which had meteoric growth in the 1930s.

The newly independent but weak Union government's treasury reported annual revenue of £334 million in 1950. In contrast, Nizam Asaf Jah VII of south India was widely reported to have a fortune of almost £668 million then. About one-sixth of the national population were urban by 1950. A US Dollar was exchanged at 4.79 Rupees.

The Economy of India under the British Raj describes the economy of India during the years of the British *Raj* from 1858 to 1947.

In the second half of the 19th century, both the direct administration of India by the British crown and the technological change ushered in by the industrial revolution, had the effect of closely intertwining the economies of India and Great Britain. In fact many of the major changes in transport and communications (that are typically associated with Crown Rule of India) had already begun before the Revolt of 1857. Since Dalhousie had embraced the technological change then rampant in Great Britain, India too saw rapid development of all those technologies. Railways, roads, canals, and bridges were rapidly built in India and telegraph links equally rapidly established in order that raw materials, such as cotton, from India's hinterland could be transported more efficiently to ports, such as Bombay, for subsequent export to England. Likewise, finished goods from England, were transported back, just as efficiently, for sale in the burgeoning Indian markets. However, unlike Britain itself, where the market risks for the infrastructure development were borne by private investors, in India, it was the taxpayers—primarily farmers and farm-labourers—who endured the risks, which, in the end, amounted to £50 million. In spite of these costs, very little skilled employment was created for Indians. By 1920, with the fourth largest railway network in the world and a history of 60 years of its construction, only ten per cent of the "superior posts" in the Indian Railways were held by Indians.

The rush of technology was also changing the agricultural economy in India: by the last decade of the 19th century, a large fraction of some raw materials—not only cotton, but also some food-grains—were being exported to faraway markets. Consequently, many small farmers, dependent on the whims of those markets, lost land, animals, and equipment to money-lenders. More tellingly, the latter half of the 19th century also saw an increase in the number of large-scale famines in India. Although famines were not new to the subcontinent, these were particularly severe, with tens of millions dying, and with many critics, both British and Indian, laying the blame at the doorsteps of the lumbering colonial administrations.

Colonial rule brought a major change in the taxation environment from revenue taxes to property taxes resulting in mass impoverishment and destitution of the great majority of farmers. It also created an institutional environment that, on paper, guaranteed property rights among the colonizers, encouragedfree trade, and created a single currency with fixed exchange rates, standardized weights and measures, capital markets, a well-developed system of railways and telegraphs, a civil service that aimed to be free from political interference, and a common-law, adversarial legal system. India's colonisation by the British coincided with major changes in the world economy—industrialisation, and significant growth in production and trade. However, at the end of colonial rule, India inherited an economy that was one of the poorest in the developing world, with industrial development stalled, agriculture unable to feed a rapidly growing population, one of the world's lowest life expectancies, and low rates of literacy.

An estimate by Cambridge University historian Angus Maddison reveals that India's share of the world income fell from 22.6% in 1700, comparable to Europe's share of 23.3%, to a low of 3.8% in 1952. While Indian leaders during the Independence struggle, and left-nationalist economic historians have blamed colonial rule for the dismal state of India's economy in its aftermath, a broader macroeconomicview of India during this period reveals that there were sectors of growth and decline, resulting from changes brought about by colonialism and a world that was moving towards industrialisation andeconomic integration.

Economic impact of British imperialism

Debate continues about the economic impact of British imperialism on India. The issue was actually raised by conservative British politician Edmund Burke who in the 1780s vehemently attacked the East India Company, claiming that Warren Hastings and other top officials had ruined the Indian economy and society. Indian historian Rajat Kanta Ray (1998) continues this line of reasoning, saying the new economy brought by the British in the 18th century was a form of plunder and a catastrophe for the traditional economy of Mughal India. (Economic Drain Theory) Ray believes that British depleted the food and money stocks and imposed high taxes that helped cause the terrible famine of 1770, which killed a third of the people of Bengal.

P. J. Marshall, a British historian known for his work on the British empire, has a reinterpretation of the view that the prosperity of the formerly benign Mughal rule gave way to poverty and anarchy. Marshall argues the British takeover did not make any sharp break with the past. British control was delegated largely through regional rulers and was sustained by a generally prosperous economy for the rest of the 18th century, except the frequent famines with very high fatality rate. Marshall notes the British raised revenue through local tax administrators and kept the old Mughal rates of taxation. Instead of the Indian nationalist account of the British as alien aggressors, seizing power by brute force and impoverishing all of India, Marshall presents a British nationalist interpretation in which the British were not in full control but instead were controllers in what was primarily an Indian play and in which their ability to keep power depended upon excellent cooperation with Indian elites. Marshall admits that much of his interpretation is still rejected by many historians.

Nehruvian Socialist rate of growth

The "Nehruvian Socialist rate of growth" is used to refer to the low annual growth rate of the economy of India before 1991. It stagnated at around 3.5% from 1950s to 1980s, while per capita income growth averaged extremely low 1.3% a year. At the same time, South Korea grew by 10% and Taiwan by 12%. This phenomenon was called the "Hindu rate of growth", by the leading Indian economist Raj Krishna.

The Economic History of India and Economy of India [from 1951-1996]

Before the last decade, the 19902 s, India was probably on the short list of almost every economist outside of India of the countries with the worst economic systems. India had and probably still has a parasitical class of politicians and bureaucrats that micromanage the economy in the interests of their class. They hypocritically aver that they are doing what they are doing in the interest of the people of India. There has been some official allegiance to socialism with a goal of achieving it through Stalinist central planning. The fact that the result has been some horrible mixture of state capitalism and moribund corporatism is usually attributed to incompetence and ineptitude on the part of the bureaucracy. The Indian American economist Jagdish Baghwati of Columbia University remarked that he agreed with the view that "India's misfortune was to have brilliant economists: an affliction that the Far Eastern super-performers were spared." The policies implemented by the Government of India before the last decade were brilliant only in maintaining the power and influence of the bureaucrats. Judged with respect to an promoting the welfare of the Indian people those policies were ridiculously bad, to the point of stupidity.

The bureaucracy has been rather competent in generating excuses for the failure of their policies. One of those exceuses has been that there is a Hindu rate of growth that is significantly lower than the rate of growth that other countries could achieve. What the bureacrats dare not say is that in maintaining a pool of economic rents the bureaucrats' policies were an outstanding success.

The disappointing economic progress in India up to 1990 cannot be attributed to any shortcoming in talent among the Indian people or the impediments resulting from Indian cultures. Indians out from under the oppression of the bureaucracy of the Indian Government have succeeded spectacularly in professions and business.

Probably the misguidance of India development can be attributed to India's first prime minister, Jawarharlal Nehru. Nehru chose the goal of economic self-sufficiency with economic development to be achieved by central planning modeled on that of the Soviet Union. By cutting off imports India gave a protected market to domestic producers. India got domestic production but it was production of low quality, obsolete products. The policies stifled economic growth and India, with its high level of population and poverty, could ill afford low rates of economic growth.

The two makes of automobiles produced in India, copied from models of the British Austin and Hillman of the 19502 s, remained unchanged for more than forty years.

The planning and adminstration of the economic did not emerge full blown. The first five year plan (1951-55) called for the planned development of only a few industries, the ones that private industry had not developed for one reason or another. In the first five year plan the other industries were left to the market.

The second five year plan (1956-1961), the product of P.C. Mahalanobis' work, was more inteventionist. It tried to implement the elements of British socialism and combine them with the tenets of Mahatma Gandhi. It sought to eliminate the importation of consumer goods, particularly luxuries, by means of high tariffs and low quotas or banning some items altogether. The large enterprises in seventeen industries were nationalized. License were required for starting new companies, for producing new products or expanding production capacities. This is when India got its License Raj, the bureaucratic control over the economy. Not only did the Indian Government require businesses get bureaucratic approval for expanding productive capacity, busineeses had to have bureaucratic approval for laying off workers and for shutting down. When a business was losing money the Government would prevent them from shutting down and to keep the business going would provide assistance and subsidies. When a business was hopeless an owner might take away, illegally, all the equipment that could be moved and disappear themselves. In such cases the Government would try to keep the business functioning by means of subsidies to the employees. One can imagine how chaotic and unproductive a business would be under such conditions.

Government planning also involved requiring businesses to produce in particular areas, usually economically backward areas. It also might require the production of certain goods such as cheap cloth for the poor.

The Indian Economic Plans had to be financed and this often meant taking resources away from agriculture and giving them to pet industries that were not viable on there own. Ultimately this meant starving agriculture to feed inefficient industries the Government favored. Such a program was not likely to alleviate poverty and so in 1971, under Nehru's daughter, Indira Gandhi, the Government tried to eliminate poverty by promoting small, labor intensive enterprises.

The net effect of the Government programs was to take away resources from agriculture in the countryside to give it to favored businesses in the cities. When the effects on agriculture and the countryside became significant the plan added programs to help the countryside (labor intensive small businesses) and programs to aid agriculture such as a fertilizer subsidy. These programs to help agriculture and the countryside generally came from resources which the Government took away from agriculture and the countryside. The fertilizer subsidy may have been of greater benefit to the wealthier farmers than to the poorer farmers.

India's output did grow but not as much as did that of other countries in the region. The Government of India generally takes credit for growth, but when India's performance is compared to that of other countries one sees that the Government's contribution to growth was negative. The followi shows the magnitude of the shortfall in growth that India's oppressive system is responsible for.

With the top performers achieving a growth rate of industrial production of about ten percent while India achieved a growth rate of only at most about five percent the cost of the License Raj to India's growth rate was about five percent, or half the rate of growth.

One of the most wonderful things to happen to the world was the genetic development of high-yielding grain varieties, the Green Revolution. This development probably put an end to famine from natural causes. Between 1970 and 1989 agricultural production in India did grow but the rate of increase was only 2.1 percent per year whereas over the same per period the annual rates of growth of farm output in Indonesia, Malaysia, the Philippines and Thailand were 3.7%, 4.7%, 3.6% and 4.5%, respectively. Again the cost of the License Raj to growth in India was about half the rate of growth. The cost of the License Raj more importantly is in the slower pace of alleviating poverty.

Socialist reforms (1950–1975)

USA was the world's largest economy followed by the USSR, Japan, Germany and China. The gross domestic product of India in 1975 was estimated at about 5 per cent that of the USA.

Before independence a large share of tax revenue was generated by the land tax, which was in effect a lump sum tax on land. Since then land taxes have steadily declined as a share of revenues and completely replaced by sales taxes.

Moreover, the structural economic problems inherited at independence were exacerbated by the costs associated with the partition of British India, which had resulted in about 2 to 4 million refugees fleeing past each other across the new borders between India and Pakistan. The settlement of refugees was a considerable financial strain. Partition also divided India into complementary economic zones. Under the British, jute and cotton were grown in the eastern part of Bengal, the area that became East Pakistan (after 1971, Bangladesh), but processing took place mostly in the western part of Bengal, which became the Indian state of West Bengal in 1947. As a result, after independence India had to employ land previously used for food production to cultivate cotton and jute for its mills.

Government was assigned an important role in the process of alleviating poverty, and since 1951 a series of plans had guided the country's economic development. Although there was considerable growth in the 1950s, the long-term rates of *real* growth were less positive than India's politicians desired and much less than those of many other Asian countries.

Toward the end of Nehru's term as prime minister, India would continue to face serious food shortages despite hoped for progress and increases in agricultural production. There was mass starvation in states like Bihar due to socialist controls on the economy. Farmers as well as industrialists were ham-strung with controls (License Raj) on their freedom to run their respective businesses.

Despite such atrocious conditions in the country Nehru's popularity remained unaffected because of the larger-than-life image and the personality cult that was promoted by the state controlled mass media.

Since 1950, India ran into trade deficits that increased in magnitude in the 1960s. The Government of India had a budget deficit problem and therefore could not borrow money from abroad or from the private sector, which itself had a negative savings rate. As a result, the government issued bonds to the RBI, which increased the money supply, leading to inflation. In 1966, foreign aid, which was hitherto a key factor in preventing devaluation of the rupee was finally cut off and India was told it had to liberalise its restrictions on trade before foreign aid would again materialise. The response was the politically unpopular step of devaluation accompanied by liberalisation. The Indo-Pakistani War of 1965led the US and other countries friendly towards Pakistan to withdraw foreign aid to India, which further necessitated devaluation. Defence spending in 1965/1966 was 24.06% of total expenditure, the highest in the period from 1965 to 1989. This, accompanied by the drought of 1965/1966, led to a severe devaluation of the rupee. Current GDP per capita grew 33% in the Sixties reaching a peak growth of 142% in the Seventies, decelerating sharply back to 41% in the Eighties and 20% in the Nineties.

From FY 1951 to FY 1979, the economy grew at an average rate of about 3.1 percent a year in constant prices, or at an annual rate of 1.0 percent per capita. During this period, industry grew at an average rate of 4.5 percent a year, compared with an annual average of 3.0 percent for agriculture. They managed to tamp down on the natural business acumen and abilities of the population, yet some economists differed over the relative importance of those factors.

Structural deficiencies, such as the need for institutional changes in agriculture and the inefficiency of much of the centrally directed industrial sector, also contributed to economic stagnation. Some other excuses that were generally offered were - War with China in 1962 and with Pakistan in

1965 and 1971; a flood of refugees from East Pakistan in 1971; droughts in 1965, 1966, 1971, and 1972;currency devaluation in 1966; and the first world oil crisis, in 1973-1974, all jolted the economy.

This is a chart of trend of gross domestic product of India at market prices estimated by *Ministry of Statistics and Programme Implementation* with figures in millions of Indian Rupees. See also the IMF database.

Year	Gross Domestic Product	US Dollar Exchange	Per Capita Income (as % of USA)
1950	100,850	4.79 Indian Rupees	1.56
1955	110,300	4.79 Indian Rupees	2.33
1960	174,070	4.77 Indian Rupees	2.88
1965	280,160	4.78 Indian Rupees	3.26
1970	462,490	7.56 Indian Rupees	2.23
1975	842,210	8.39 Indian Rupees	2.18

The Union government treasury reported annual revenue of £5-6 billion in 1975 thus registering an average annual growth of almost 12 per cent during the third quarter of 20th century. Nevertheless, prime minister Indira proclaimed emergency and suspended the Constitution in 1975. About one-fifth of the national population were urban by 1975.

1975 - 2000

Economic liberalization in India in the 1990s and first decade of the 21st century led to large changes in the economy.

This is a chart of trend of gross domestic product and foreign trade of India at market prices estimated by*Ministry of Statistics and Programme Implementation* with figures in millions of Indian Rupees. See also the IMF database.

Year	Gross Domestic Product	Exports	Imports	US Dollar Exchange	Inflation Index (2000=100)	Per Capita Income (as % of USA)
1975	842,210			8.39 Indian Rupees		2.18

Conted.

Year	Gross Domestic Product	Exports	Imports	US Dollar Exchange	Inflation Index (2000=100)	Per Capita Income (as % of USA)
1980	1,380,334	90,290	135,960	7.86 Indian Rupees	18	2.08
1985	2,729,350	149,510	217,540	12.36 Indian Rupees	28	1.60
1990	5,542,706	406,350	486,980	17.50 Indian Rupees	42	1.56
1995	11,571,882	1,307,330	1,4[illegible]9,530	32.42 Indian Rupees	69	1.32
2000	20,791,898	2,781,260	2,975,230	44.94 Indian Rupees	100	1.26

About one-fourth of the national population was urban by 2000.

2000 - present

The gross domestic product of India in 2007 was estimated at about 8 per cent that of the USA. National Democratic Alliance led by Bharatiya Janata Party (BJP), was in helm of economic affairs from 1998 to 2004. During this period there were two finance ministers, viz., Yashwant Sinha (1998–2003) and Jaswant Singh (2003–2004). The main economic achievement of the government was the universal license in telecommunication field, which allows CDMA license holders to provide GSM services and vice versa. NDA started off the Golden Quadrilateral road network connecting main metros of Delhi, Chennai, Mumbai and Kolkata. The project, still under construction, was one of the most ambitious infrastructure projects of independent India. Simultaneously, North-South and East-West highway projects were planned and construction was started.

The top 3 per cent of the population still contribute 50 per cent of the GDP and benefits of economic growth have not trickled down. Education for all is still an unrealised dream in India. This was made a fundamental right by amending the constitution of India and huge amount of money was pumped into the project under the name of Sarva Shiksha Abhiyan. This project met with limited success. Graduate unemployment was estimated at 34 million nationwide.

Currently, the economic activity in India has taken on a dynamic character which is at once curtailed by creaky infrastructure, for example dilapidated roads and severe shortages of electricity, and cumbersome justice system yet at the same time accelerated by the sheer enthusiasm and ambition of industrialists and the populace. The upward economic cycle in India is expected in short time to effectively address the shortcomings and bottlenecks of the infrastructure. The fast changing, seemingly chaotic and unsettled situation is much more hopeful and reassuring than the socialist morass that was the Nehru and Indira Gandhi legacy.

This is a chart of trend of gross domestic product and foreign trade of India at market pricesestimated by *Ministry of Statistics and Programme Implementation* with figures in millions of Indian Rupees. See also the IMF database.

Year	Gross Domestic Product	Exports	Imports	US Dollar Exchange	Inflation Index (2000=100)	Per Capita Income (as % of USA)
2000	20,791,898	2,781,260	2,975,230	44.94 Indian Rupees	100	1.26
2005	34,195,278			44.09 Indian Rupees	121	1.64
2010	66,911,800			45.83 Indian Rupees	126	2.01

For purchasing power parity comparisons, the US Dollar is exchanged at 9.46 Rupees only. Despite steady growth and continuous reforms since the Nineties, Indian economy is still mired in bureaucratic hurdles from coast to coast. This was confirmed by a World Bank report published in late 2006 ranking Pakistan (at 74th) well ahead of India (at 134th) based on ease of doing business.

The Union government treasury reported annual revenue of £51-52 billion in 2005 thus registering an average annual growth of almost 22 per cent since 2000. India imported about 85 per cent of oil and 22 per cent of gas consumption by 2003.

CHAPTER-3

FEATURES OF INDIAN ECONOMY

The Indian economy continues to grow as a global economic powerhouse. India's development is particularly impressive given the considerable obstacles in fostering economic growth. These obstacles are truly epic with widespread poverty, limited natural resources, and one of the largest populations. While this growth is impressive, India continues to have hundreds of millions in abject poverty and much of the economic prosperity has been fairly localized to specific regions and sectors. The booming software and technology sector receives daily world attention, however those languishing in poverty remain largely ignored. Thus, it is important to understand whether the nascent economic prosperity has also caused an increase in income inequality. Economic theories vary on both the causes and implications of income equality, however empirical evidence indicates that India has been able to maintain low income inequality during periods of significant economic growth. It is important to not, that India's economic miracle is a recent phenomenon and that future prospects are far from certain. How well the Indian people and government will be able to channel current growth into long-term prosperity remains to be seen.

India is an underdeveloped economy. Its is a vast country having an area of 3.3 million sq. km. It has almost 5,76,000 villages. The population of India is widely scattered over villages and towns.

Nearly 75% of the population lives in rural & semi urban areas, while the rest lives in towns. There is doubt that the bulk of its population lives in conditions of misery. Poverty is not only acute but is also a chronic malady in India. At the same time, there exist unutilized natural resources.

It is, therefore, quite important to understand the basic characteristics of the Indian economy, treating it as one of the underdeveloped but developing economies of the world.

Low Per Capita

India's per capita income (nominal) is $ 1219, ranked142nd in the world, while its per capita purchasing power parity(PPP) of US$ 3,608 is ranked 129th. It is estimated that India's Per Capita Income will register an average growth rate of 13% during 2011-20 so as to reach $ 4,200 by 2020. In the year 2020 India's real GDP is projected to be at $ 5 trillions & per capita Nominal GDP would be at $ 3,650. India's per capita purchasing power parity(PPP) will be at $ 12,800 in the year 2020. States of India have large disparities. One of the critical problems facing India's economy is the sharp and growing regional variations among India's different states and territories in terms of per capita income, poverty, availability of infrastructure and socio-economic development. Although income inequality in India is relatively small (Gini coefficient: 32.5 in year 1999- 2000) it has been increasing of late. Wealth distribution in India is fairly uneven, with the top 10% of income groups earning 33% of the income. Despite significant economic progress, a quarter of the nation's population earns less than the government-specified poverty threshold of $0.40/day. 27.5% of the population was living below the poverty line in 2004–2005.

Between 1999 and 2008, the annualized growth rates for Maharashtra (9.0%) Gujarat (8.8%),Haryana (8.7%), or Delhi (7.4%) were much higher than for Bihar (5.1%), Uttar Pradesh (4.4%), orMadhya Pradesh (3.5%). By 2010, economically backward states start to catchup up with developed states with Bihar with an impressive 11 percent growth rate. This is said to be due to better governance.

According to a World Bank paper *Development Policy Review*, $1 a day poverty rates in rural Orissa(43%) and rural Bihar (40%) are some of the highest in the world. Seven low-income states -Bihar, Chhattisgarh, Jharkhand, Madhya Pradesh, Orissa, Rajasthan, and Uttar Pradesh - are home to more than half of India's population. Bihar's 80 million people are by far the poorest in India.

On the other hand, rural Haryana (5.7%) and rural Punjab (2.4%) compare well with middle-income countries.

Rural-urban Gap

Like in other countries, cities provide better standard of living.

Towns and cities make more than two thirds of the Indian GDP, even though less than a third lives in them.

India has a high rate of migration from Rural areas to Urban Cities.A major reason for the massive migration to cities was the Partition of India.More than half of the refugees from Pakistan settled In Urban areas such as Delhi. It is estimated that up to 590 million people,or 40 % of the Indian Population will be living in cities by 2030,much higher than the current 28 %.Also,it is estimated that five states,including Tamil Nadu, West Bengal, Gujarat, Maharashtra, Karnataka,and Punjab will have more than half of their total population living in Urban areas by 2030.

In India, Urban Areas have seen a much higher growth rate as compared to Rural Areas. Despite up to three-fourths of the population living in Rural Areas, Rural Areas contribute to only one-thirds of the National Income. The Main reason for Rural India's poor performance in terms of Income is the fact that Rural India is mostly dependent on agriculture. The Agriculture sector In India grew at a rate of only 1.6% in 2008-09, while the Indian Economy grew at a rate of 6.7%,despite the 2008 Financial Crisis. An Extremely slow rate of growth in the agriculture sector of the Indian Economy has a serious Implication for the Rural-Urban Divide, both in terms of Income and GDP. Some estimates say that that the average income of a person living in an urban are may be upto 4 times higher than that of a person living in a rural area. The rising levels of Urbanization in India are a major reason for the rising levels of Income Disparity in the country. Despite the fact that up to four-fifths of Indian houselholds save money, almost one-fourth of them spend more than they earn.

The overall poverty ratio may have declined to 21.8% in 2004-05 from 26.1% in 1999-2000 as per the report of National Sample Survey (NSS) released by the Planning Commission but the per capita income per month is still as low as Rs 292.95 in rural Andhra Pradesh against the national average of Rs 356.30 and Rs 378.84 in urban Assam against the national average of Rs 538.60.

The per capita income in rural areas is maximum at Rs 478.02 in Uttarakhand while the highest per capita income in urban areas is Maharashtra and also in Dadra and Nagar Haveli and Goa at Rs 665.90. The tie among the three territories is because the report has used the same estimation for the three of them. Another interesting fact that the figures in the report show is that though Uttarakhand has the highest per capita income in rural areas it has as many as 27.11 lakh people living below poverty line in rural areas at 40.8% which is almost double the national average of 28.3%.

The state has the fourth largest number of people living below poverty line at 39.6% both in rural and urban areas in 2004-05.

Bridging the Urban-Rural Gap

In India, the Government has taken steps to Bridge the Urban-Rural Gap. This Includes setting up of Council for Advancement of People's Action and Rural Technology (CAPART),by the Ministry of Rural Development. CAPART helps in Providing assistance to various organizations which help in Developmental Activities. There is a constantly widening rift between Rural and Urban India, not only in terms of Income, but other social measures too. There is an Urgent need to strengthen the agriculture sector in India, bring about reforms in labour laws, and provide Education.

Low Standard of Living

With one of the fastest growing economies in the world, clocked at a growth rate of 8.3% in 2010, India is fast on its way to becoming a large and globally important consumer economy. The Indian middle class, estimated to be 150 million people, by McKinsey is fast becoming used to Western culture. It will reach 600 million by 2030. According to Deutsche Research the estimates are nearly 300 million people for all Middle Class. If current trends continue, Indian per capita purchasing power parity will significantly increase from 4.7 to 6.1 percent of the world share by 2015. In 2006, 22 percent of Indians lived under the poverty line. India aims to eradicate poverty by 2020.

According to NCAER, India's middle class population to touch 267 million in 5 yrs. Further ahead, by 2025-26 the number of middle class households in India is likely to more than double from the 2015-16 levels to 113.8 million households or 547 million individuals. .

The standard of living in India shows large disparity. For example, rural areas of India exist with very basic (or even non-existent) medical facilities, while cities boast of world class medical establishments. Similarly, the very latest machinery may be used in some construction projects, but many construction workers work without mechanisation in most projects.

In 2010, the per capita PPP-adjusted GDP for India was US$3,608.

Poverty in India

A 24.3% of the population earned less than $1 (PPP, around $0.25 in nominal terms) a day in 2005, down from 42.1% in 1981. 41.6% of its population is living below the new international poverty line of $1.25 (PPP) per day, down from 59.8% in 1981. The World Bank further estimates that a third of the global poor now reside in India.

On the other hand, the Planning Commission of India uses its own criteria and has estimated that 27.5% of the population was living below the poverty line in 2004–2005, down from 51.3% in 1977–1978, and 36% in 1993-1994. The source for this was the 61st round of the National Sample Survey (NSS) and the criterion used was monthly per capita consumption expenditure below Rs. 356.35 for rural areas and Rs. 538.60 for urban areas. 75% of the poor are in rural areas, most of them are daily wagers, self-employed householders and landless labourers.

Although Indian economy has grown steadily over the last two decades, its growth has been uneven when comparing different social groups, economic groups, geographic regions, and rural and urban areas. Between 1999 and 2008, the annualized growth rates for Gujarat (8.8%), Haryana (8.7%), orDelhi (7.4%) were much higher than for Bihar (6%), Uttar Pradesh (7%), or Madhya Pradesh (5%). Poverty rates in rural Orissa (43%) and rural Bihar (41%) are higher than in the world's poorest countries such as Malawi.

Since the early 1950s, successive governments have implemented various schemes, under planning, to alleviate poverty, that have met with partial success. Programmes like *Food for work* and *National Rural Employment Programme* have attempted to use the unemployed to generate productive assets and build rural infrastructure. In August 2005, the Indian parliament passed the *Rural Employment Guarantee Bill*, the largest programme of this type, in terms of cost and coverage, which promises 100 days of minimum wage employment to every rural household in 200 of India's 600 districts. The Indian government is planning to bring in more economic reforms which can help farmers and unskilled labourers transition into industrialized sectors.

Life expectancy in India by States in year 2003

State	Total	Male	Female
Andhra Pradesh	63.1	61.6	64.1
Assam	57.2	57.1	57.6

Conted.

State	Total	Male	Female
Bihar	60.2	60.7	58.9
Gujarat	62.8	61.9	63.7
Haryana	64.5	64.1	65.0
Himachal Pradesh	65.6	65.1	65.8
Karnataka	64.0	62.4	65.5
Kerala	73.5	70.6	76.1
Madhya Pradesh	56.4	56.5	56.2
Maharastra	65.8	64.5	67.0
Orissa	57.7	57.6	57.8
Punjab	68.1	66.9	69.1
Rajastan	60.5	59.8	60.9
Tamil Nadu	64.6	63.7	65.7
Uttar Pradesh	58.4	58.9	57.7
West Bengal	63.4	62.8	64.3
India	**61.7**	**60.8**	**62.5**

Poverty is widespread in India, with the nation estimated to have a third of the world's poor. According to a 2005 World Bank estimate, 26.1% of the total Indian population falls below the international poverty line of US$ 1.25 a day (PPP, in nominal terms ₹21.6 a day in urban areas and 14.3 in rural areas). A recent report by the Oxford Poverty and Human Development Initiative states that 8 Indian states have more poor than 26 poorest African nations combined which totals to more than 410 million poor in the poorest African countries. According to a new UN Millennium Development Goals Report, as many as 320 million people in India and China are expected to come out of extreme poverty in the next four years, while India's poverty rate is projected to drop to 22% in 2015. The report also indicates that in Southern Asia, however, only India, where the poverty rate is projected to fall from 51% in 1990 to about 22% in 2015, is on track to cut poverty in half by the 2015 target date.

The 2011 Global Hunger Index (GHI) Report ranked India 45th, amongst leading countries with hunger situation. It also places India amongst the three countries where the GHI between 1996 and 2011 went up from 22.9 to 23.7, while 78 out of the 81 developing countries studied, including Pakistan, Nepal, Bangladesh, Vietnam, Kenya, Nigeria, Myanmar, Uganda, Zimbabwe and Malawi, succeeded in improving hunger condition.

Physical infrastructure

Since independence, India has allocated nearly half of the total outlay of the five-year plans for infrastructural development. Much of the total outlay was spent on large projects in the area of irrigation, energy, transport, communications and social overheads. Development of infrastructure was completely in the hands of the public sector and was plagued by corruption, bureaucratic inefficiencies, urban-bias and an inability to scale investment. Calcutta city was the first city in India to boast of a metro-system.Today the calcutta metro is considered among the world's best in terms of service and infrastructure. India's low spending on power, construction, transportation, telecommunications and real estate, at $31 billion or 6% of GDP in 2002 has prevented India from sustaining a growth rate of around 8%. This has prompted the government to partially open up infrastructure to the private sector allowing foreign investment. India holds second position in the world in roadways' construction.

As of 31 December 2005, there were an estimated 835,000 broadband lines in India. Low tele-density is the major hurdle for slow pickup in broadband services. Over 76% of the broadband lines were via DSL and the rest via cable modems.

A 2007 study by the Asian Development Bank showed that in 20 cities the average duration of water supply was only 4.3 hours per day. No city had a continuous water supply. The longest duration of supply was 12 hours per day in Chandigarh, and the lowest was 9 hours per day in Rajkot.

Regional imbalance

One of the critical problems facing India's economy is the sharp and growing regional variations among India's different states and territories in terms of per capita income, poverty, availability of infrastructure and socio-economic development. For instance, the difference in growth rate between the forward and backward states was 0.3% (5.2% & 4.9%) during 1980–81 to 1990–91, but had grown to 3.3% (6.3% & 3.0%) during 1990–91 to 1997–98. Per Capita Income in India varies drastically. As of 2010, New Delhi had a Per Capita Income of $ 3,020 whereas Bihar's Per Capita Income was at a paltry $ 445.

The five-year plans have attempted to reduce regional disparities by encouraging industrial development in the interior regions, but industries still tend to concentrate around urban areas and port cities. Even the industrial townships in the interiors, Bhilai for instance, resulted in very little development in the surrounding areas. After liberalisation, the disparities have grown despite the efforts of the union government in reducing them. Part of the reason being that manufacturing and services and not agriculture are the engines of growth. The more advanced states are better placed to benefit from them, with infrastructure like well developed ports, urbanisation and an educated and skilled workforce which attract manufacturing and service sectors. The union and state governments of backward regions are trying to reduce the disparities by offering tax holidays, cheap land, etc., and focusing more on sectors like tourism, which although being geographically and historically determined, can become a source of growth and is faster to develop than other sectors.

Effect of Poverty on Indian Economy

In 1947, the average annual income in India was US$439, compared with US$619 for China, US$770 for South Korea, and US$936 for Taiwan. By 1999, the numbers wereUS$1,818; US$3,259; US$13,317; andUS$15,720, respectively. (numbers are in 1990 international Maddison dollars) In other words, the average income in India was not much different from South Korea in 1947, but South Korea became a developed country by 2000s. At the same time, India was left as one of the world's poorer countries.

License Raj refers to the elaborate licenses, regulations and the accompanying red tape that were required to set up and run business in Indiabetween 1947 and 1990. The License Raj was a result of India's decision to have a planned economy, where all aspects of the economy are controlled by the state and licenses were given to a select few. Corruption flourished under this system.

The labyrinthine bureaucracy often led to absurd restrictions - up to 80 agencies had to be satisfied before a firm could be granted a licence to produce and the state would decide what was produced, how much, at what price and what sources of capital were used.

—BBC

India had started out in the 1950s with: high growth rates, openness to trade and investment, a promotional state, social expenditure awareness and macro stability but ended the 1980s with: low growth rates, closure to trade and investment, a license-obsessed, restrictive state (License Raj), inability to sustain social expenditures and macro instability, indeed crisis.

Poverty has decreased significantly since reforms were started in the 1980s.

Liberalization policies and their effects

Other points of view hold that the economic reforms initiated in the early 1990s are responsible for the collapse of rural economies and the agrarian crisis currently underway. As journalist and the Rural Affairs editor for The Hindu, P Sainath describes in his reports on the rural economy in India, the level of inequality has risen to extraordinary levels, when at the same time, hunger in India has reached its highest level in decades. He also points out that rural economies across India have collapsed, or on the verge of collapse due to the neo-liberal policies of the government of India since the 1990s. The human cost of the "liberalisation" has been very high. The huge wave of farm suicides in Indian rural population from 1997 to 2007 totaled close to 200,000, according to official statistics. That number remains disputed, with some saying the true number is much higher. Commentators have faulted the policies pursued by the government which, according to Sainath, resulted in a very high portion of rural households getting into the debt cycle, resulting in a very high number of farm suicides. As professor Utsa Patnaik, India's top economist on agriculture, has pointed out, the average poor family in 2007 has about 100 kg less food per year than it did in 1997.

Government policies encouraging farmers to switch to cash crops, in place of traditional food crops, has resulted in an extraordinary increase in farm input costs, while market forces determined the price of the cash crop. Sainath points out that a disproportionately large number of affected farm suicides have occurred with cash crops, because with food crops such as rice, even if the price falls, there is food left to survive on. He also points out that inequality has reached one of the highest rates India has ever seen. In a report by Chetan Ahya, Executive Director at Morgan Stanley, it is pointed out that there has been a wealth increase of close to US$1 Trillion in the time frame of 2003-2007 in the Indian stock market, while only 4-7% of the Indian population hold any equity. During the time when Public investment in agriculture shrank to 2% of the GDP, the nation suffered the worst agrarian crisis in decades, the same time as India became the nation of second highest number of dollar billionaires. Sainath argues that

Farm incomes have collapsed. Hunger has grown very fast. Public investment in agriculture shrank to nothing a long time ago. Employment has collapsed. Non-farm employment has stagnated. (Only the National Rural Employment Guarantee Act has brought some limited relief in recent times.) Millions move towards towns and cities where, too, there are few jobs to be found.

In one estimate, over 85 per cent of rural households are either landless, sub-marginal, marginal or small farmers. Nothing has happened in 15 years that has changed that situation for the better. Much has happened to make it a lot worse.

Those who have taken their lives were deep in debt – peasant households in debt doubled in the first decade of the neoliberal "economic reforms," from 26 per cent of farm households to 48.6 per cent. Meanwhile, all along, India kept reducing investment in agriculture (standard neoliberal procedure). Life was being made more and more impossible for small farmers.

As of 2006, the government spends less than 0.2% of GDP on agriculture and less than 3% of GDP on education. However, some government schemes such as the mid-day meal scheme, and the NREGA have been partially successful in providing a lifeline for the rural economy and curbing the further rise of poverty.

Economic Growth and Income Inequality in India

India has made significant economic progress over the last ten years and is rapidly emerging as a major economic force. Overall economic growth has continued at an impressive rate while specific sectors, most notably software and related services, are recording exponential rates of growth. This growth is all the more impressive, even if the significant obstacles inherent in the Indian economy remain to be overcome. These obstacles include: a high rate of poverty (primarily in absolute but also in relative terms); the lack of significant natural resources, administrative hassles, low rate of educational progress, income inequality and a very large population of 1.2 billion people, second only to China. However, it is suspected that because of the specific localization of the nascent economic growth, the benefits have been realized by a relative minority, while hundreds of millions continue to live in abject poverty. This could result in significant increases in income equality; a situation that may have significant repercussions.

Economists and social scientists have dedicated significant effort to the study of income equality. The topic has waxed and waned in importance over the years, with many academics and policy experts choosing to focus more on absolute poverty than overall income distribution. However, income equality is important because of the implications for social and political development. It is widely understood that income equality can provide stability for a nation, which can only help in fostering long-term economic growth. More directly, income equality enables many more individuals to participate more fully in the economy. This is due to income equality providing opportunities for employment, product consumption, access to borrowing, and the ability to invest and save.

Therefore, it is necessary to understand the income distribution effects in India, with a primary emphasis on the last fifteen years when India began significant market reforms. India has had a relatively short history as an independent nation and during that time, has embarked on a variety of economic development strategies. Moreover, India is an incredibly diverse nation with widely varying cultural, economic, political, and religious norms. Thus, the implications for income equality are indeed significant in maintaining stability in such a large and diverse nation.

By comparing India's economic growth and income equality, one can determine whether the recent economic prosperity has been realized by many or relatively few individuals. This will aid in understanding the implications for other dimensions of development, including those pertaining to social and political aspects. The paper first documents the historical context of India's development over the last several decades. Second, an examination of the existing theories concerning economic growth and income equality is provided. Third, the empirical evidence for India is provided and the existing theories tested. Finally, conclusions from the results of the empirical test, as well as future implications are discussed.

It is important to note that India's economic growth is a relatively recent phenomenon and the current global economic environment is increasingly more complex.

The dynamic nature of global economic integration has rendered many traditional economic theories irrelevant in several situations.

Income distribution refers to the spread of a country's income percentage throughout its population and yields a ratio between income of the richest in a country to the poorest. When income is not proportionally distributed, it is called income inequality. While many would argue it is a very much necessary part of natural economics, as in many other countries, India's increasing income inequality continues to pose a significant threat. In most cases, income inequality plays a big role in the amount of crime a country has because "as the rich get richer and the poor get poorer" it promotes unhappiness.

A great portion of India's population is a victim of rising monetary deficits, most of which has crossed well under the poverty threshold.

While the top 10% of India's population enjoys 31.1% of the country's income, the lowest 10% suffers with merely 3.6%. The following data portrays how India's Inequality measures ratio compares to that of other countries:

India	8.6
United Kingdom	13.8
United States	15.9
Sierra Leone	87.2
Austria	6.9
Slovenia	5.9

The graph depicts how great the distance is between the upper 20% and lower 40% in both rural and urban areas. To look specifically at urban statistics (squares and circles that are not shaded), as we approach the early years of the century, the income level of the upper 20%, which was previously at a diminutive spread shot up drastically as the country grew technologically.

In the debate over growth and equality, and comparisons of India and China, proponents of India's path to development make much of the fact that income inequality in India is relatively low. The UN Human Development Report 2006 estimates the Gini Index for India to be 32.5 (in 2000). Yes, India's income distribution is relatively less unequal. But inequality is rising – fast.. For observers of the India-China debate, indeed for observers of economic growth, this plot is illustrative because growth has not reduced inequality. Instead, income inequality has exacerbated considerably, rising from a historic low of 29.6 in 1990 to 32.5 in 2000 (a rise of 9.7%). This ignores the high of 36 seen in 1999 (I exclude the Gini of 37.8 recorded in 1997, as that is from a separate data series). The rate at which India achieved improvements in life expectancy slowed considerably in the post-reform era. There are two reasons for this:

1. As GNP rises, the resulting income inequality may be impacting overall life expectancy. As fewer people earn more the GNP rises, but the large majority that gets relatively poorer are worse off.
2. Another ugly truth may well be that a market-oriented India and China provide far less for its people than did socialist India and China. Under the guise of reform, governments in both countries are not only withdrawing from the market but also from public services.

This observation of increasing income inequality seems to strengthen at least the first of these hypothesis. Of course, a correlation between growth and inequality does not by itself disprove the need for economic growth. Economists still argue that growth is a necessary condition for reducing poverty, and in India it has indeed brought millions out of poverty. But it may also have made many worse off. Now if only the economists could come up with a solution for that conundrum.

The moderate increase in inequality recorded over the past two decades hides a larger underlying trend. In developed countries, governments have been taxing more and spending more to offset the trend towards more inequality – they now spend more on social policies than at any time in history. Of course, they need to spend more because of the rapid ageing of population in developed countries – more health care and pensions expenditures are necessary. The redistributive effect of government expenditures dampened the rise in poverty in the decade from the mid-1980s to the mid-1990s, but amplified it in the decade that followed, as benefits became less targeted on the poor. If governments stop trying to offset the inequalities by either spending less on social benefits, or by making taxes and benefits less targeted to the poor, then the growth in inequality would be much more rapid. Relying on taxing more and spending more as a response to inequality can only be a temporary measure. The only sustainable way to reduce inequality is to stop the underlying widening of wages and income from capital. In particular, we have to make sure that people are capable of being in employment and earning wages that keep them and their families out of poverty. This means that developed countries have to do much better in getting people into work, rather than relying

on unemployment, disability and early retirement benefits, in keeping them in work and in offering good career prospects.

There are a number of objections that people might make in response to the previous paragraphs. They might, for example, point to the following considerations:

- What matters is not just income. Public services such as education and health can be powerful instruments in reducing inequality.
- Some people who have low incomes nevertheless have lots of assets, so they should not be considered poor.
- We should not care unduly about poverty at a point in time – only if people have low incomes for a long period are they likely to be seriously deprived.
- A better way of looking at inequality is seeing if people are deprived of key goods and services, such as having enough

food to eat, or being able to afford a television or a washing machine.

- A society in which income was distributed perfectly equally would not be a desirable place either. People who work harder, or are more talented than others, should have more income.

What matters, in fact, is equality of opportunity, not equality of outcomes.

Factors that have driven changes in income inequality and poverty over time

- Changes in the structure of the population are one of the causes of higher inequality. However, this mainly reflects the rise in the number of single-adult households rather than population ageing per se.
- Earnings of full-time workers have become more unequal in most OECD countries. This is due to high earners becoming even more so. Globalisation, skill-biased technical change and labour market institutions and policies have all probably contributed to this outcome.
- The effect of wider wage disparities on income inequality has been offset by higher employment. However, employment rates among less-educated people have fallen and household joblessness remains high.
- Capital income and self-employment income are very unequally distributed, and have become even more so over the past decade. These trends are a major cause of wider income inequalities.
- Work is very effective at tackling poverty. Poverty rates among jobless families are almost six times higher than those among working families.
- However, work is not sufficient to avoid poverty. More than half of all poor people belong to households with some earnings, due to a combination of low hours worked during the year and/or low wages. Reducing in-work poverty often requires in-work benefits that supplement earnings.

Economic Growth and Income Inequality in India

Economic growth is defined as "the steady process by which the productive capacity of the economy is increased over time to bring about rising levels of national output and income". Economic growth is generally gauged by a variety of Gross Domestic Product (GDP) measures, where GDP represents the total output or production of an economy. GDP, while strictly a measure of output, is also understood to be total income as well. There are a variety of limitations to using GDP as a measure of output or income. Most notably, differences in inflation, population size, and purchasing power can cause significant variances when comparing GDP. However, overall GDP given in 2000 US dollars (i.e. inflation adjusted) is a relatively robust figure for measuring growth, especially in relation to income equality. Income equality is the distribution of total income amongst the representative population. In a nation with perfect income equality, each and every individual has an equal share of the total income. This is contrasted with perfect ncome inequality, where one individual has all of the total income. Of course, neither of these extreme situations exists in any national economy. In practice, nations maintain income distributions somewhere between the two extremes. Income equality can be compared internally for a given nation, as well as externally between multiple nations.

Unemployment and Underemployment in India

Open unemployment is not a true indicator of the gravity of the unemployment problem in an economy such as India, characterised as it is by large-scale underemployment and poor employment quality in the unorganised sector, which accounts for over 90 per cent of the total employment. The organised sector contributes only about 9 per cent to the total employment.

Underemployment in various segments of the labour force is quite high.

For instance, though open unemployment was only 2 per cent in 1993-94, the incidence of under-employment and unemployment taken together was as much as 10 per cent that year. This, in spite of the fact that the incidence of underemployment was reduced substantially in the decade ending 1993-94.

According to the Planning Commission, the States which face the prospect of increased unemployment in the post-Ninth Plan period (2002-2007) are Bihar, Rajasthan, Uttar Pradesh, Kerala and Punjab.

Employment generation has been one of the important objectives of development planning in India. The problem of employment is closely interlinked with the eradication of poverty. There are three main aspects of the employment problem in India. They are the problem of proportion of labour to total population, problem of productivity of labour and problem of unemployment and underemployment of labour. These three aspects are interrelated. There is low rate participation of labour in India. Low rate of employment among women is a striking feature in India. There has almost been no change in LFPR (labour force participation rate). The dependency rate is quite high in India. Problem of unemployment and underemployment is the chronic feature of the Indian economy. It is the main cause of poverty in India. Unemployment in India is mostly structural. The rate of unemployment is different in different states. Sector wise unemployment in India is rural and urban unemployment.

Urban unemployment is of two types viz, industrial unemployment and educated unemployment. Rural unemployment is more than 70% as rural population is more than 70% of the total population in India. There are various types of unemployment in India. They are seasonal, structural, frictional, technological, involuntary and disguised. The productivity criterion refers to disguised unemployment. It is mainly found in agriculture. It is a kind of underemployment. It involves both zero marginal productivity of man hour and zero marginal productivity of labour. It implies too many persons on too little land. Educated unemployment is one variant of open unemployment. It is mainly due to the defective educational system. Underemployment is one variant of open unemployment.

It is mainly due to the defective educational system. Underemployment may be visible or invisible. The ratio between unemployed workers and total labour force is called unemployment rate. Low productivity of employment is the third aspect of the employment problem. Productivity of labour in India is low due to many factors. The essential of the employment policy is to increase production, control population growth, reform the education system, emphasize cottage and small scale industrial units to tackle the problem of seasonal, frictional, structural, technological and disguised unemployment and effectively do manpower planning etc. There have been various schemes to solve the problem of educated unemployment.

A series of anti poverty employment programmes like PMRY have been launched for the solution of the problem of educated unemployment. Poverty and inequality are interlinked. Poverty can be defined as subsistence, inequality and externality. In the absolute sense, it relates to subsistence. It relates to the minimum standard -of living. In the relative sense, poverty means difference in the relative standard of living of the people. It relates to inequality in the level of living. We in India are mostly concerned with absolute poverty. The concept of poverty line has been used to know the extent of poverty in a country. People below the poverty line suffer from absolute poverty. Control of population growth, higher economic growth and income redistribution etc. are the most important measures of eradication of poverty. Various anti poverty measures have been taken during the plan period starting from the first to the 9th five year plan. Various special anti poverty employment programmes. Like JRY, NRY etc. have been launched from time to time. Various social security measures like NOPS, ESIC etc. have been launched.

Inequality exists both in developing and developed economies. Economic inequality is one of the causes of mass poverty, Inequality is basically due to mal distribution of national income. There are three forms of economic inequality. They are inequality of assets, inequality of income and consumption and regional inequality. These three major forms of inequalities are inextricably interlinked and reinforcing. Inequality and poverty are also interconnected and like poverty inequality is also bad. Suitable measures should be taken with a view to reducing existing economic inequality if not removing it.

Dualistic Economy

A dualistic economy is the existence of two separate economic sectors within one country, divided by different levels of development, technology, and different patterns of demand.

A dual economy is the existence of two separate economic sectors within one country, divided by different levels of development, technology, and different patterns of demand. The concept was originally created by Julius Herman Boeke to describe the coexistence of modern and traditional economic sectors in a colonial economy.

Dual economies are common in less developed countries, where one sector is geared to local needs and another to the global export market. Dual economies may exist within the same sector, for example a modern plantation or other commercial agricultural entity operating in the midst of traditional cropping systems. Sir Arthur Lewisused the concept of a dualistic economy as the basis of his labour supply theory of rural-urban migration. Lewis distinguished between a low-income, rural, subsistence sector with surplus population, and an expanding urban capitalist sector. The urban economy absorbed labour from rural areas (holding down urban wages) until the rural surplus was exhausted.

Globalization and Rural India

The process of liberalization and industrialization, fast gained importance in India in the 1980s. However it was only in 1990s, after the phenomenon of globalization gaining momentum in India, that the Indian economy truly opened up. Globalization has led to increased opportunities to the average Indian - an increase in employment, income, output, investment and also to a rapid expansion of the banking and financial sector, telecom sector, growth in export potential and social sector projects.

The government implemented the new industrial policy in 1991. There was a regard that the benefits of policy implementation would trickle down to the lower sections of the population.

The rural economy comprises 71% of the total population of India. Agriculture and allied activities are the main sources of income and this primary sector contributes to almost 25% of India's GDP. The advantages of globalization, as envisioned by the government, have not trickled down to the rural poor. There has been no evidence of positive growth in the unorganized sector of the economy. Globalization, it is said, is adversely affecting the rural Indian.

The opening up of the economy signifies cheaper imports in a country where agricultural prices are constantly fluctuating. This hampers the producers and leads to further losses. The producers might be hesitant to produce the same crops next year and also, multiple cropping is not common in India. Thus, farmers cannot shift from food grains to more marketable crops.

Farmers, artisans, unskilled labor and workers bear the impact of losses due to increased competition and comparative advantage enjoyed by the more developed countries. The critics of globalization also affirm that Multi-national Corporations (MNCs) have penetrated the economy only to gobble up Indian enterprises and also to gain a foothold in one of the largest and fastest growing economies of the world.

India is characterized as a dualistic economy, where a modern economy exists side by side with a traditional one. This technological dualism is further exaggerated owing to globalization. The disparity between the rural and urban rich and poor is widening at a greater pace than ever before. However, this disparity is not evident at the initial stages and will show up when the gap is extended.

India is a labor surplus country facing an acute problem of population explosion. Most of India's population comprises the rural people. Increased investment and growth in capital or adopting technology that is capital intensive will lead to unemployment. Governmental schemes and measures to control poverty and unemployment in rural India are deficient due to bureaucracy and widespread corruption. Thus, inequalities in rural India are exceedingly difficult to tackle.

Due to the failure of the trickle down effect, the rural Indian suffers his miserable fate at the hands of globalization. The MNCs and investors are also unlikely to bring about development due to regional disparity and lack of development in the financial sector.

The recent spate of suicide of farmers in the Vidharbha region and the attacks on retail outlets in rural areas bears testimony to this ugly reality. Without adequate improvement in the government's delivery mechanism, the despair of the average rural Indian will be prolonged.

15 Essential features of Indian Economy

Following are the 15 essential features of Indian Economy:

1. Indian Economy-Underdeveloped

On the eve of independence, Indian economy was underdeveloped economy. As an underdeveloped economy, Indian economy had the following features:

(i) Low Per Capita Income: Underdeveloped economies have low per capita income. India has no exception to it. In 1947-48, per capita income was Rs. 230. People were poor. They were not getting fair square meals a day. They had no shelter and clothing. Most of the people were unemployed.

(ii) Poor Infrastructure: On the eve of independence infrastructural development which comprised of communication and transport and electricity etc. was very poor. In 1948, power generation capacity was nearly 2100 MW; length of railway lines was 53,596 Kms.

(iii) Dependence on Imports: The country had to heavily depend on imports. Armed forces of the country also depended on foreign imports. Moreover, several consumer goods like sewing machines, medicines, oil, bicycles etc. were imported from abroad.

(iv) Illiteracy: Illiteracy was both cause and effect of poverty. Due to illiteracy, people were unable to use new techniques in agriculture and industry. They were unable to organize trade and commerce on modern lines. In 1948, rate of illiteracy was 18%. Thus 82% of the population was illiterate.

(v) Agricultural economy: Indian economy was predominantly agricultural. In 1948, about 70% population was engaged in agriculture. Moreover, agriculture constituted 50% of national income. But agriculture itself was backward. Regarding productivity, it was 110 kg/hectare for rice in 1947 as against 748 kg in Japan.

(vi) Low Development of Industries: There was very little development of industries. Large industries used to produce consumer goods. Basic and key industries were very less in number. In 1947, cement production was 26 lakh tonnes, of sugar 10 lakh tonnes and that of cloth just 421 crore meter.

2. *Stagnant Economy*

During the British period, Indian economy remained almost stagnant. There was very slow growth of economy. This was clear from the fact that for almost a century, the average annual growth rate of per capita income in India was not more than 0.5%.

The high growth rate of population tended to make it difficult to maintain even the proposed growth rate. In fact poverty was widespread and about 40% people were living below poverty line.

The causes of stagnation and backwardness are laissez faire, commercialization of agriculture, neglect of irrigation, destruction of cottage and handicraft and economic drainage and discriminatory tariff policy.

3. *Semi-Feudal Economy*

During the British rule, Indian economy had a mixed mode of production. Feudalism was more prominent than other modes of production.

A substantial developed capitalistic sector had emerged. Handicraftsmen had lost their independent status and were engaged in a simple commodity production. Bonded labour force was prevalent in agriculture. Primitive social organizations existed in areas inhabited by the tribals.

4. *Depreciated Economy*

On the eve of Independence Indian economy was depreciated. In every economy, extensive use of factors of production, inevitably leads to their wear and tear. If no arrangements are made to replace the depreciated factors then the stock of gross capital declines.

This results into the fall in production capacity. Such an economy is called depreciated economy. After World War II Indian economy also turned into depreciated economy.

During World War II India had supplied large quantity of goods to Britishers. India was paid for it in terms of sterling. But due to lack of real capital, its production capacity declined.

5. *Pre-dominance of Agriculture*

Agriculture is the main sector of Indian economy, which is in total contrast to the economic structure of a developed economy. More than 70 per cent of the total population is engaged in agricultural activities while the picture is absolutely different in advanced countries.

According to Dr. Cloustone, "India has depressed classes, the tool has depressed industries and unfortunately, agriculture is one of them" Therefore, the essence of Indian economy is an agrarian economy.

6. Underutilized Natural Resources

It has been rightly stated that India is a rich country inhabited by poor people. It means that the country possesses abundant stock of natural resources but the problem is that these resources are not fully utilized for the production of material goods and services. The result is poverty of the people. The vicious circle of poverty moves for year to year together.

7. Heavy Population Pressure

Population is a major factor influencing the nature of a country's economy. Over-population creates complex economic problems.

The income per capita is low, the efficiency of labour is not satisfactory and there is an acute housing shortage. Unemployment and low standard of living dominate the scene. In India, the rate of growth of population was about 1.25% per annum during 1941-51.

8. Capital Deficiency

Deficiency of capital is another basic characteristic of Indian economy. In case of physical capital, its total stock is not adequate for equipping well to the entire labour force and full utilization of natural resources.

Similarly, human capital is far from satisfaction. The major reasons of low level of capital formation in India were (i) low inducement to invest and (ii) low propensity and capacity to save.

9. Famines

In the pre-British period famines had been occurring. These famines showed an unbridled increase in the 18th and 19th centuries. Between 1765-1858 the country experienced 12 famines and 4 scarcities. Similarly, between 1860-1908, 20 famines spread their wings.

In 1943 Bengal famine shook the foundation of the country. William Digby estimated that during 1854-1901, 28.8 million persons died due to famines. In the famine of 1899-1900 2.5 million persons died of starvation.

10. Industrial Backwardness

On the eve of independence Indian economy was backward from industrial point of view there was deficiency of basic and heavy industries. Among heavy industries, there was Tata Iron and Steel industry.

The production of machines in the country was negligible. Statistics reveal that in 1947 total production of iron & steel was 9 lakh tonnes.

11. Low Levels of Living

India has been, and even today is one among the poorest countries of the world. Barma few rich, the common masses forced to lead a miserable life. Almost half of country's population is below the poverty line.

Quantity of goods available per head of population is meager and the quality is invariably indifferent. Nutritional content of consumption is grossly inadequate and hunger, starvation and disease are fairly widespread.

12. Lack of Social Overhead Capital

Social Overhead Capital comprises of such industries which help in the growth of other industries. Social overhead capital or infrastructure as it is now called, includes such industries like railways and other means of transport, electricity and other sources of energy, communication, banking etc.

Unfortunately not much attention was paid to this during the British rule and consequently the development of industries in India remained slow and tardy.

13. Widespread Unemployment

Unemployment in India is a direct outcome of rapidly increasing population. More people need more jobs but the underdeveloped economy of India cannot accommodate them. This naturally leads to widespread unemployment. Thus unemployment becomes an all round problem in the country.

14. Income Disparities

The gap between wealth and poverty is exceedingly wide in India. A handful of rich persons get a relatively large share of the total income while the large mass of poor population gets a relatively small portion of it.

Inequalities of income distribution are to be observed both in the rural and urban sectors of the economy. Inequalities of income are to be seen in the form of unequal distribution of land in the agricultural sector and concentration of economic power in non-agricultural sector.

15. Absence of Enterprise and Initiative

In India, enterprise and initiative are inhibited by the social system which denies opportunities for creative faculties.

The force of custom, the rigidity of status, absence of intellectual curiosity and distrust of new ideas, combine to create an atmosphere inimical to enterprise, experimentation and innovation. Whatever little entrepreneurship exists tends to become monopolistic and quasi-monopolistic.

SECTORS OF THE INDIAN ECONOMY

There are Following Sectors in Indian Economy

Primary Sector

When the economic activity depends mainly on exploitation of natural resources then that activity comes under the primary sector. Agriculture and agriculture related activities are the primary sectors of economy.

Secondary Sector

When the main activity involves manufacturing then it is the secondary sector. All industrial production where physical goods are produced come under the secondary sector.

Tertiary Sector

When the activity involves providing intangible goods like services then this is part of the tertiary sector. Financial services, management consultancy, telephony and IT are good examples of service sector.

Primary Sector Based to Tertiary Sector Based

During early civilization all economic activity was in primary sector. When the food production became surplus people's need for other products increased. This led to the development of secondary sector. The growth of secondary sector spread its influence during industrial revolution in nineteenth century.

After growth of economic activity a support system was the need to facilitate the industrial activity. Certain sectors like transport and finance play an important role in supporting the industrial activity. Moreover, more shops were needed to provide goods in people's neighbourhood.

Ultimately, other services like tuition, administrative support developed.

Interdependency of Sectors

To understand this interdependency, let us take an example of a cold drink. A cold drink contains water, sugar and artificial flavour. Suppose if there is no sugarcane production then procuring sugar will become difficult and costly for the cold drink manufacturer. Now to transport sugarcane to sugar mills and sugar to the cold drink plant needs the services of a transporter. A person or system of persons is required to maintain and monitor all these movements of goods from farm to factory to shop in different locations. That is where role of administrative staffs comes. Let us go back to the farmer. He also needs feritlisers and seeds which is processed in some factory and which will be delivered to his doorstep by some means of transportation.

To top it all at every step of these activities we require the proper monetary and banking system. So, in a nutshell this describes how interrelated all sectors of an economy are.

Growth and Status of Different Sectors in India

Closely observe the given graphs. The first graph shows the rupeewise turnover of various sectors in 1973 and 2003. The second graph shows the share of three sectors in the GDP during these 20 years and last graph shows share in providing employment.

The first graph shows a massive increase in turnover for all these sectors during 20 years, which shows the way our economy grew. The second graph shows that share of agriculture decreased substantially and that of industry remained static and share of services grew. Particularly the growth of share of services sector was phenomenal from 35% to 55%. Now the third graph paints a distressing picture. The share in providing employment was not in tune with the share in GDP. The agriculture provided employment to 75% workers and this decreased to 60% in 2000, which is not as big a drop as agriculture's drop in GDP contribution. On the other hand the growth in employment provided by other two sectors was substantially low.

Meaning of this:

1. Majority of people are still employed in agricultural activities. As agriculture provides seasonal employment during cropping season so chances of hidden employment are big. Moreover, as history suggests a developed nation's dependency shifts from primary sector towards tertiary sector in all aspects of economic development, so it can be said that India is still way behind because majority still depend on agriculture.
2. Secondary and Tertiary Sector have failed to generate enough employment opportunities making a pressure on primary sector. Although educated and skilled workforce do get employed in secondary and tertiary sector but for unskilled and semi-skilled workers there is still shortage of employment avenues.

Other Classifications of Economy

Organised Sector

The sector which carries out all activity through a system and follows the law of the land is called organized sector. Moreover, labour rights are given due respect and wages are as per the norms of the country and those of the industry. Labour working organized sector get the benefit of social security net as framed by the Government.

Certain benefits like provident fund, leave entitlement, medical benefits and insurance are provided to workers in the organized sector. These security provisions are necessary to provide source of sustenance in case of disability or death of the main breadwinner of the family. Otherwise the dependents will face a bleak future.

Unorganised Sector

The sector which evade most of the laws and don't follow the system come under unorganized sector. Small shopkeepers, some small scale manufacturing units keep all their attention on profit making and ignore their workers basic rights. Workers don't get adequate salary and other benefits like leave, health benefits and insurance are beyond the imagination of people working in unorganized sectors.

Public Sector

Companies which are run and financed by the Government comprise the public sector. After independence India was a very poor country. India needed huge amount of money to set up manufacturing plants for basic items like iron and steel, aluminium, fertilizers and cements. Additionally infrastructure like roads, railways, ports and airports also require huge investment. In those days Indian entrepreneur was not cash rich so government had to start creating big public sector enterprises like SAIL (Steel Authority of India Limited), NGC(Oil & Natural Gas Comission).

Private Sector

Companies which are run and financed by private people comprise the private sector. Companies like Hero Honda, Tata are from private sectors. Government Aided Schemes to Fight Unemployment Government, from time to time, announces and implements various employment scheme to fight unemployment or hidden employment to help the weaker section of society. Shcemes like NREG (National Rural Employment Guarantee) is the latest announced by the UPA government in 2004. This programme guarantees a minimum of 100 days of employment to at least one person from every rural household. This is part of government's effort to ensure the 'Right to Work' to the rural poor citizen.

Agriculture in India

The agriculture sector, for so long the mainstay of the Indian **Economy**, now accounts for only about 20 per cent of GDP, yet employs over 50 per cent of the population. For some years after independence, India depended on foreign aid to meet its food needs, but in the last 35 years, food production has risen steadily, mainly due to the increase in irrigated areas and widespread use of high-yield seeds, fertilizers, and pesticides. The **Country** has large grain stockpiles (around 45 million tons) and is a net exporter of food grains.

Cash crops, especially tea and coffee, are the major export earners. **India** is the world's largest producer of tea, with annual production of around 470 million tons, of which 200 million tons is exported. **India** also holds around 30 per cent of the world spice market, with exports around 120,000 tons per year.

With a view to strengthening the sector, building infrastructure for handling, transportation, and storage of food grains has been granted "infrastructure status" and will be eligible for a tax holiday. Further, processors of food and vegetables are exempt from excise duty.

Agriculture in India has a significant history. Today, India ranks second worldwide in farm output. Agriculture and allied sectors like forestry and fisheries accounted for 16.6% of the GDP in 2009, about 50% of the total workforce. The economic contribution of agriculture to India's GDP is steadily declining with the country's broad-based economic growth. Still, agriculture is demographically the broadest economic sector and plays a significant role in the overall socio-economic fabric of India.

Per 2010 FAO world agriculture statistics, India is the world's largest producer of many fresh fruits and vegetables,milk, major spices, select fresh meats, select fibrous crops such as jute, several staples such as millets and castor oilseed. India is the second largest producer of wheat andrice, the world's major food staples. India is also the world's second or third largest producer of several dry fruits, agriculture-based textile raw materials, roots and tuber crops, pulses, farmed fish, eggs, coconut, sugarcane and numerous vegetables. India ranked within the world's five largest producers of over 80% of agricultural produce items, including many cash crops such as coffee and cotton, in 2010. India is also one the world's five largest producers of livestock and poultry meat, with one of the fastest growth rates, as of 2011.

One report from 2008 claimed India's population is growing faster than its ability to produce rice and wheat. Other recent studies claim India can easily feed its growing population, plus produce wheat and rice for global exports, if it can reduce food staple spoilage, improve its infrastructure and raise its farm productivity to those achieved by other developing countries such as Brazil and China.

In fiscal year ending June 2011, with a normal monsoon season, Indian agriculture accomplished an all time record production of 85.9 million tons of wheat, a 6.3 percent increase from a year earlier. Rice output in India also hit a new record at 95.3 million tons, a 7% increase from the year earlier. Lentils and many other food staples production also increased year over year. Indian farmers, thus produced about 71 kilograms of wheat and 80 kilograms of rice for every member of Indian population in 2011. The per capita supply of rice every year in India is now higher than the per capita consumption of rice every year in Japan.

India exported about 2 billion kilograms each of wheat and rice in 2011 to Africa, Nepal, Bangladesh and other regions of the world.

Aquaculture and catch fishery is amongst the fastest growing industries in India. Between 1990 and 2010, Indian fish capture harvest doubled, while aquaculture harvest tripled. In 2008, India was the world's sixth largest producer of marine and freshwater capture fisheries, and the second largest aquaculture farmed fish producer. India exported 600,000 metric tonnes of fish products to nearly half of all the world's countries.

India has shown a steady average nationwide annual increase in the kilograms produced per hectare for various agricultural items, over the last 60 years. These gains have come mainly from India's green revolution, improving road and power generation infrastructure, knowledge gains and reforms. Despite these recent accomplishments, agriculture in India has the potential for major productivity and total output gains, because crop yields in India are still just 30% to 60% of the best sustainable crop yields achievable in the farms of developed as well as other developing countries. Additionally, losses after harvest due to poor infrastructure and unorganized retail cause India to experience some of the highest food losses in the world.

Indian agriculture policy since 1947

Over 50 years since its independence, India has made immense progress towards food security. Indian population has tripled, but food-grain production more than quadrupled: there has thus been substantial increase in available food-grain per capita.

Prior to the mid-1960s India relied on imports and food aid to meet domestic requirements. However, two years of severe drought in 1965 and 1966 convinced India to reform its agricultural policy, and that India could not rely on foreign aid and foreign imports for food security. India adopted significant policy reforms focused on the goal of food grain self-sufficiency. This ushered in India's Green Revolution. It began with the decision to adopt superior yielding, disease resistant wheat varieties in combination with better farming knowledge to improve productivity. The initial increase in production was centred on the irrigated areas of the Indian states of Punjab, Haryana and western Uttar Pradesh. With both the farmers and the government officials focusing on farm productivity and knowledge transfer, India's total food grain production soared. A hectare of Indian wheat farms that produced an average of 0.8 tons in 1948, produced 4.7 tons of wheat in 1975 from the same land. Such rapid growths in farm productivity enabled India to become self-sufficient by the 1970s. It also empowered the smallholder farmers to seek further means to increase food staples produced per hectare. By 2000, Indian farms were adopting wheat varieties capable of yielding 6 tons of wheat per hectare.

With agricultural policy success in wheat, India's Green Revolution technology spread to rice. However, since irrigation infrastructure was very poor, Indian farmer innovated with tube-wells, to harvest ground water. When gains from the new technology reached their limits in the states of initial adoption, the technology spread in the 1970s and 1980s to the states of eastern India — Bihar, Orissa and West Bengal. The lasting benefits of the improved seeds and new technology extended principally to the irrigated areas which account for about one-third of the harvested crop area. In the 1980s, Indian agriculture policy shifted to "evolution of a production pattern in line with the demand pattern" leading to a shift in emphasis to other agricultural commodities like oilseed, fruit and vegetables. Farmers began adopting improved methods and technologies in dairying, fisheries and livestock, and meeting the diversified food needs of India's growing population. As with Rice, the lasting benefits of improved seeds and improved farming technologies now largely depends on whether India develops infrastructure such as irrigation network, flood control systems, reliable electricity production capacity, all season rural and urban highways, cold storage to prevent food spoilage, modern retail, and competitive buyers of produce from the Indian farmer. This is increasingly the focus of Indian agriculture policy.

India's agricultural economy is undergoing structural changes. Between 1970 and 2011, the GDP share of agriculture has fallen from 43 to 16 percent. This isn't because of reduced importance of agriculture, or a consequence of agricultural policy. This is largely because of the rapid economic growth in services, industrial output, and non-agricultural sectors in India between 2000 to 2010.

The effect of Indian government's agricultural policy is limited because India is a federal state and most agricultural issues are dealt with at the state level. Uniform institutional change is far more difficult to achieve in India than in China.

Indian agriculture policy is aimed essentially at improving food self sufficiency and alleviating hunger through food distribution. Aside from investing in agricultural infrastructure, the government supports agriculture through measures including minimum support prices (MSP) for the major agricultural crops, farm input subsidies and preferential credit schemes.Under the price support policy, MSPs are set annually for basic staples to protect producers from sharp price falls, to stabilise prices and to ensure adequate food stocks for public distribution. In the past guaranteed prices have been below the prevailing market prices, according to the International Food Policy Research Institute (IFPRI) in 2007.At the same time subsidies on farm inputs including fertilisers, electrical power and irrigation water have led to inefficient use of inputs and indirectly subsidise income. IFPRI concluded that "support for agriculture (from 1985-2002) has been largely counter cyclical to world prices".

Financial Sector

An extensive financial and banking sector supports the rapidly expanding Indian **Economy. India** boasts of a wide and sophisticated banking network. The sector also has a number of national and state level financial institutions. These include foreign and institutional investors, investment funds, equipment leasing companies, venture capital funds, etc. Further, the **Country** has a well-established stock market, comprising 23 stock exchanges, with over 9,000 listed companies. Total market capitalization, on the two dominant stock exchanges, the Bombay Stock Exchange (BSE) and the National Stock Exchange (NSE), stood at Rs. 6,926 billion and Rs. 7,604 billion respectively, at the end of December 2000. The Indian capital markets are rapidly moving towards a market that is modern in terms of infrastructure as well as international best practices such as derivative trading with stock index futures, addition to the list of compulsory Demat trading and rolling settlement in certain specified shares, commencement of internet based trading, etc.

The last year witnessed several Indian companies, mobilizing resources by tapping the world market through the ADR/GDR route. So as to improve the liquidity in the ADR/GDR market and to give opportunity to Indian shareholders to divest their shareholding in the ADR/GDR market abroad, measures such as two-way fungibility in ADR/GDR issues of Indian companies has been introduced and sponsorship of ADR/ GDR offerings against existing shareholding. In addition to the above, 26 per cent foreign equity has been allowed in the insurance sector and investment and divestment by venture capital funds and companies registered with SEBI has been simplified.

FII inflows were USD 2.34 billion (January 2001 to June 2001) compared to USD 1.5 billion for 2000, showing an upward trend despite depressed stock market indices. Net cumulative FII inflows crossed USD 14 billion (June 2001).

The Indian money market is classified into: the organised sector (comprising private, public and foreign owned commercial banks and cooperative banks, together known as *scheduled banks*); and the unorganised sector (comprising individual or family owned indigenous bankers or money lenders andnon-banking financial companies (NBFCs)). The unorganised sector and microcredit are still preferred over traditional banks in rural and sub-urban areas, especially for non-productive purposes, like ceremonies and short duration loans.

Prime Minister Indira Gandhi nationalised 14 banks in 1969, followed by six others in 1980, and made it mandatory for banks to provide 40% of their net credit to priority sectors like agriculture, small-scale industry, retail trade, small businesses, etc. to ensure that the banks fulfill their social and developmental goals. Since then, the number of bank branches has increased from 10,120 in 1969 to 98,910 in 2003 and the population covered by a branch decreased from 63,800 to 15,000 during the same period. The total deposits increased 32.6 times between 1971 to 1991 compared to 7 times between 1951 to 1971. Despite an increase of rural branches, from 1,860 or 22% of the total number of branches in 1969 to 32,270 or 48%, only 32,270 out of 5 lakh (500,000) villages are covered by a scheduled bank.

Since liberalisation, the government has approved significant banking reforms. While some of these relate to nationalised banks (like encouraging mergers, reducing government interference and increasing profitability and competitiveness), other reforms have opened up the banking and insurance sectors to private and foreign players.

As of 2007, banking in India is generally mature in terms of supply, product range and reach-even, though reach in rural India still remains a challenge for the private sector and foreign banks. In terms of quality of assets and capital adequacy, Indian banks are considered to have clean, strong and transparent balance sheets relative to other banks in comparable economies of Asia. The Reserve Bank of India is an autonomous body, with minimal pressure from the government. The stated policy of the Bank on the Indian Rupee is to manage volatility but without any fixed exchange rate.

Insurance is a subject listed in the concurrent list in the Seventh Schedule to the Constitution of India where both centre and states can legislate. The insurance sector has gone through a number of phases and changes. Since 1999, when the government opened up the insurance sector by allowing private companies to solicit insurance and also allowing foreign direct investment of up to 26%, the insurance sector has been a booming market. However, the largest life-insurance company in India is still owned by the government. In India, insurance has a deep-rooted history. Insurance in various forms has been mentioned in the writings of Manu (Manusmrithi), Yagnavalkya (Dharmashastra) and Kautilya (Arthashastra). The fundamental basis of the historical reference to insurance in these ancient Indian texts is the same i.e. pooling of resources that could be re-distributed in times of calamities such as fire, floods, epidemics and famine. The early references to Insurance in these texts has reference to marine trade loans and carriers' contracts. Currently India is a US$41 billion industry. Currently, in India only two million people (0.2 % of the total population of 1 billion) are covered under Mediclaim, whereas in developed nations like USA about 75 % of the total population are covered under some insurance scheme. With more and more private companies in the sector, the situation may change soon.

Banking in India originated in the last decades of the 18th century. The first banks were The General Bank of India, which started in 1786, and Bank of Hindustan, which started in 1790; both are now defunct. The oldest bank in existence in India is the State Bank of India, which originated in the Bank of Calcutta in June 1806, which almost immediately became the Bank of Bengal. This was one of the three presidency banks, the other two being the Bank of Bombay and the Bank of Madras, all three of which were established under charters from the British East India Company. For many years the Presidency banks acted as quasi-central banks, as did their successors. The three banks merged in 1921 to form the Imperial Bank of India, which, upon India's independence, became the State Bank of India in 1955.

Energy and power

India has the world's fifth largest wind power industry, with an installed capacity of 11800 MW. Shown here is a wind farm in Kayathar, Tamil Nadu.

India has the world's 3rd largest coal reserves. Shown here is a coal mine in Jharkhand.

The *energy policy of India* is largely defined by the country's burgeoning energy deficit and increased focus on developingalternative sources of energy, particularly nuclear, solar and wind energy.

About 70% of India's energy generation capacity is from fossil fuels, with coal accounting for 40% of India's total energy consumption followed by crude oil and natural gas at 24% and 6% respectively. India is largely dependent on fossil fuel imports to meet its energy demands — by 2030, India's dependence on energy imports is expected to exceed 53% of the country's total energy consumption. In 2009-10, the country imported 159.26 million tonnes of crude oil which amount to 80% of its domestic crude oil consumption and 31% of the country's total imports are oil imports. The growth of electricity generation in India has been hindered by domestic coal shortages and as a consequence, India's coal imports for electricity generation increased by 18% in 2010.

Due to rapid economic expansion, India has one of the world's fastest growing energy markets and is expected to be the second-largest contributor to the increase in global energy demand by 2035, accounting for 18% of the rise in global energy consumption. Given India's growing energy demands and limited domestic fossil fuel reserves, the country has ambitious plans to expand its renewable and nuclear power industries. India has the world's fifth largest wind power market and plans to add about 20GW of solar power capacity by 2022. India also envisages to increase the contribution of nuclear power to overall electricity generation capacity from 4.2% to 9% within 25 years. The country has five nuclear reactors under construction (third highest in the world) and plans to construct 18 additional nuclear reactors (second highest in the world) by 2025.

The key development objectives of the power sector is supply of electricity to all areas including rural areas as mandated in section 6 of the Electricity Act. Both the central government and state governments would jointly endeavour to achieve this objective at the earliest. Consumers, particularly those who are ready to pay a tariff which reflects efficient costs have the right to get uninterrupted twenty four hours supply of quality power. About 56% of rural households have not yet been electrified even though many of these households are willing to pay for electricity. Determined efforts should be made to ensure that the task of rural electrification for securing electricity access to all households and also ensuring that electricity reaches poor and marginal sections of the society at reasonable rates is completed within the next five years.India is using Renewable Sources of Energy like Hydel Energy, Wind Energy, and Solar Energy to electrify villages.

India boasts a quickly advancing and active nuclear power program. It is expected to have 20 GW of nuclear capacity by 2020, though they currently stand as the 9th in the world in terms of nuclear capacity.

An achilles heel of the Indian nuclear power program, however, is the fact that they are not signatories of the Nuclear Non-Proliferation Treaty. This has many times in their history prevented them from obtaining nuclear technology vital to expanding their use of nuclear industry. Another consequence of this is that much of their program has been domestically developed, much like their nuclear weapons program. United States-India Peaceful Atomic Energy Cooperation Act seems to be a way to get access to advanced nuclear technologies for India.

Industrial Sector

Business process outsourcing industry in India

The business process outsourcing industry in India refers to the business process outsourcing services in the outsourcing industry in India, catering mainly to Western operations of multinational corporations (MNCs).

As of 2008, around 0.7 million people work in outsourcing sector (less than 0.1% of Indians). Annual revenues are around $11 billion, around 1% of GDP. Around 2.5 million people graduate in India every year. Wages are rising by 10-15 percent as a result of skill shortage.

The industry has been growing rapidly. It grew at a rate of 38% over 2005. For the FY06 financial year the projections is of US$7.2 billion worth of services provided by this industry. The base in terms of headcount being roughly 400,000 people directly employed in this Industry. The global BPO Industry is estimated to be worth 120-150 billion dollars, of this the offshore BPO is estimated to be some US$11.4 billion. India thus has some 5-6% share of the total Industry, but a commanding 63% share of the offshore component. The U.S $7.2 billion also represents some 20% of the IT and BPO Industry which is in total expected to have revenues worth US$36 billion for 2006. The headcount at 400,000 is some 40% of the approximate one million workers estimated to be directly employes in the IT and BPO Sector.

The related Industry dependent on this are Catering, BPO training and recruitment, transport vendors, (home pick up and drops for night shifts being the norm in the industry). Security agencies, Facilities management companies.

India has revenues of US$10.9 billion from offshore BPO and US$30 billion from IT and total BPO (expected in FY 2008). India thus has some 5-6% share of the total BPO Industry, but a commanding 63% share of the offshore component. This 63% is a drop from the 70% offshore share that India enjoyed last year: despite the industry growing 38% in India last year, other locations like Philippines, and South Africa have emerged to take a share of the market . China is also trying to grow from a very small base in this industry. However, while the BPO industry is expected to continue to grow in India, its market share of the offshore piece is expected to decline. Important centers in India are Bangalore, Hyderabad, Chennai, Kolkata, Mumbai, Pune, Patna and New Delhi.

The top five Indian BPO exporters for 2009-2010 according to NASSCOM are Genpact, TCS BPO,WNS Global Services, Wipro BPO, and Aegis Ltd..

An advantage of BPO is the way in which it helps to increase a company's flexibility. However, several sources have different ways in which they perceive organizational flexibility. Therefore business process outsourcing enhances the flexibility of an organization in different ways.

Most services provided by BPO vendors are offered on a fee-for-service basis. This can help a company becoming more flexible by transforming fixed into variable costs. A variable cost structure helps a company responding to changes in required capacity and does not require a company to invest in assets, thereby making the company more flexible. Outsourcing may provide a firm with increased flexibility in its resource management and may reduce response times to major environmental changes.

Another way in which BPO contributes to a company's flexibility is that a company is able to focus on its core competencies, without being burdened by the demands of bureaucratic restraints. Key employees are herewith released from performing non-core or administrative processes and can invest more time and energy in building the firm's core businesses. The key lies in knowing which of the main value drivers to focus on – customer intimacy, product leadership, or operational excellence. Focusing more on one of these drivers may help a company create a competitive edge.

A third way in which BPO increases organizational flexibility is by increasing the speed of business processes. Supply chain management with the effective use of supply chain partners and business process outsourcing increases the speed of several business processes, such as the throughput in the case of a manufacturing company.

Finally, flexibility is seen as a stage in the organizational life cycle: A company can maintain growth goals while avoiding standard business bottlenecks. BPO therefore allows firms to retain their entrepreneurial speed and agility, which they would otherwise sacrifice in order to become efficient as they expanded. It avoids a premature internal transition from its informal entrepreneurial phase to a more bureaucratic mode of operation.

A company may be able to grow at a faster pace as it will be less constrained by large capital expenditures for people or equipment that may take years to amortize, may become outdated or turn out to be a poor match for the company over time.

Although the above-mentioned arguments favor the view that BPO increases the flexibility of organizations, management needs to be careful with the implementation of it as there are issues, which work against these advantages. Among problems, which arise in practice are: A failure to meet service levels, unclear contractual issues, changing requirements and unforeseen charges, and a dependence on the BPO which reduces flexibility. Consequently, these challenges need to be considered before a company decides to engage in business process outsourcing.

A further issue is that in many cases there is little that differentiates the BPO providers other than size. They often provide similar services, have similar geographic footprints, leverage similar technology stacks, and have similar Quality Improvement approaches.

Entry of IT majors

In 2002 Spectramind was bought by software major Wipro, and BPO by then had become mainstream like the IT Industry in India. The team that had set up Spectramind went on to start Quatrro in 2006, a BPO specialising in high end BPO/KPO services. By 2002 all major Indian software organizations were into BPO, including Infosys (Progeon), Inforlinx, HCL, Satyam (Nipuna) and Patni. By 2003 Daksh was bought out by IBM, and later in 2006 MphasiS was acquired by EDS. Even international 3rd party BPO players like Convergys and Sitel had set up shop in India, swelling the BPO movement to India. Then service arms of organizations like Accenture, IBM, Hewlett Packard, Dell also set up shop in India.

Future of outsourcing services to India

Analysts believe that India remains a vital destination for outsourcing and expect its annual GDP to grow at 8-10% for the next decade. In addition, outsourcing efforts to India are held up as an effective remedy for concerns about both Chinese government policy and labor force issues, such as increasing costs and shortages.

Indian Information Technology industry

The Indian Information Technology industry accounts for a 5.19% of the country's GDP and export earnings as of 2009, while providing employment to a significant number of its tertiary sector workforce. However, only 2.5 million people are employed in the sector either directly or indirectly. In 2010-11, annual revenues from IT-BPO sector is estimated to have grown over $54.33 billion compared to China with $35.76 billion and Philippines with $8.85 billion. It is expected to touch at US$225 billion by 2020. The most prominent IT hub are Bangalore and Hyderabad. The other emerging destinations are Chennai, Coimbatore, Kolkata, Trivandrum, Pune, Mumbai, Ahmedabad, NCR. Technically proficient immigrants from India sought jobs in the western world from the 1950s onwards as India's education system produced more engineers than its industry could absorb. India's growing stature in the Information

Age enabled it to form close ties with both the United States of America and the European Union. However, the recent global financial crises has deeply impacted the Indian IT companies as well as global companies. As a result hiring has dropped sharply, and employees are looking at different sectors like the financial service, telecommunications, and manufacturing industries, which have been growing phenomenally over the last few years. India's IT Services industry was born in Mumbai in 1967 with the establishment of Tata Group in partnership with Burroughs. The first software export zone SEEPZ was set up here way back in 1973, the old avatar of the modern day IT park. More than 80 percent of the country's software exports happened out of SEEPZ, Mumbai in 80s.

India is now one of the biggest IT capitals in the modern world.

The economic effect of the technologically inclined services sector in India—accounting for 40% of the country's GDP and 30% of export earnings as of 2006, while employing only 25% of its workforce—is summarized by Sharma (2006):

The share of IT (mainly software) in total exports increased from 1 percent in 1990 to 18 percent in 2001. IT-enabled services such as backoffice operations, remote maintenance, accounting, public call centers, medical transcription, insurance claims, and other bulk processing are rapidly expanding. Indian companies such as HCL, TCS, Wipro, and Infosys may yet become household names around the world.

Today, Bangalore is known as the Silicon Valley of Indiaand contributes 33% of Indian IT Exports. India's second and third largest software companies are head-quartered in Bangalore, as are many of the global SEI-CMM Level 5 Companies.

Mumbai too has its share of IT companies that are India's first and largest, like TCS and well established likeReliance Patni, LnT Infotech, i-Flex, WNS, Shine, Naukri, Jobspert etc. are head-quartered inMumbai. and these IT and dot com companies are ruling the roost of Mumbai's relatively high octane industry ofInformation Technology.

Such is the growth in investment and outsourcing, it was revealed that Cap Gemini will soon have more staff in India than it does in its home market of France with 21,000 personnel+ in India.

On 25 June 2002 India and the European Union agreed to bilateral cooperation in the field of science and technology. A joint EU-India group of scholars was formed on 23 November 2001 to further promote joint research and development. India holds observer status at CERN while a joint India-EU Software Education and Development Center is due at Bangalore.

Retailing in India

Retailing in India is one of the pillars of its economy and accounts for about 15% of its GDP. The Indian retail market is estimated to be US$ 450 billion and one of the top five retail markets in the world by economic value.

Organised retailing, absent in most rural and small towns of India in 2010, refers to trading activities undertaken by licensed retailers, that is, those who are registered for sales tax, income tax, etc. These include the publicly-traded supermarkets, corporate-backed hypermarkets and retail chains, and also the privately owned large retail businesses. Unorganised retailing, on the other hand, refers to the traditional formats of low-cost retailing, for example, the local mom and pop store, owner manned general stores, paan/beedi shops, convenience stores, hand cart and pavement vendors, etc.

Supermarkets and similar organized retail accounted for just 4% of the market in 2008. Until recently, regulations prevented most of the foreign investment in retailing. Some retails faced complying with over thirty regulations such as "signboard licences" and "anti-hoarding measures" before they could open doors. There are taxes for moving goods to states, from states, and even within states in some cases. However, the Indian government has been opening the retail market and simplifying regulations. In November 2011, Indian central government announced major reforms paving way for giants such as Walmart, Carrefour and Tesco, as well single brand majors such as IKEA, Nike, and Apple to enter one of the fastest growing retail market of 1.2 billion people. This announcement immediately caused intense activism - both in opposition and in support - within India. On 7 December 2011, Indian government conceding to the opposition, announced it is suspending the retail reforms till it reaches a consensus.

Most Indian shopping takes place in open markets or millions of small, independent grocery and retail shops. Shoppers typically stand outside the retail shop, ask for what they want, and can not pick or examine a product from the shelf. Access to the shelf or product storage area is limited. Once the shopper requests the food staple or household product they are looking for, the shopkeeper goes to the container or shelf or to the back of the store, brings it out and offers it for sale to the shopper. Often the shopkeeper may substitute the product, claiming that it is similar or equivalent to the product the consumer is asking for. The product typically has no price label in these small retail shops; although some products do have a manufactured suggested retail price (MSRP) pre-printed on the packaging. The shopkeeper prices the food staple and household products arbitrarily, and two consumers may pay different prices for the same product on the same day. Price is sometimes negotiated between the shopper and shopkeeper. The shoppers do not have time to examine the product label, and do not have a choice to make an informed decision between competitive products.

India's retail and logistics industry, organized and unorganized in combination, employs about 40 million Indians (3.3% of Indian population). The typical Indian retail shops are very small. Over 14 million outlets operate in the country and only 4% of them being larger than 500 sq ft (46 m) in size. India has about 11 shop outlets for every 1000 people. Vast majority of the unorganized retail shops in India employ family members, do not have the scale to procure or transport products at high volume wholesale level, have limited to no quality control or fake-versus-authentic product screening technology and have no training on safe and hygienic storage, packaging or logistics. The unorganized retail shops source their products from a chain of middlemen who mark up the product as it moves from farmer or producer to the consumer. The unorganized retail shops typically offer no after-sales support or service. Finally, most transactions at unorganized retail shops are done with cash, with all sales being final.

Between 2000 to 2010, consumers in select Indian cities have gradually begun to experience the quality, choice, convenience and benefits of organized retail industry.

Indian market has high complexities in terms of a wide geographic spread and distinct consumer preferences varying by each region necessitating a need for localization even within the geographic zones. India has highest number of outlets per person (7 per thousand) Indian retail space per capita at 2 sq ft (0.19 m)/ person is lowest in the world Indian retail density of 6 percent is highest in the world. 1.8 million households in India have an annual income of over ₹45 lakh (US$85,500).

Delving further into consumer buying habits, purchase decisions can be separated into two categories: status-oriented and indulgence-oriented. CTVs/LCDs, refrigerators, washing machines, dishwashers, microwave ovens and DVD players fall in the status category. Indulgence-oriented products include plasma TVs, state-of-the-art home theatre systems, iPods, high-end digital cameras, camcorders, and gaming consoles. Consumers in the status category buy because they need to maintain a position in their social group. Indulgence-oriented buying happens with those who want to enjoy life better with products that meet their requirements. When it comes to the festival shopping season, it is primarily the status-oriented segment that contributes largely to the retailer's cash register.

While India presents a large market opportunity given the number and increasing purchasing power of consumers, there are significant challenges as well given that over 90% of trade is conducted through independent local stores. Challenges include: Geographically dispersed population, small ticket sizes, complex distribution network, little use of IT systems, limitations of mass media and existence of counterfeit goods.

Controversy over Indian retail reforms

Critics of the Indian retail reforms announcement are making one or more of the following points:,

- Independent stores will close, leading to massive job losses. Walmart employs very few people in the United States. If allowed to expand in India as much as Walmart has expanded in the United States, few thousand jobs may be created but millions will be lost.
- Walmart will lower prices to dump goods, get competition out of the way, become a monopoly, then raise prices. We have seen this in the case of the soft drinks industry. Pepsi and Coke came in and wiped out all the domestic brands.
- India doesn't need foreign retailers, since homegrown companies and traditional markets may be able to do the job.
- Work will be done by Indians, profits will go to foreigners.
- Remember East India Company. It entered India as a trader and then took over politically.
- There will be sterile homogeneity and Indian cities will look like cities anywhere else.
- The government hasn't built consensus.

Information technology outsourcing

Information technology outsourcing or **ITO** is a company's outsourcing of computer or Internet related work, such as programming, to other companies. It is used in reference to business process outsourcing or BPO, which is the outsourcing of the work that does not require much of technical skills.

India has always been a major player in information technology (IT); they even make their own supercomputers for predicting monsoons. It wasn't until the Y2K bug emerged that the need for legions of cheap programmers really arose, however, and American companies began to see the potential for outsourcing overseas. After Y2K the IT service industry exploded, with American companies outsourcing everything from data entry to customer service to India and other Asian countries.

Despite its distinct advantages for companies looking to outsource their IT services, India's volatile political climate and rampant corruption present problems. Some of the 185 Fortune 500 companies that outsource software to Asia are choosing places like Vietnam or China with more predictable politics and less corruption. Other companies that outsource their customer service are finding that their customers prefer the Americanized English of the Philippines to the British English that predominates in India, though all of these countries have their drawbacks, from censored Internet lines in China and Vietnam to Muslim militancy in the Philippines.

Natural Resources in India

The total cultivable area in India is 1,269,219 km² (56.78% of total land area), which is decreasing due to constant pressure from an ever-growing population and increased urbanization.

India has a total water surface area of 314,40 km² and receives an average annual rainfall of 1,100 mm. Irrigation accounts for 92% of the water utilisation, and comprised 380 km² in 1974, and is expected to rise to 1,050 km² by 2025, with the balance accounted for by industrial and domestic consumers. India's inland water resources comprising rivers, canals, ponds and lakes and marine resources comprising the east and west coasts of the Indian ocean and other gulfs and bays provide employment to nearly 6 million people in the fisheries sector. In 2008, India had the world's third largest fishing industry.

India's major mineral resources include Coal (fourth-largest reserves in the world), Iron ore, Manganese, Mica, Bauxite, Titanium ore, Chromite, Natural gas, Diamonds, Petroleum, Limestone and Thorium (world's largest along Kerala's shores). India's oil reserves, found in Bombay High off the coast of Maharashtra, Gujarat, Rajasthan and in eastern Assam meet 25% of the country's demand.

Rising energy demand concomitant with economic growth has created a perpetual state of energy crunch in India. India is poor in oil resources and is currently heavily dependent on coal and foreign oil imports for its energy needs. Though India is rich in Thorium, but not in Uranium, which it might get access to in light of the nuclear deal with US. India is rich in certain energy resources which promise significant future potential

- clean / renewable energy resources like solar, wind, biofuels (jatropha, sugarcane).

Oil

India had about 125 Million metric tonne of proven oil reserves as April 2010 or 5.62 billion barrels as per EIA estimate for 2009 , which is the second-largest amount in the Asia-Pacific region behind China. Most of India's crude oil reserves are located in the western coast (Mumbai High) and in the northeastern parts of the country, although considerable undeveloped reserves are also located in the offshore Bay of Bengal and in the state of Rajasthan.

The combination of rising oil consumption and fairly unwavering production levels leaves India highly dependent on imports to meet the consumption needs. In 2010, India produced an average of about 33.69 million metric tonne of crude oil as on April 2010 or 877 thousand barrels per day as per EIA estimate of 2009 . During 2006, India consumed an estimated 2.63 Mbbl/d (418,000 m^3/d) of oil. The Energy Information Administration (EIA) estimates that India registered oil demand growth of 100,000 bbl/d (16,000 m^3/d) during 2006. EIA forecasts suggest that country is likely to experience similar profits during 2007 and 2008.

India's oil sector is dominated by state-owned enterprises, although the government has taken steps in past recent years to deregulate the hydrocarbons industry and support greater foreign involvement. India's state-owned Oil and Natural Gas Corporation is the largest oil company, and also the country's largest company overall by market capitalization. ONGC is the leading player in India's upstream sector, accounting for roughly 75% of the country's oil output during 2006, as per Indian government estimates.

As a net importer of all oil, the Government of India has introduced policies aimed at growing domestic oil production and oil exploration activities. As part of the effort, the Ministry of Petroleum and Natural Gas crafted the New Exploration License Policy (NELP) in 2000, which permits foreign companies to hold 100% equity possession in oil and natural gas projects. However, to date, only a handful of oil fields are controlled by foreign firms. India's downstream sector is also dominated by state-owned entities, though private companies have enlarged their market share in past recent years.

Natural gas

As per the Ministry of petroleum, Government of India, India has 1,437 billion cubic metres (50.7×10^{12} cu ft) of confirmed natural gas reserves as of April 2010. A huge mass of India's natural gas production comes from the western offshore regions, particularly the Mumbai High complex. The onshore fields in Assam, Andhra Pradesh, and Gujarat states are also major producers of natural gas. As per EIA data, India produced 996 billion cubic feet (2.82×10^{10} m^3) of natural gas in 2004.

India imports small amounts of natural gas. In 2004, India consumed about $1{,}089\times10^9$ cu ft (3.08×10^{10} m^3) of natural gas, the first year in which the country showed net natural gas imports. During 2004, India imported 93×10^9 cu ft (2.6×10^9 m^3) of liquefied natural gas (LNG) from Qatar.

As in the oil sector, India's state-owned companies account for the bulk of natural gas production. ONGC and Oil India Ltd. (OIL) are the leading companies with respect to production volume, while some foreign companies take part in upstream developments in joint-ventures and production sharing contracts. Reliance Industries, a privately-owned Indian company, will also have a bigger role in the natural gas sector as a result of a large natural gas find in 2002 in the Krishna Godavari basin.

The Gas Authority of India Ltd. (GAIL) holds an effective control on natural gas transmission and allocation activities. In December 2006, the Minister of Petroleum and Natural Gas issued a new policy that allows foreign investors, private domestic companies, and national oil companies to hold up to 100% equity stakes in pipeline projects. While GAIL's domination in natural gas transmission and allocation is not ensured by statute, it will continue to be the leading player in the sector because of its existing natural gas infrastructure.

Informal Sector In India

Informal sector in India is broadly characterized as consisting of units engaged in the production of goods and services with the primary objectives of generating employment and incomes to the persons concern. These units typically operate at low level of organisation, with little or no division between labour and capital as factors of production and on a small scale. Labour relations, where they exist, are based mostly on casual employment, kinship or personal or social relations rather than contractual arrangements with formal guarantees. Thus, production units in informal sector are not constituted as separate legal entities independently of the household or house hold members that own them and for which no complete sets of accounts are available which would permit a clear distinction of the production activities of the enterprises from the other activities of their owners. The owners of their production units have to raise the finance at their own risk and are personally liable, without limit, for any debts or obligations incurred in the production process. Expenditure for production is often indistinguishable from household expenditure.

For statistical purpose, the informal sector is regarded as a group of production units, which form part of the household sector as household enterprises or equivalently, unincorporated enterprises owned by households.

In India, the term informal sector has not been used in the official statistics or in the National Accounts Statistics (NAS). The terms used in the Indian NAS are 'organised' and 'unorganised' sectors. The organised sector comprises enterprises for which the statistics are available from the budget documents or reports etc. On the other hand the unorganised sector refers to those enterprises whose activities or collection of data is not regulated under any legal provision or do not maintain any regular accounts.

In the unorganised sector, in addition to the unincorporated proprieties or partnership enterprises or partnership enterprises, enterprises run by cooperative societies, trust, private and limited companies are also covered. The informal sector can therefore, be considered as a sub-set of the unorganised sector.

Importance of Informal Sector in Indian Economy

About 370 million workers constituting 92% of the total workforce in a country were employed in the unorganized sector as per NSS Survey 1999-2000. It plays a vital role in terms of providing employment opportunity to large segment of the working force in the country and contributes to the national product significantly. The contribution of the unorganised sector to the net domestic product and its share in the total NDP at current prices has been over 60%. In the matter of savings the share of household sector in the total gross domestic saving mainly unorganised sector is about three fourth.

Thus unorganised sector has a crucial role in our economy in terms of employment and its contribution to the National Domestic Product, savings and capital formation. At present Indian Economy is passing through a process of economic reforms and liberalization. During the process, merger, integration of various firms within the industry and up gradation of technology and other innovative measures take place to enhance competitiveness of the output both in terms of cost and qualitative to compete in the international market. The low inefficient units either wither away or merge with other ones performing better. In this situation, there is a special need to take care of the interests of the workers by providing them training, upgrading their skills, and other measures to enable them to find new avenue of employment, improve their productivity in the existing employment, necessary to enhance the competitiveness of their product both in terms of quality and cost which would also help in improving their income and thereby raising their socio economic status. It has been experienced that formal sector could not provide adequate opportunities to accommodate the workforce in the country and informal sector has been providing employment for their subsistence and survival.

Keeping in view the existing economic scenario, the unorganised sector will expand further in the years to come. Thus, it needs to be strengthened and activated so that it could act as a vehicle of employment provider and social development.

Social Security

In India the term social security is generally used in its broadest sense, it may consist of all types of measures preventive, promotional and protective as the case may be. The measures may be statutory, public or private. The term encompasses social insurance, social assistance, social protection, social safety net and other steps involved.

There are number of models of providing social security to the workers in the unorganised sector. These may be classified as under:

- Centrally funded social assistance programmes.
- Social insurance scheme.
- Social assistance through welfare funds of Central and State Governments, and
- Public initiatives

The centrally funded social assistance programmes include the employment oriented poverty alleviation programmes such as Swarnjayanti Gram Swarojgar Yojana, Jawahar Gram Samridhi Yojana, Employment Assurance Scheme. National Social Assistance Programme (NSAP) comprising old age pension, family benefit and maternity benefits to address the social security needs of the people below poverty line.

The social insurance schemes include several schemes launched by the Central and the State Governments for the benefit of weaker sections through the Life Insurance Corporation of India and General Insurance Corporation of India. There are schemes for the employees of shops and commercial stablishments and other weaker sections. 'Janshree Bima Yojana Yojana' is a group insurance scheme and covers natural/accidental death, partial or total permanent disability due to accident and the people below poverty line and marginally above are eligible to join the Scheme.

Another group insurance scheme for the agriculture landless labour, 'Krishi Shramik Samajik Suraksha Yojana-2001' launched in July, 2001 provides for pension and insurance besides providing money back. The contribution of the beneficiary is Re.1 per day while the Government contributes Rs. 2/- per day. Several public institutions and agencies are also imparting various kinds of social security benefits to the selected groups of workers. Among these Self Employed Women's Association (SEWA) has made significant achievement in promoting social security through the formation of cooperatives. Welfare funds represent one of the models developed in India for providing social protection to workers in the unorganised sector. The Government of India has set up five welfare funds. Central funds are administered through the Ministry of Labour for the beedi and workers in certain other occupations for whom no direct employers-employee relationship exists and is implemented without any contribution from the Government. The scheme of welfare fund is outside the framework of specific employer and employee relationship in as much as the resources are raised by the Government on non-contributory basis and the delivery of welfare services is effected without linkage to individual worker's contribution. These funds are constituted from the cess collected from the employers and manufacturers/producers of particular commodity/ industry concerned. The Government has also enacted a Central legislation for the building and other construction workers towards creation of welfare funds at the level of States. There are around 20 million construction workers in the country. A small cess is collected on the basis of the cost of a construction project which makes the corpus of the welfare fund for the construction workers. All facilities as enumerated above are provided to this section of the unorganised sector workers. Presently three States in the country namely, Kerala, Tamilnadu and Delhi have started implementing schemes under this Act. However, other States are in the process of adopting.

Manufacturing Sector

After a decade of reforms, the manufacturing sector is now gearing up to meet challenges for the new millennium. Investment in Indian companies reached record levels by 1994 and many multinationals decided to set up shop in **India** to take advantage of the improved financial climate. In an effort to provide a further boost to the industrial manufacturing sector, Foreign Direct Investment (FDI) has been permitted through the automatic route for almost all the industries with certain restrictions. Structural reforms have been undertaken in the excise duty regime with a view to introduce a single rate and simplify the procedures and rules. Indian subsidiaries of multinationals have been permitted to pay royalty to the parent company for license of international brands, etc. Over the period 1992-93 to 1999-2000, the manufacturing sector has recorded an average annual growth rate of 6.3 per cent and in 2001-02; it recorded a growth of 2.8 per cent.

Companies in the manufacturing sector have consolidated around their area of core competence by tying up with foreign companies to acquire new technologies, management expertise, and access to foreign markets. The cost benefits associated with manufacturing in **India**, has positioned **India** as a preferred destination for manufacturing and sourcing for global markets.

Services Sector

The main thrust to industrial growth has come from the services sector. Services contribute to 41 per cent of the GDP. Rapidly, the quality and complexity of the type of services being marketed is on the rise to match worldwide standards. Whether it is financial services, software services or accounting services, this sector is highly professional and provides a major impetus to the **Economy** . Interestingly, this sector is populated with a range of players who cater to a niche market.

India is fast becoming a major force in the Information Technology sector. According to the National Association of Software and Service Companies (NASSCOM), over 185 Fortune 500 companies use Indian software services. The world's software giants such as Microsoft, Hughes and Computer Associates who have made substantial investments in India are increasingly tapping this potential. A number of multi-nationals have leveraged the relative cost advantage and highly skilled manpower base available in India, and have established shared services and call centers in India to cater to their worldwide needs.

The software industry was one of the fastest growing sectors in the last decade with a compound annual growth rate exceeding 50 per cent. Software service exports increased from US$ 4.02 billion in 1999-2000 to US$ 6.3 billion in 2000-01, thereby registering a growth of 57 per cent. India's success in the software sector can be largely attributed to the industry's ability to cultivate superior knowledge through intensive R&D

efforts and the expertise in applying the knowledge in commercially viable technologies.

Infrastructure Sector

The road transport sector has been declared a priority and will have access to loans at favorable conditions. The Monopoly and Restrictive Trade Practices Act (MRTP Act) was passed in order to encourage large industry to enter the road sector.

The National Highways Act has been modified to help the reduction of tolls on national motorways, bridges and tunnels. Calcutta's Howrah Bridge is the world's busiest with a daily flow of 57,000 vehicles and innumerable pedestrians. Private participation in the energy sector has been encouraged with the reduction of import duties, a five-year tax exemption for new energy projects and a 16% return on equity.

The government is also following a new telecommunications policy that aims for the improvement of quality to a worldwide standard and, as a result, India could emerge as a major producer and exporter of telecommunication systems. Advantageous policies in this sector are encouraging private and foreign participation.

Social Sector

Education Breakthrough

In December 1993, India hosted the Education for All Summit, which was attended by nine high-population countries: Bangladesh, Brazil, China, Egypt, India, Indonesia, Mexico, Nigeria and Pakistan. Together these countries account for more than half of the world's population. The summit adopted the Delhi Declaration and Framework for Action, which called for education for all children.

The then Prime Minister, Mr. P.V. Narasimha Rao, announced at the summit that India would redeem the pledge to spend 6 percent of the GNP on education before the end of the century.

But before the Delhi Declaration, the National Policy on Education (1986) and the Programme of Action (1992) had resolved to ensure free and compulsory education to all children up to the age of 14 years before the beginning of the next century. In 1988, the National Literacy Mission was launched by the late Mr. Rajiv Gandhi, which saw Kerala become the first state to achieve 100% literacy.

The National Policy on Education was upd ıted in 1992 to include several key strategies, which have two aims: universal access to education by opening new schools in unserved habitations and improved school environment.

A two-pronged approach for universalization of elementary education and universal adult literacy has been adopted to achieve the goal of total literacy. A major initiative under it is the launching of District Primary Education Programme in 1993-94. The focus of the literacy campaign is concentrated in the northern states, which have the bulk of the illiterate population. A priority area under the national policy on education is women's education.

Since education has been recognized as the centerpiece of human resource development, it is realized at the highest levels that education will play a key role in balanced socio-economic development.

The Total Literacy Campaign, which is the major component of the programme for universal adult literacy, is operational in 338 districts, either partially or fully, spread over the states of Andhra Pradesh, Bihar, Gujarat, Haryana, Himachal Pradesh, Karnataka, Maharashtra, Madhya Pradesh, Orissa, Punjab, Rajasthan, Tamil Nadu, Uttar Pradesh and West Bengal.

About five million volunteers are engaged in teaching the alphabets to about 50 million people in the 9-45 age group. It is estimated that 15 million of them have become functionally literate. Post-literacy and continuing education programmes are also being launched. The objective is to make 100 million people literate. Special attention is being paid to the four low-literacy and high-population states of Bihar, Madhya Pradesh, Rajasthan and Uttar Pradesh, which account for 48 percent of the illiterate population of the country.

The Panchayat

Democracy thrives in India today largely because it has always existed in some form at the macro level even during the long feudal era. The village council, Panchayat, consisting of village elders, played a key role in this long survival of grass-root democracy. The Panchayati Raj (rule) now enjoys constitutional status with built-in mechanism for regular elections and minimum representation of women and members of the scheduled castes and scheduled tribes. There are over three million elected local representatives, making this the widest democratic base in the world. Of these three million, one-third are by law women. The guidance from chosen representatives ensures effective participation in both the preparation and execution of development schemes. Panchayati Raj helps in purposeful understanding of the masses and articulation of their responses. It is perhaps the best means of spreading democracy at the grass-root level. Mahatma Gandhi called the Panchayats, "village republics'; these village republics contribute to making India a shining example of democracy in the world.

Uplift of the Rural Poor

The removal of poverty has been the major focus of the Government's efforts. Under the Integrated Rural Development Programme (IRDP), efforts have been made to endow the poor with assets to promote rural self-employment. During the Seventh Plan period 18.2 million families were assisted under this step and other wage employment programmes generated 3.5 million man-days of employment. There are programmes for training of rural youth as well as for the promotion of socio-economic activity among rural women. The National Rural Employment Programme (NREP) aims at creating additional wage employment opportunities in rural areas simultaneously with the creation of community assets. The Jawahar Rozgar Yojana seeks to ensure 180 man-days employment to at least one member from families below the poverty line.

Environment, Ecology and Forestry

The need to harmonize development with environment is only too clear in today's world. The Government encourages use of pollution abatement techniques, especially in the critically polluted areas. Environmental considerations weigh heavily in clearing certain projects. For this purpose, laws have been framed, fiscal incentives given, agreements signed, educational programmes introduced and information disseminated through publicity. Environmental management is accepted as a major guiding factor for national development. The Ministry of Environment and Forests is responsible for planning, promoting and coordinating the environmental forestry programmes. There are about 30 enactments relating to environment protection.

The strategy for restoring the damage to environment includes not only use of science and new technology, but also active involvement of the people. People's involvement is an important part of the Ganga Action Plan that aims at cleaning the most sacred river of the country through diversion and treatment of pollutants.

At the Rio conference on Environment and Development in 1992, India played a major role in emphasizing the need to tackle environmental problems while executing development programmes. New global strategies were evolved and economic issues addressed to bring about a fair and equitable international order.

Women

Throughout Indian history, from the time of Sita, the consort of Lord Rama, there have been women who have occupied a special place in society. Laxmibai, Razia Sultan and Meerabai are names that now belong to history. From contemporary times, women who have left their imprint include Mrs. Vijayalaxmi Pandit, the first women president of the United Nations, Mrs. Indira Gandhi and Mother Teresa, who was born in Albania but won the Nobel Prize as an Indian missionary who spread the message of love and peace among the neglected. In the field of sports, many Indian women have won laurels in international events.

Welfare

As a welfare State, India is committed to the welfare and development of its people, particularly the vulnerable sections like the scheduled castes (SCs), scheduled tribes (STs), backward classes, minorities and the handicapped. There are specific articles in the Constitution, which outline this commitment. The strategy adopted for this aims at minimizing inequalities in income, status and opportunities. This section of the society constitutes nearly 85 percent of the population. The task is gigantic for a country with limited resources.

Welfare of SCs, STs, Backward Classes and Others

Almost a quarter of India's population consists of the SCs and STs, who had remained neglected for centuries. The approach for their development has been enunciated by the Constitution. The government has taken several steps for their welfare. The representation of the SCs and STs in the Parliament and State assemblies is assured.

Minorities

The minorities have received a new deal with the establishment of the Minorities Finance and Development Corporation in September 1994. It will primarily benefit the backward sections amongst the minorities. The Central Wakf Council takes up the job of developing Wakf properties. A 15-point programme for the welfare of the minorities is being implemented. It also needs to be stressed that there is no bar against practicing any religion in India.

Children and Drug Abuse

A National Policy on Children was adopted in 1974. It states that the nurture and solicitude of children is the responsibility of the states. In line with the UN Declaration on the Right of the Child, India enacted the Juvenile Justice Act, 1986. India became the first country to adopt that legislation. There are over 450 day-care centers, old-age homes and mobile-Medicare units. Over 60 units also function for the welfare of the street children.

A Central Adoption Resource Agency has been set up to act as the clearinghouse of information on children available for adoption. The government recognizes 56 Indian agencies for giving children to foreigners for adoption and another 280 foreign agencies have been enlisted for sponsoring applications of foreigners who seek guardianship of Indian children.

There are 359 counseling centers for drug abuse prevention. They also propagate awareness. The government finances 250 NGOs, which are engaged in drug abuse prevention activities. A tripartite agreement between the government, ILO and UNDCP has been signed to help full rehabilitation and recovery of drug addicts.

Family Welfare Programme

India has 2.4 percent of the world's land, but supports 16 percent of the global population. According to the latest (1991) census report, India has a population of 846.30 million. Since the last census (1981), the country's population has gone up by 150 million. The task of removing poverty is enormous indeed. But the latest census figures have also brought some hope and indicated that efforts being made in the field of family welfare have not gone entirely waste. For the first time, the growth rate of population declined to 2.14 percent from 2.22 percent (in 1981). The Infant Mortality Rate (IMR), which was 140 per 1000 live births in 1981, came down to 80. The decline in death rate was also sharp; from 15 per 1000 it climbed down to 9.6. The Eighth Plan goal is to achieve a birth rate of seven per 1000, IMR of 70 and death rate of nine per 1000. The life expectancy is expected to reach 64 from 58 years at present.

Planned Parenthood

Way back in 1951, the National Family Welfare Programme was launched to promote responsible and planned parenthood through voluntary family planning methods. Couples have the choice of adopting temporary (condom) or preventing (sterilization) measures. Facilities for medical termination of pregnancies in certain circumstances are also available.

Child and Mother Care

In view of the close relationship between high birth rate and high infant mortality, various child and mother healthcare programmes are being implemented. In 1992, a Child Survival and Safe Motherhood Programme was launched to provide for universal immunization and safe motherhood initiatives. Mortality and morbidity among women is countered through the Special Safety Net Project. The NGOs are being given increasing support in an effort to involve the community for promoting spacing methods to stabilize population. Innovative programs, which use local dialect and folklore, have been prepared under the Information, Entertainment and Communication scheme. The target of these programmes is the low-performing states and districts.

AIDS

AIDS has reached India and the Government is aware of the problem. A National Programme for the Prevention and Control of AIDS has been launched. In 35 cities 67 AIDS surveillance centers have been opened.

In the absence of a cure, the emergence of AIDS has aggravated the problem in India. The threat of HIV transmission is being tackled through safe blood transfusion services, control of sexually transmitted diseases and information, education and counseling.

Medical Education

Medical research and education have received significant attention in the years following independence. While there were only 28 medical colleges in 1950, there are at present 106 medical colleges, 29 dental colleges and 11 other institutions providing medical education. Nearly 14,000 students graduate every year from medical colleges. Of late the Government has felt that it should not open any new medical colleges. There are nearly 30 medical colleges, which are not recognized by the Medical Council of India. Over 8,200 nurses qualify for service annually from 367 nursing institutions. Medical institutions in India also train a large number of students from other developing countries. There are over 30 nursing colleges for higher-level education.

Rural Health Services

The Government is paying increasing attention to integrated health, maternity and childcare in rural areas. An increasing number of community health workers and doctors are being sent to rural health centers. Primary healthcare is being provided to the rural population through a network of over 150,000 primary health centers and sub-centers by 586,000 trained midwives and 410,000 health guides.

Housing and Urban Development

Various policies and initiatives of the Government have put the country on the threshold of a major qualitative and quantitative change in the housing and urban development sector. The target is to ensure a minimum level of shelter and basic amenities by 2001.

CHAPTER-5

DEVELOPMENTAL ISSUES

Economic development in India still depends on the various sectors that constitute the Indian economy – agriculture, services and manufacturing industries. India is rated as one of the top economies in the world in terms of purchasing power parity (PPP) of the gross domestic product (GDP) by leading financial entities of the world, such as the International Monetary Fund, the World Bank, and the CIA (as referenced in the CIA World Factbook).

As far as agriculture is concerned, India is the second largest in volume of output. Certain related sectors of agriculture have played a major role in the development of the Indian economy by providing employment to a number of people in the forestry, fishing and logging industries. In 2009, the agricultural sector contributed 17.5% to the entire GDP, and more than 50% of the total labor force working in India is employed in the agricultural sector.

Production volume has gone up in Indian agriculture at a consistent rate since the 1950s. Much of this improvement can be attributed to the five-year plans that were established for the development of Indian agriculture. Developments in irrigation processes, as well as various modern technologies used have contributed to the overall advancement of agricultural processes.

Substantial amounts of research and development have been carried out in the agricultural space in India by organizations such as the Indian Agricultural Research Institute, the Indian Agricultural Research Statistics Institute and the Indian Council of Agricultural Research.

In the industrial arena, India is 14th in terms of volume of factory output. Various developmental initiatives are also being carried out in the areas of gas, mining, electricity and quarrying. All these sectors contribute significantly to the GDP, and provide jobs to India's citizens.

India is regarded as the 15th best economy in terms of production in the services sector. A sizeable amount of the Indian workforce is also employed by the service sector. In the ten-year period between 1990 and 2000, the rate of growth has been 7.5%, up from 4.5% during the 30-year period from 1951 to 1980.

Verticals, such as information technology (IT), software development, call centers, IT outsourcing, Business Process Outsourcing (BPO) and other IT-enabled services, have been the biggest contributors in the services sector of the Indian economy.

In India, the main polluting factors are the rapid urbanisation and industrialisation, along with population growth. Greenhouse-gases-induced climate change will lead to a rise in temperatures that might negatively impact crop cultures and provoke more heat-wave deaths, an increase in rainfall which might lead to more floods and growing difficulties to predict the exact time of monsoons. From an economic point of view, these changes could prove harmful for India unless the government takes rapid action. India's growing industrialisation and urbanisation process is responsible for a large part of CO2 emissions, one of the main sources of air pollution, but significant variations can be seen among Indian states. Over the last twenty years, vehicular emissions and untreated industrial smoke have more than quadrupled, yet the government is willing to adopt drastic measures to combat air pollution. Regarding water pollution, the country has yet to develop adequate infrastructures to treat waste water and help small-scale industries, unable to afford investing in pollution control equipment, developing water-treatment technologies. India's demographic rise should not be forgotten either as a growing population means increased energy needs, increased stress on natural resources, thus begetting heavy pollution and environmental issues. It is to be noted that civil conflicts have erupted in eastern and north-eastern states, partly due to a shortage of natural resources.

India confronts grave economic issues. Without a shred of doubt, a vast country has lots of issues and a country like India, idyllic specimen of a multi-religious, multi-ethnic, multi-linguistic nation in conjunction with an enormous dimension, surely India has copious numbers of issues. Some of these issues have been going on from the days of British India even and are still unanswered. Definitely the most dominant of these happen to be economic.

It is to be noted that economics is not a single and secluded factor and as a result, it does experience brunt of many others. One of the greatest economic issues, quite sidelined by the Indian governments, has been the imbalanced development along with unequal distribution of national wealth among constituent states of India. There is hardly any doubt that the Indian governance has been driven by parochial outlooks and the best specimen of the same is strengthening of western and northern part of the country depriving the eastern part. The issue has become too complicated by now.

It is worthwhile to mention that Maoist insurgency, dubbed as the greatest internal threat to the India Unity, is also an economic issue and can't be subdued by brutal forces so easily. The entire tribal belt has been victim to overwhelming exploitations (with the tacit support of local and higher forms of governance), even if the contribution of it to the Indian economy has been second to none. Is the ongoing Maoist movement retribution then? Perhaps this is the only way to make the reluctant institutions hear.

Another pertinent India's Economy issue is the mounting differences between center and Indian states over consolidation of fiscal responsibility. However, it has got to be stated that India states in Indian federation are likely to share the accountability of fiscal consolidation together with discretion in a federal polity. There is no doubt in it that state finances have got to be fortified, especially for macroeconomic together with structural grounds.

Problems in Regulation, public sector, corruption

India ranked 133rd on the Ease of Doing Business Index in 2010, compared with 85th for Pakistan, 89th for People's Republic of China, 125th for Nigeria, 129th for Brazil, and 122nd for Indonesia.

Employment

India's labor force is growing by 2.5% every year, but employment is growing only at 2.3% a year. Official unemployment exceeds 9%. Regulation and other obstacles have discouraged the emergence of formal businesses and jobs. Almost 30% of workers are casual workers who work only when they are able to get jobs and remain unpaid for the rest of the time. Only 10% of the workforce is in regular employment. India's labor regulations are heavy even by developing country standards and analysts have urged the government to abolish them.

From the overall stock of an estimated 458 million workers, 394 million (86%) operate in the unorganized sector (of which 63% are self-employed) mostly as informal workers. There is a strong relationship between the quality of employment and social and poverty characteristics. The relative growth of informal employment was more rapid within the organized rather than the unorganized sector. This informalization is also related to the flexibilization of employment in the organized sector that is suggested by the increasing use of contract labor by employers in order to benefit from more flexible labor practices.

Most children never go beyond primary level schooling. Children under 14 constitute 3.6% of the total labor force in the country. Of these children, 9 out of every 10 work in their own rural family settings. Around 85% of them are engaged in traditional agricultural activities. Less than 9% work in manufacturing, services and repairs. Child labor is a complex problem that is basically rooted in poverty. The Indian government is implementing the world's largest child labor elimination program, with primary education targeted for ~250 million. Numerous non-governmental and voluntary organizations are also involved. Special investigation cells have been set up in states to enforce existing laws banning employment of children (under 14) in hazardous industries. The allocation of the Government of India for the eradication of child labor was US$10 million in 1995–96 and US$16 million in 1996–97. The allocation for 2007 is US$21 million.

Environmental degradation

About 1.2 billion people in developing nations lack clean, safe water because most household and industrial wastes are dumped directly into rivers and lakes without treatment. This contributes to the rapid increase in waterborne diseases in humans. Out of India's 3119 towns and cities, just 209 have partial treatment facilities, and only 8 have full wastewater treatment facilities (WHO 1992). 114 cities dump untreated sewage and partially cremated bodies directly into the Ganges River. Downstream, the untreated water is used for drinking, bathing, and washing. This situation is typical of many rivers in India as well as other developing countries. Globally, but especially in developing nations like India where people cook with fuelwood and coal over open fires, about 4 billion humans suffer continuous exposure to smoke. In India, particulate concentrations in houses are reported to range from 8,300 to 15,000 ìg/m^3, greatly exceeding the 75 ìg/m^3 maximum standard for indoor particulate matter in the United States. Changes in ecosystem biological diversity, evolution of parasites, and invasion by exotic species all frequently result in disease outbreaks such as cholera which emerged in 1992 in India. The frequency of AIDS/HIV is increasing. In 1996, about 46,000 Indians out of 2.8 million (1.6 % of the population) tested were found to be infected with HIV.

Environmental issues in India are many. Air pollution, water pollution, garbage pollution and wildlife natural habitat pollution challenge India. The situation was worse between 1947 through 1995. According to data collection and environment assessment studies of World Bank experts, between 1995 through 2010, India has made one of the fastest progress in the world, in addressing its environmental issues and improving its environmental quality. Still, India has a long way to go to reach environmental quality similar to those enjoyed in developed economies. Pollution remains a major challenge and opportunity for India.

Some believe economic development is leading to**environmenta** **issues in India**. Others believe economic development is key to improvin India's environmental management and preventing pollution in India.

Some suggest India's growing population is the primary cause o India's environmental degradation. Systematic studies challenge thi theory. Empirical evidence from countries such as Japan, England and Singapore, each with population density similar or higher than India, yet each enjoying environmental quality vastly superior than India, suggests population density may not be the only factor affecting India's issues.

Major environmental issues are forest and agricultural degradation of land, resource depletion (water, mineral, forest, sand, rocks etc.), environmental degradation, public health, loss of biodiversity, loss ofresilience in ecosystems, livelihood security for the poor.

The major sources of pollution in India include the rampant burning of fuelwood and biomass such as dried waste from livestock as the primary source of energy, lack of organized garbage and waste removal services, lack of sewage treatment operations, lack of flood control and monsoon water drainage system, diversion of consumer waste into rivers, cremation practices near major rivers, government mandated protection of highly polluting old public transport, and continued operation by Indian government of government owned, high emission plants built between 1950 to 1980.

India's water supply and sanitation issues are related to many environmental issues.

Environmental issues are one of the primary causes of disease, health issues and long term livelihood impact for India.

Major issues

Air pollution, poor management of waste, growing water scarcity, falling groundwater tables, water pollution, preservation and quality of forests, biodiversity loss, and land/soil degradation are some of the major environmental issues India faces today.

India's population growth adds pressure to environmental issues and its resources.

Environmental issues in India include various natural hazards, particularly cyclones and annual monsoon floods. An estimated 60% of cultivated land suffers from soil erosion, waterlogging, and salinity. It is also estimated that between 4.7 and 12 billion tons of topsoil are lost annually from soil erosion.

The Indian Agricultural Research Institute of Parvati has estimated that a 3 °C rise in temperature will result in a 15 to 20% loss in annual wheat yields. These are substantial problems for a nation with such a large population depending on the productivity of primary resources and whose economic growth relies heavily on industrial growth. Civil conflicts involving natural resources—most notably forests and arable land—have occurred in eastern and northeastern states.

Population Growth and Environmental Quality

There is a long history of study and debate about the interactions between population growth and the environment. According to the British thinker Malthus, for example, a growing population exerts pressure on agricultural land, causing environmental degradation, and forcing the cultivation of land of poorer and poorer quality. This environmental degradation ultimately reduces agricultural yields and food availability, causes famines and diseases and death, thereby reducing the rate of population growth. Population growth, because it can place increased pressure on the assimilative capacity of the environment, is also seen as a major cause of air, water, and solid-waste pollution. The result, Malthus theorized, is an equilibrium population that enjoys low levels of both income and environmental quality. Malthus suggested positive and preventative forced control of human population, along with abolition ofpoor laws.

Corruption

Corruption in many forms has been one of the pervasive problems affecting India. For decades, the red tape, bureaucracy and the *Licence*

Raj that had strangled private enterprise. The economic reforms of 1991 cut some of the worst regulations that had been utilized in corruption.

Corruption is still large. A 2005 study by Transparency International (TI) India found that more than half of those surveyed had firsthand experience of paying a bribe or peddling influence to get a job done in a public office. The chief economic consequences of corruption are the loss to the exchequer, an unhealthy climate for investment and an increase in the cost of government-subsidised services. The TI India study estimates the monetary value of petty corruption in 11 basic services provided by the government, like education, healthcare, judiciary, police, etc., to be around ₹21,068 crore (US$4 billion). India still ranks in the bottom quartile of developing nations in terms of the ease of doing business, and compared with China, the average time taken to secure the clearances for a startup or to invoke bankruptcy is much greater.

The Right to Information Act (2005) and equivalent acts in the states, that require government officials to furnish information requested by citizens or face punitive action, computerisation of services and various central and state government acts that established vigilance commissions have considerably reduced corruption or at least have opened up avenues to redress grievances. The 2006 report by Transparency International puts India at 70th place and states that significant improvements were made by India in reducing corruption.

Political, bureaucratic, corporate and individual corruption in India are major concerns. A 2005 study conducted byTransparency Internationalin India found that more than 55% of Indians had first-hand experience of paying bribes or influence peddlingto get jobs done in public offices successfully.

Transparency International estimates that truckers pay US$5 billion in bribes annually. In 2010 India was ranked 87th out of 178 countries in Transparency International's Corruption Perceptions Index.

In the book 'Corruption in India: The DNA and RNA' authored by Professor Bibek Debroy and Laveesh Bhandari say that the public officials in India may be cornering as much as Rs.92,122 crore ($18.42 billion), or 1.26 per cent of the GDP, through corruption. The books estimates that corruption has virtually envelopedIndia growing annually by over 100 percent and most bribery is accrued from the transport industry, real estate and "other public services". On March 31, 2010 theComptroller and Auditor General of India said that unutilised committed external assistance was of the order of Rs.1,05,339 crore."

"The recent scams involving unimaginably big amounts of money, such as the 2G spectrum scam, are well known. It is estimated that more than trillion dollars are stashed away in foreign havens, while 80% of Indians earn less than 2$ per day and every second child is malnourished. It seems as if only the honest people are poor in India and want to get rid of their poverty by education, emigration to cities, and immigration, whereas all the corrupt ones, are getting rich through scams and crime. It seems as if India is a rich country filled with poor people", the organisers of Dandi March II in the United States said.

A 2005 study done by Transparency International (TI) in India found that more than 50% of the people had firsthand experience of paying bribe or peddling influence to get a job done in a public office. Taxes and bribes are common between state borders; Transparency International estimates that truckers pay annually US$5 billion in bribes. A 2009 survey of the leading economies of Asia, revealed Indian bureaucracy to be not just least efficient out of Singapore, Hong Kong, Thailand, South Korea, Japan, Malaysia, Taiwan, Vietnam, China, Philippines and Indonesia; further it was also found that working with India's civil servants was a "slow and painful" process.

Land and Property

Officials often steal state property. In cities and villages throughout India, consisting of municipal and other government officials, elected politicians, judicial officers, real estate developers and law enforcement officials, acquire, develop and sell land in illegal ways.

Tendering processes and awarding contracts

Government officials having discretionary powers in awarding contracts engage in preferential treatment for selected bidders and display negligence in quality control processes '*Bold text*'. Many state-funded construction activities in India, such as road building, are dominated by construction mafias, which are groupings of corrupt public works officials, materials suppliers, politicians and construction contractors. Shoddy construction and material substitution result in roads and highways being dangerous, and sometimes simply washed away when India's heavy monsoon season arrives.

Medicine

In Government Hospitals, corruption is associated with non availability of medicines, getting admission, consultations with doctors and availing diagnostic services.

Income tax Department

There have been several cases of collusion of officials of the income tax department of India for a favorable tax treatment in return for bribes.

Preferential award of public resources

As detailed earlier, land in areas with short supply is relatively common with government entities awarding public land to private concerns at negligible rates. Other examples include the award ofmining leases to private companies without a levy of taxes that is proportionate to the market value of the ore.

Problems of Poverty and Development in India

As India prepares to enter a new millenium, the degraded state of India's natural environment cannot escape comment or analysis. Some believe that the deterioration in the environment is of such magnitudc that all development must cease for the planet to survive. Others dismiss the entire environmental movement as comprised of loony troublemakers who have no right to interefere with the sanctity of private property and private enterprise. Still others berate the environmental movement for being an exclusively middle-class movement that is irrelevant to the class struggle.

Lost in the middle of these antagonistic positions are those who see environmental pollution as a serious issue that affects people cutting across class lines but also recognize the unfairness of the existing order in which the earth's resources and benefits of modern technology are monopolized by a minority of the rich on this planet. For them, issues of environmental degradation must be tackled on a war-footing, but they reject solutions that preserve the unfair distribution of the world's products and natural resources. For them, fairness and justice - the idea that there must be progress for all, cannot be sacrificed in the name of "saving the environment". For them, environmental concerns must be integrated into the general class struggle, and against the tendency of private interests to violate and exploit both people and the environment. Their world-view is in sharp contrast with those environmental elitists who wish to enjoy all the fruits of modern industrial development while denying those same benefits to the proletarian masses who must struggle and survive under the most primitive of human conditions.

One-third of India's population (roughly equivalent to the entire population of the United States) lives below the poverty line and India is home to one-third of the world's poor people.

Though the middle class has gained from recent positive economic developments, India suffers from substantialpoverty. According to the new World Bank's estimates on poverty based on 2005 data, India has 456 million people, 41.6% of its population, living below the new international poverty line of $1.25 (PPP) per day. The World Bank further estimates that 33% of the global poor now reside in India. Moreover, India also has 828 million people, or 75.6% of the population living below $2 a day, compared to 72.2% for Sub-Saharan Africa.

Wealth distribution in India is fairly uneven, with the top 10% of income groups earning 33% of the income. Despite significant economic progress, 1/4 of the nation's population earns less than the government-specified poverty threshold of $0.40/day. Official figures estimate that 27.5% of Indians lived below the national poverty line in 2004–2005. A 2007 report by the state-run National Commission for Enterprises in the Unorganized Sector (NCEUS) found that 25% of Indians, or 236 million people, lived on less than 20 rupees per day with most working in "informal labor sector with no job or social security, living in abject poverty."

Air and Water Pollution in Delhi

Take the issue of air and water pollution in Delhi and the recent supreme-court rulings in that regard. Few can deny that Delhi's air is deadly to breathe. By some estimates, one in three is now afflicted with chronic breathing ailments. Almost a sixth of all children are reputed to suffer from lead induced mental retardation. Gastro-epidemics (resulting from water-borne pollutants) have been all too frequent in recent years, with children being especially vulnerable. Yet, for some industrialists this is not a "serious" enough problem to warrant further regulation or even ensure the implementation of existing regulations. Curiously, some unionists have adopted the absurd position that this is not a "class" issue, as if the poor and the working class don't suffer from lung diseases or water contamination. If anything, it is the other way around. The poor are the first to suffer from the effects of air and water pollution. While the rich can limit their exposure to air-borne toxics by driving around in air-conditioned cars, the poor who must walk to work, or use bicycles or public transport simply can't escape the ill-effects. The rich can buy bottled spring water or distilled water, but the poor usually can't afford anything but tap water. Rather than dismiss such concerns, unionists and others involved in the class-struggle ought to be the first to take up the battle against air and water pollution.

Instead, this aloof attitude has led to solutions that don't go far enough, and are decidedly unfair to the poor. For instance, the Supreme Court has ruled that "polluting industries" must be relocated out of Delhi. Does that mean that these polluting industries are now free to destroy the health of residents in Ghaziabad, Meerut or Rohtak? Does the Indian Supreme Court only care about the health of those who reside in the nation's capital? And what of the hapless employees of those industrial units that were given the orders to relocate? How are they supposed to cope with unemployment and lack of income?

Shouldn't the real solution have been to insist upon correcting manufacturing processes so that they didn't pollute in the first place? Of course, one of the obstacles to any environmental regulation is that businesses will scream that it hurts their "bottom line". When the right to profits is supreme there is little arguing with such views. Yet, not many in the environmental movement consider public ownership of industry as a possible solution where environmental regulations could be enforced across the board, without the risk of corruption or lobbying by private business interests.

Lack of proper sanitation is a major concern for India. Statistics conducted by UNICEF have shown that only 31% of India's population is using improved sanitation facilities as of 2008. It is estimated that one in every ten deaths in India is linked to poor sanitation and hygiene. Diarrhoea is the single largest killer and accounts for one in every twenty deaths. Around 450,000 deaths were linked to diarrhoea alone in 2006, of which 88% were deaths of children below five. Studies by UNICEF have also shown that diseases resulting from poor sanitation affects children in their cognitive development.

Without proper sanitation facilities in India, people defecate in the open or rivers. One gram of faeces could potentially contain 10 million viruses, one million bacteria, 1000 parasite cysts and 100 worm eggs. The Ganges river in India has a stunning 1.1 million litres of raw sewage being disposed into it every minute. The high level of contamination of the river by human waste allow diseases like cholera to spread easily, resulting in many deaths, especially among children who are more susceptible to such viruses.

A lack of adequate sanitation also leads to significant economic losses for the country. A Water and sanitation Program (WSP) study The Economic Impacts of Inadequate Sanitation in India (2010) showed that inadequate sanitation caused India considerable economic losses, equivalent to 6.4 per cent of India's GDP in 2006 at US$53.8 billion (Rs.2.4

trillion). In addition, the poorest 20% of households living in urban areas bore the highest per capita economic impacts of inadequate sanitation.

Recognising the importance of proper sanitation, the Government of India started the Central Rural Sanitation Program (CRSP) in 1986, in hope of improving the basic sanitation amenities of rural areas. This program was later reviewed and, in 1999, the Total Sanitation Campaign (TSC) was launched. Programs such as Individual Household Latrines (IHHL), School Sanitation and Hygiene Education (SSHE), Community Sanitary Complex, Anganwadi toilets were implemented under the TSC.

Through the TSC, the Indian Government hopes to stimulate the demand for sanitation facilities, rather than to continually provide these amenities to its population. This is a two-pronged strategy, where the people involved in this program take ownership and better maintain their sanitation facilities, and at the same time, reduces the liabilities and costs on the Indian Government. This would allow the government to reallocate their resources to other aspects of development. Thus, the government set the objective of granting access to toilets to all by 2017. To meet this objective, incentives are given out to encourage participation from the rural population to construct their own sanitation amenities. In addition, the government has set out to educate its people on the importance and benefits of proper sanitation through mass communication and interpersonal communication techniques. This is done through mass and print media to reach out to a larger audience and through group discussions and games to better engage and interact with the individual.

A significant source of pollution in India's cities are vehicles - cars, two-wheelers, three-wheelers, trucks and buses. Although there have been small steps in moving towards unleaded fuel, little has been done to improve and encourage the use of public transportation. Railways have been neglected and buses for commuters are poorly maintained. Private bus, tempo and truck manufacturers have largely gotten away with producing poor quality vehicles that routinely exceed emission norms. In a socialist economy, private cars would not be a priority. Expanding the rail network and improving the quality of buses and goods transport vehicles would instead, get their due importance. Unfortunately, a majority in the environmental movement are unable to break from their affinity with private ownership and support of private enterprise. As a result, society makes little, or very slow progress in solving these pressing issues.

The Issue of "Big Dams" and National Sovereignty

Another divisive issue for India has been the growing controversy over "big dams". Over the years, critics of India's dams have presented a host of damning evidence pointing to the deplorable neglect of displaced people - especially poor tribal communities. Critics have also correctly pointed out how many dams are started but never completed, or else poorly constructed. Corruption and mismanagement have often led to huge cost overruns, and too often, there is a lack of follow-up in building adequate feeder canals, or else, the canals that are built are not properly maintained.

But rather than calling for the rectification of such grievious errors, many have adopted an idealogical and blanket opposition to all hydro-projects. This has led to grave consequences for the nation. By increasing the nation's reliance on thermal power stations, it has created chaos in the national grid. Thermal power stations are much less suited to handling fluctuating demand. Given the poor quality of India's coal, and the long distances it has to be transported, India's thermal power plants are more polluting, relatively expensive to maintain, and prone to frequent tripping. What is even worse is that the neglect of hydro-power is leading to a growing reliance on even more expensive imported fuel based power plants of the Enron-type. *Not only are these very costly (and also entail environmental risks), they involve a grave loss of national independence.*

While it is not surprising that US-based anti-dam groups might encourage the shift to oil and gas-based energy, it is tragic how some Indian environmentalists are falling into that trap. As it is, India's oil import bill is too large for the country to afford. By building more oil and gas based power plants, India will become even more vulnerable to pressure from the US, which has a virtual stranglehold on the world's oil trade.

It is important to note that historically, manipulating water resources has been a powerful tool for political conquerers. When Mandu was conquered by invaders from the North-West, Bhojpur's dams were destoyed so as to demoralize and weaken the local peasantry and destroy the legitimacy of the Parmar rulers. The Parmar Rajahs of Bhojpur were particularly renowned builders and admired and venerated for their acumen as great architects and civil engineers. By destroying Bhojpur's dams, Mandu's Afghan conquerers were able to hasten their defeat. Several centuries later, India's British colonial rulers, through a policy of deliberate and wanton neglect, destroyed Bengal's traditional water-works, thus compromising the region's ability to feed and defend itself. It is therefore, not surprising that powerful neo-colonial interests in the West would wish to keep India energy deficient, and dependant on imported sources.

The negative reation to India's nuclear tests, and the resistance to India's nuclear power policy, stems at least partially from the desire of some to constrict India's development. Even though India's nuclear power plants use resources that are locally available, and have a safety record that matches the highest international standards, India's nuclear policy has been severely criticized in major international fora. International groups are particularly hypocritical in their condemnation of India's nuclear efforts when in fact, it is the rich industrialized countries like France, Sweden, Japan (and many others) who are the biggest users of nuclear energy. Although new technologies reduce the problem of nuclear waste-management, and make it much more manageable, many in the West prefer to foist oil-based energy use in oil-poor countries like India.

"Independence in the energy sector is central to the national sovereignty and national well-being for an oil importing and developing country like India". This was the view expressed recently by Dr S. K. Chopra, Senior Advisor to the Ministry of Non-Conventional Energy Sources. Dr Chopra was speaking after making a presentation on "Energy Policy for India - Towards Energy Independence" in Delhi. A strong advocate of alternative energy, he spoke against the oil intensification of the Indian economy. He pointed out that there was inadequate use of renewable sources of energy which must be stepped up. *"We are one of the leaders in harnessing wind energy, but must widen our net"*, he remarked. On the atomic energy front, Dr Chopra stated that India and France had begun harnessing atomic power at the same time. But while France was getting 80 per cent of its energy needs from atomic power today, its contribution in India was only 2.35 per cent of the entire need.

Energy Management

Ideally, India should do far more to manage the demand for power. Sections of Indian industry are extremely wasteful in their use of energy. India's homes could be better designed to be cooler in the summer and warmer in the winter. More could be done to strengthen the national power-grid, minimize transmission losses and rebuild and improve outdated power plants. Non-polluting alternative power sources such as wind, solar and tidal power need far more national support and funding. These should be particularly useful in residential use and in electrifying remote and poorly connected villages of the country.

But these alternatives cannot replace conventional sources of energy production entirely. It should be noted that the development of "alternative energy resources" presumes highly developed conventional energy sources. *Wind-turbines require manufacturing that would be impossible without energy supplied by conventional power plants. Solar panels also need advanced high-energy industrial manufacturing.* Hence, it would be naive to argue that India could simply abandon the development of conventional energy resources and suddenly switch to alternative sources. Those who advocate 'small decentralized plants' seem unaware of the heavy requirements of modern industrial production.

The transition to alternative sources will take several decades. In order for India to expand it's use of non-polluting alternatives to thermal or oil/gas based power, it will also have to expand the production of conventional energy in that interim period. Moreover, for energy alternatives to became fully viable, considerably more research and seed capital will be necessary. This is unlikely to come from private sources, and will require greatly increased state-funding.

Dialectics of Development and Environmental Preservation

Ultimately, the strength of India's environmental movement will depend on how it builds alliances with popular movements and sympathizes with the concerns of all of India's down-trodden. There is a great deal to be done in terms of cleaning and protecting the environment. But it cannot be done by simply ignoring the poverty that results from under-development. Neither would it be correct to espouse environmental concerns in a manner that preserves the right of the rich to every modern luxury even as the poor huddle in slums in the heat and cold.

Take the "Narmada Bachao Andolan". Activists involved with Narmada Bachao rightly bring up the issue of *"development for whom?"*. Who pays the price, and who garners the benefits of "development" are extremely important issues facing India as a nation. But is the final answer that all development must cease - *or that development must be structured differently?* Is the problem of developmental inequality a cause or more a symptom of existing class relations in society?

At present there is a huge chasm between opponents and proponents of the Narmada dam. Some argue that the dam should have never been built. Others point to how it has already succeeded in preventing the frequently recurring flooding that occurred along the banks during heavy monsoon years. In Gujarat, support for the dam is almost universal and even extends to popular NGOs. The problems of the dam oustees are real and exceedingly important. But so too are the drinking water problems of Gujarat's poor. While the rich can buy water from tankers, or buy Bisleri (or it's equivalent) for drinking, Gujarat's rural and urban poor have far fewer options. In a bad year, dalit and tribal women often bear the biggest burden in trudging miles to find water for their families. Although much more could be done to augment rain-water harvesting in Gujarat, it is important to recognize that most of Gujarat's ground water is extremely brackish. Without any major all-weather rivers of it's own, it is little wonder that the Narmada project is defended with such passion in the state.

Many of India's environmental controversies are a result of the high density of India's population. Unlike Europe, which was able to ease the pressure of it's burgeoning population through colonial conquests in America and Australia, India has few options when countries like the US and Australia have limited immigration to a trickle. Partition further aggravated the situation for India when the best naturally irrigated lands went to Pakistan and Bangladesh. Even a cursory look at the map will demonstrate how Pakistan and Bangladesh are blessed with a unique natural network of rivers. Pakistan is ideally situated for the construction of modern dams and is a power surplus nation but it's unyielding hostility towards India means that India cannot avail of those natural resources.

There is also tremendous undeveloped hydro potential in Nepal and the Indian North-East. While India can do little about the opposition to joint development of water resources with India in Nepal - the North-East is fairly sparsely populated, and at least some of the hydro-potential could be harnessed without too much controversy. The Brahmaputra which is prone to deadly flooding urgently needs new check dams if nothing else. But the lack of a national water-management and power policy, the reluctance to support state-investment in new projects and the headlong rush towards privatization prevents some of the best hydro-resources in the sub-continent from being carefully developed.

The problems of development in India are exceedingly complex. Class inequities, geographical and political limitations greatly compound India's environmental situation. But with greater sensitivity towards basic human needs, one hopes that India's future development will be harmonized and reconciled with environmental contradictions. But without a doubt, that will entail restrictions on the "freedom" of private capital to use land and mineral resources at will. It will also entail curtailments on the lifestyles of India's rich and powerful. It will require India's environmentalists to embrace the class struggle, and require India's activists for the oppressed to embrace environmental concerns.

Educational Issues

While many schools were built, they had poor infrastructure and inadequate facilities. Schools in the rural areas were especially affected.

According to District Information System for Education (DISE) in India in 2009, only about 51.5% of all schools in India have boundary walls, 16.65% have computers and 39% have electricity. Of which, only 6.47% of primary schools and 33.4% of secondary schools have computers, and only 27.7% of primary schools have electricity. Learning in poorly furnished schools was not conducive, resulting in poor quality education.

Furthermore, the absence rates of teachers and students were high, while their retainment rates low. The incentives for going to school were not apparent, while punishment for absence was not enforced. Despite the government's decree on compulsory education and the child labour ban, many children were still missing classes to go to work. The government did not interfere even when children missed school.

Also, online country studies publications by the Federal Research Division of the Library of Congress stated that "it was not unusual for the teacher to be absent or even to subcontract the teaching work to unqualified substitutes". This exacerbates the problems of the lack of qualified teachers. Currently, the student-teacher ratio remains high at around 32, which is not much of an improvement since 2006 when the ratio was 34.

Economic and social disparities also plague the fundamentals of the education system. Rural children are less able to receive education because of greater opportunity costs, since rural children have to work to contribute to the family's income. According to the Annual Status of Education in 2009, the average attendance rate of students in the rural states is about 75%. Though this rate varies significantly, states like Uttar Pradesh and Bihar had more than 40% absentees during a random visit to their schools. In the urban states, more than 90% of the students were present in their schools during a visit

Issues and its Priorities in Indian Economy

The sharp slowdown in India's GDP and export growth following three years of high growth in each case, are two central areas of concern. Export growth decelerated sharply in 1996-97 and 1997-98, accompanied by a marked deceleration in industrial growth. The level of concern regarding the fiscal deficit and infrastructure problems continues to rise with each passing year.

Higher growth is the best antidote for removing mass poverty and unemployment, and for generating revenues needed to supply public goods and other vital government services. Therefore, it is imperative to put back the economy on a higher growth path of the order 7 to 8 per cent per annum.

This would necessitate raising of the country's savings rate to about 30 per cent of GDP through a reduction of government dissavings, an improvement in the performance of non-traded infrastructure (energy, transport and communications) and restoration of export growth to respectable levels. The slippage on the fiscal front during 1997- 98 is a cause of concern.

Continuing high deficits have a number of adverse consequences. Lack of fiscal flexibility complicates the task of preserving macroeconomic stability, as it puts a heavy burden on monetary policy. Pre-emption of credit by the government is likely to crowd out credit to private sector and raise interest rates. This in turn would dampen the recovery of private production and investment. It could also constrain the pace of financial liberalisation.

India's earlier experience shows that high levels of government expenditure and fiscal deficits can also put pressure on the current account deficit in the balance of payments. This is particularly important at a time when export growth has slowed. Among the reasons for the slow down in export growth is the slower growth of world trade, the real appreciation of the rupee vis-à-vis the country's trading partners, and the very sharp depreciation of the currencies of some of our potential competitors in Asia. It is therefore essential to maintain a market-responsive exchange rate determined by fundamental demand-supply factors, while containing any excessive short-term volatility.

Further, as FDI is the most stable form of capital flow, the share of FDI in total capital flows must be raised progressively. FDI also has the additional benefit of introducing new technology, techniques and practices into the economy. ECB, FII and FDI norms and procedures have been substantially liberalised in past years to facilitate the flow of funds for production and investment. Greater procedural simplifications are however still necessary in the area of FDI.

The states of the Indian federation are also expected to share the responsibility of fiscal consolidation and prudence in a federal polity. State finances need to be strengthened, for both macroeconomic and structural reasons. An expansion in revenue expenditure by states raises the revenue deficit while leaving little fund . for developmental expenditures, especially for the key area of human resource development. Inadequate infrastructure (irrigation, electricity, roads etc) and human capital formation (expenditures on education, basic health etc.) where states shoulder major responsibilities have large costs not only to the states concerned but beyond their borders. Similarly, inefficient state taxes can limit the benefits accruing from the reform of central taxes.

Though the rate of growth in non-food credit of 14.2 per cent in 1997-98 was higher then that in 1996-97 (10.9 per cent), it was much lower than that in 1995-96 (22.5 per cent). The slow growth in non-food credit remained a source of concern in view of deceleration in industrial production. However, the significant expansion in bank investment commercial papers and other debt instruments like bonds and debentures of both PSUs and private corporates has complemented non-food credit. Nevertheless, measures need to be taken to induce banks to step up delivery of non-food credit to medium and small industrial units. At the same time, considering the prevailing low rate of inflation, real interest rates are high, making the cost of institutional funds expensive. The banking system has to be reformed so that interest rates come done due to competitive pressures, greater efficiency and lower implicit taxation of the banking sector. Access of companies to debt markets also needs to be improved by deepening and widening these markets.

Despite several policy initiatives taken by the SEBI, the primary market remained subdued in 1997-98. Resource mobilisation through public issues from the primary market in 1997- 98 is estimated to have slowed down to one-third of the amount mobilised in 1996-97. The depressed situation prevailing in the capital markets may be at least partially responsible for low investment. Corporations found it difficult to mobilise resources for industrial investment. It is necessary to address this issue and make the capital market a stronger instrument for mobilising funds. Confidence seems to be returning gradually to the market in 1998-99. Further measures are needed to bring back small investors to the capital market by raising the transparency and accountability of listed companies as well as that of capital market intermediaries. Efforts must also continue to modernise and improve India's regulatory and payments systems to get them on par with developed countries.

As world inflation rates are currently of the order of 0 to 3 per cent, 4 to 6 per cent inflation rate could be regarded as an acceptable level for India at present. In 1997-98 the annual rate of increase in prices was confined to this range. Inflationary pressures tend to build up either on account of supply side shortfalls in primary products, which later get reflected in the manufacturing sector or due to pressures on the demand side. Where as the former is dealt with through timely and judicious supply management policies often involving government market intervention through liberal trade policy, the latter is dealt with through appropriate macro-economic policies involving control of money supply and fiscal deficit. The year 1998-99 may require special efforts at supply management in order to offset the possible shortfall in food-grains, sugar and cotton production.

Barring 1996-97, when food-grains output peaked at 199.3 million tonnes, the growth in food-grains output during nineties has been just about 1.73 per cent per annum. The yield rates appear to have reached a plateau in major wheat and rice growing areas. Hence attention would have to shift to those regions where productivity is well below the national average. Eastern Uttar Pradesh, Bihar and Orissa could be target areas where higher investment in rural infrastructure by way of improved water conservation and delivery system, fertiliser use and credit availability should receive special focus.

The pace of industrial growth and investment has slackened markedly since the middle of 1996-97 for a variety of reasons. Some of the factors are cyclical and can be expected to correct themselves. Others are the result of some of the policies followed in the past. On the policy side, therefore, measures should embrace a broad array and include: steps to boost export growth, to revive the primary capital market, to encourage higher private and public investment to relieve infrastructure bottlenecks and boost demand for core industrial sectors, and fiscal and monetary policies aimed at moderating real rates of interest and ensuring adequate availability of productive capital to industry. The climate for industrial investment and growth can also be greatly enhanced through bold economic policy initiatives. Economic reforms play a vital role not only by directly stimulating higher productivity and efficiency, but also by keeping confidence high and boosting investment intentions of entrepreneurs.

Reform of inappropriate policies, unproductive government programmes and inefficient public organisations and projects can generate hope and confidence in a more productive future.

Almost 20 years ago a High Level Government Committee made wide-ranging recommendations for replacement of controls and licenses by fiscal and other indirect policy instruments. While there has been substantial progress with delicencing industry and foreign trade, the "controls mind-set" remains influential and the "inspector raj" continues to flourish. Fresh initiatives are necessary to reduce the role of these factors in industry, agriculture, trade, infrastructure, finance and social services in order to unleash the productive energies and capacities of economic agents in all these areas. At the same time, new emphasis must be accorded to improve rating and certification systems, self-regulatory organisations and (in areas of natural monopoly such as some infrastructure services) independent regulatory authorities.

With the revival of economic growth, the demand for key infrastructure services such as power, telecom, railways, roads and ports, will press harder against existing supply constraints. The strategy to relieve infrastructure bottlenecks must encompass both the creation of additional capacity in various sectors as well as initiatives to induce much better capacity utilisation. The strategy must also encourage both private and public provision of infrastructure services in a competitive environment and with an appropriate and transparent regulatory framework. This broad approach calls for an acceleration of sector-specific reforms to tackle existing lacunae in the design and implementation of policies.

To illustrate, low capacity utilisation and high transmission and distribution losses, unrealistic tariff policies and non-commercial approaches of State Electricity Boards (SEBs) constrain both the levels of generation and distribution from the existing power network as well as the flow of fresh investment into this sector. The railways and postal services continue to suffer from substantial operational losses in their provision of subsidised service. In the case of railways, the heavy cross-subsidy of passenger traffic by freight traffic has led to a situation where India's comparative advantage in key sectors such as coal and steel has been severely eroded. Indian ports suffer from problems of outdated organisational modes and low productivity of labour and equipment in comparison to many other Asian ports. The level of investment in new roads and the quality of maintenance of existing networks is far below requirement. All these issues and problems need to be tackled urgently.

As India approaches the 21st century, the shortcomings in its social sectors — such as education, health, water supply and sanitation, housing — in relation to both our own aspirations as well as performance levels achieved by other Asian countries becomes increasingly stark and unacceptable. The constitutional provision of making primary education free and compulsory up to fifth standard should be implemented as soon as feasible. The provision of free education for girls will not only empower women but also help in controlling population growth and improving the quality of life of our children.

The achievement of health for all requires greater focus on epidemic diseases and better water supply, sewage and sanitation systems. In the social sectors, Central and State Governments must clearly play a leading role in ensuring universal provision of basic minimum services. However, policies should be designed to encourage private provision of services as well. It is noteworthy that the south Indian state of Kerala's oft-commended achievements in the fields of education and literacy are substantially dependent on a long history of private schools at all levels.

The government wants that the ongoing economic reform process be re-appraised and revitalised to give the entire national development effort a more humane face.

The eradication of poverty and unemployment is the abiding goal of India's development policies and programmes. The achievement of this goal will require sustained and rapid economic growth combined with well functioning public programmes for social services, rural development and employment generation to provide an effective safety net for all those millions at the margins of the growth process.

Problems Facing Indian Economy

1. *Inflation*

Fuelled by rising wages, property prices and food prices inflation in India is an increasing problem. Inflation is currently between 6-7%. A record 98% of Indian firms report operating close to full capacity (2)With economic growth of 9.2% per annum inflationary pressures are likely to increase, especially with supply side constraints such as infrastructure. The wholesale-price index (WPI), rose to an annualised 6.6% in Janu 2007.

2. *Poor educational standards*

Although India has benefited from a high % of English speakers. (important for call centre industry) there is still high levels of illiteracy amongst the population. It is worse in rural areas and amongst women. Over 50% of Indian women are illiterate

3. *Poor Infrastructure*

Many Indians lack basic amenities lack access to running water. Indian public services are creaking under the strain of bureaucracy and inefficiency. Over 40% of Indian fruit rots before it reaches the market; this is one example of the supply constraints and inefficiency's facing the Indian economy.

4. *Balance of Payments deterioration*

Although India has built up large amounts of foreign currency reserves the current account deficit has deteriorate in recent months. This deterioration is a result of the overheating of the economy. Aggregate Supply cannot meet Aggregate demand so consumers are sucking in imports. Excluding workers remittances India's current account deficit is approaching 5% of GDP.

5. High levels of debt

Buoyed by a property boom the amount of lending in India has grown by 30% in the past year. However there are concerns about the risk of such loans. If they are dependent on rising property prices it could be problematic. Furthermore if inflation increases further it may force the RBI to increase interest rates. If interest rates rise substantially it will leave those indebted facing rising interest payments and potentially reducing consumer spending in the future.

6. Inequality has risen rather than decreased

It is hoped that economic growth would help drag the Indian poor above the poverty line. However so far economic growth has been highly uneven benefiting the skilled and wealthy disproportionately. Many of India's rural poor are yet to receive any tangible benefit from the India's economic growth. More than 78 million homes do not have electricity. 33% (268million) of the population live on less than $1 per day. Furthermore with the spread of television in Indian villages the poor are increasingly aware of the disparity between rich and poor.

7. Large Budget Deficit

India has one of the largest budget deficits in the developing world. Excluding subsidies it amounts to nearly 8% of GDP. Although it is fallen a little in the past year. It still allows little scope for increasing investment in public services like health and education.

8. Rigid labour Laws

As an example Firms employing more than 100 people cannot fire workers without government permission. The effect of this is to discourage firms from expanding to over 100 people. It also discourages foreign investment. Trades Unions have an important political power base and governments often shy away from tackling potentially politically sensitive labour laws.

Indian Economy & Economic Issues

Economics experts and various studies conducted across the globe envisage India and China to rule the world in the 21st century. For over a century the United States has been the largest economy in the world but major developments have taken place in the world economy since then, leading to the shift of focus from the US and the rich countries of Europe to the two Asian giants - India and China.

The rich countries of Europe have seen the greatest decline in global GDP share by 4.9 percentage points, followed by the US and Japan with a decline of about 1 percentage point each. Within Asia, the rising share of China and India has more than made up the declining global share of Japan since 1990. During the seventies and the eighties, ASEANcountries and during the eighties South Korea, along with China and India, contributed to the rising share of Asia in world GDP.

India is slated to become the third largest economy with a share of 14.3 per cent of global economy by 2015 and graduate to become the "third pole" and growth driver by 2035.

As the share of USA in World GDP falls from 21 to 18 per cent and that of India rises from 6 to 11 per cent in 2025, the latter emerges as third pole in the global economy, according to ADB India Economic Bulletin.

India, which is now the fourth largest economy in terms of purchasing power parity, will overtake Japan and become third major economic power within 10 years.

A growth rate of above 8% was achieved by the Indian economy during the year 2003-04 and in the advanced estimates for 2004-05, Indian economy has been predicted to grow at a level of 6.9 %. Growth in the Indian economy has steadily increased since 1979, averaging 5.7% per year in the 23-year growth record. Many factors are behind this robust performance of the Indian economy in 2004-05. High growth rates in Industry & service sector and a benign world economic environment provided a backdrop conducive to the Indian economy. Another positive feature was that the growth was accompanied by continued maintenance of relative stability of prices. There is a paramount need to move Indian agriculture beyond its centuries old dependency on monsoon. This can be achieved by bringing more area under irrigation and by better water management.

In spite of measures taken to attract Foreign Direct Investment (FDI), the inflow was below expectations in the last five years. A significant achievement of the economy in the external sector has been the steady and sustained improvement in the balance of payment position. Another notable development was the decline in the inflation rate during the five years.

Value-Added Tax (VAT), one of the most radical reforms to be proposed for the Indian economy, has been approved by 21 Indian States.

Over 120 countries worldwide have introduced VAT over the past three decades and India is amongst the last few to introduce it.

The Government has set up several committees with a view to pursue economic reforms that enable higher economic growth and generate more employment, while making the Indian economy more globally competitive. The Government has also taken several steps to revitalize the public sector and increase public investment. Two important institutional innovations have been the creation of the National Committee on Infrastructure, chaired by the Prime Minister, and the Investment Commission, chaired by Shri Ratan Tata.

The economy is expected to grow at close to 7 per cent. To step up the rate of growth further, requires more investment in infrastructure and in agriculture and an improvement in government finances.

High-energy costs continue to exert pressure on the price front. While work on the national highways project has been speeded up, port and rail modernization has acquired a much higher profile recently. Public and private investment in both areas has been stepped up sharply. A financial Special Purpose Vehicle has been created to channelize funds for investment in the infrastructure sector.

Economic reforms began in earnest only in July 1991. The reforms of the last 10 years have gone a long way toward freeing up the domestic economy from state control. Progress has also been made in many areas that were previously off limits to reforms. Insurance has been opened to private investors, both domestic and foreign. Diesel oil and gas prices have undergone some increases. At least symbolic reductions have also been made in fertilizer and food subsidies. The value-added tax has undergone substantial rationalization. These reforms have paid handsomely. The economy has grown at more than 6 percent coupled with full macroeconomic stability.

Economic reforms of the last decade have virtually bypassed agriculture. Besides fertilizers among others, farmers need adequate supply of water and electricity. Financial sector reforms, particularly the reform of banking, remain a distant goal.

While foreign banks are now allowed freely to open branches in India, they have not yet moved in aggressively. Banking sector privatization will take time but large efficiency gains could be achieved if labor laws are reformed to restore the hire and fire policy.

The most important area of reforms is perhaps India's power sector. Virtually no sector of the economy — industry, agriculture, or services — can achieve successful transformation without adequate supply of power. Infrastructure is another important area of reforms. Roads, railways, and ports all need expansion as well as improvement in the quality of service. Fertilizer and food subsidies pose yet another challenge. As much as 0.7 percent of GDP goes into fertilizer subsidies. Finally, the reform of bureaucracy is essential. The problem of a bloated bureaucracy and the need for downsizing it is well recognized. Moreover, the success of the reforms in delivering growth and poverty reduction must make the road to future reforms less bumpy.

In India for almost four decades the country was pursuing a path of development in which public sector was expected to be the engine of growth. However, the public sector had overgrown itself and their shortcomings started manifesting in the shape of low capacity utilization and low efficiency due to over manning and poor work ethics, over capitalization due to substantial time and cost overruns, inability to innovate, take quick and timely decisions, large interference in decision making process etc.

The Government started to deregulate the areas of its operation and subsequently, the disinvestment in Public Sector Enterprises (PSEs) was announced. The process of deregulation was aimed at enlarging competition and allowing new firms to enter the markets. The market was thus opened up to domestic entrepreneurs / industrialists and norms for entry of foreign capital were liberalized.

Due to the current revenue expenditure on items such as interest payments, wages and salaries of Government employees and subsidies, the Government is left with hardly any surplus for capital expenditure on social and physical infrastructure. While the Government would like to spend on basic education, primary health and family welfare, large amount of resources are blocked in several non-strategic sectors such as hotels, trading companies, consultancy companies, textile companies, chemical and pharmaceuticals companies, consumer goods companies etc. Additionally, the continued existence of the PSEs is forcing the Government to commit further resources for the sustenance of many non-viable PSEs. The Government continues to expose the taxpayers' money to risk, which it can readily avoid. To top it all, there is a huge amount of debt overhang, which needs to be serviced and reduced before money is available to invest in infrastructure. All this makes disinvestment of the Government stake in the PSEs absolutely imperative.

Current Problems of Indian Economy

On the week ending 11th June 2011, the inflation rate for primary commodities was 12.62%, while that of food articles was 9.13%. The inflation rate for fuel and power is 12.84%, within which the inflation rate for LPG is 11.31%, petrol 33.23% and high speed diesel 5.64%. The current hike in the above-mentioned commodities is sure to further increase the inflation rate of the economy, thereby causing even more misery for the people.

The inflation rate of the economy as a whole has been consistently high over the last two years. Even if we look at the figures for this year, we will find that in December 2010, the inflation rate (WPI) was 9.45%, which increased to 9.68% in March 2011 and subsequently declined to 9.06% in May 2011. If we look at week-on-week inflation rate, then also it is seen that the inflation rate for primary products which was 10.94% on 7th May 2011 has increased to 12.62% on 11 June 2011. In this period while the inflation rate remained more than 9%, the government of India increased the price of petroleum products twice in two months. High inflation and the incapacity of the government to deal with it is a major problem in today's Indian economy. Far from dealing with the problem, the government with these measures is further accentuating it.

The government's response on the issue of inflation is two fold. The first argument from the government about the inflationary episode in India, is that the global inflation of food prices has had an adverse impact on the food inflation in India. It is undoubtedly the case that there is an international inflation of food prices, which is sure to have some adverse effect on the food inflation in India. However, this volatility in the world food market is impacting India mainly because of opening up Indian agriculture to the international market, a policy which is aggressively advocated by the government. Now to blame international food inflation for higher inflation in India, must logically result in a rethink of the policies of globalization, which is vehemently ruled out by the government. The fact of the matter is that the government is only saying a half truth. If we look at the following table, it is obvious that the inflation rate in India is the highest amongst major developing countries, except Russia. This shows that putting the blame of higher inflation on international factors is plain wrong.

Table 1: Inflation Rate according to Consumer Price Index (CPI) in Selected Countries

Country	Inflation Rate (CPI), March 2011
Brazil	6.3
India	8.8

Conted.

Country	Inflation Rate (CPI), March 2011
China	5.4
Indonesia	6.7
Russia	9.4
South Africa	4.1

Source: RBI Bulletin, May 2011

The main factors driving the food inflation in the economy is basically a prolonged neglect of Indian agriculture, whereby the growth rate of agriculture has come down, so much so that the growth rate of food grains during 1993-94 to 2003-04 was only 0.69% which further reduced to 0.32% during 2004-05 to 2009-10. Such a slowdown in the growth rate of food grain production, is a result of two decades of following neo-liberal policies of decreasing public investment in agriculture, a drying up of agricultural credit, withdrawal of extension services of the government, etc. It is this decline in the production of food-grains which is the real driving force of the inflationary tendencies in the economy. This tendency is further strengthened by speculation through forward trading in food-grains and liberalization of the agricultural sector to world price fluctuations. In other words, the prevailing high food inflation in India is a structural problem and hence will continue unless these problems are overcome.

The other issue with regard to inflation, as repeatedly pointed out by the government is the issue of higher crude prices in the international market, because of which it has to increase the domestic prices of petroleum products. Again, it is true that there has been an increase in the prices of crude oil in the international market. But to deregulate the prices of petroleum products was incorrect for at least two reasons. First, any increase in the international price of oil is basically like a tax levied on the domestic economy by outsiders. The government does not want this extra levy to be imposed on the country. This can be done by keeping the import bill constant, through a reduction in the demand of oil. The price of petroleum products is increased, assuming that the demand for oil is a negative function of price. This is however not the case because oil being a necessary commodity of immense importance, the demand for oil is price inelastic. What essentially results with increasing the price of oil is cost-push inflation, which further adds to the already existing inflationary situation in the country. Moreover, the victims of such inflation are those whose wages do not rise with a rise in inflation, who are essentially the unorganized workers and the poor. In other words, the marginalized section of the poor becomes adversely affected. Thus with price deregulation, neither will the import bill of the government decrease, nor will it lead to any decrease in inflationary pressures. Secondly, the entire argument of under-recoveries of the oil-companies because of which the prices are increased is again a lie. The fact of the matter is that the total revenue collected from the government in 2008-09 from petroleum sector is Rs 161798 crore, while the total subsidy and under-recovery from this sector was Rs 105980 crore[2], which is less than the total revenue collected.

Faced with such inflationary trends in the economy, the RBI has been raising interest rates, through an increase in the repo rate (the rate at which banks borrow from the RBI), with the hope that this will result in a decrease in demand in the economy, which will result in a decrease in inflationary trends. Even in June 2011, the repo rate was increased from 7.25% to 7.5%, with the explicit aim of reigning in inflation. The question is whether such monetary policy measures will result in a decline in inflation or not.

The basic idea behind increasing the repo rate is that with such an increase, the banks will increase their rate of interest which will result in a decline in investment, demand for real estate and other such loans, thereby decreasing demand in the economy and hence inflation. This is however not a correct assumption to make in case of the current inflationary episode in India. The main ingredients of the current inflationary situation are food inflation and primary commodities inflation, and fuel and power inflation. Now, the problem with food inflation, as has been already discussed is that it is a structural problem resulting from a decline in food-grains production. Secondly, most of the people of the country do not buy food by taking loans from banks. Hence, with increase in interest rate, neither is there a positive impact on food production nor is there an impact on food consumption, since the demand for food is independent of interest rate. On the other hand, the rise in inflation for fuel and power has been mainly administered by the government through raising the price of oil and gas. Any increase in the interest rate does not decrease the price of oil, since it is mainly administered.

Let us however try and look at the macroeconomics of India to look at a more serious problem. The output of any economy can be written in the following form:

$$Y=C+I+G+X-M$$

where, C=consumption

I=Investment

G=Government Expenditure, net of taxes

X=Exports
M=Imports
Y=Output

Now, with the policies of neo-liberalism fiscal deficit cannot increase. Hence G does not rise. If we look at the external sector of India, we find that India runs a current account deficit such that (X-M) is negative. With a rise in the prices of international crude oil, the import bill of India has increased resulting in a further downward pressure on the current account. However, the export situation of India is not expected to improve drastically in the recent future. Therefore, there is not much that will change in India's current account. Therefore, the impact of G and (X-M) on the output is negative. Therefore, for Y to increase, C and/or I has to increase.

In India, neo-liberalism has also entailed an increase in inequality with the income distribution tilting towards the rich and elite. With such a pro-rich tilt in income distribution, the growth rate should have had a tendency to come down, since the consumption propensity of the rich is less than that of the poor. However, this did not happen because the growth rate of the economy was mainly sustained by a high consumption of the rich and the elites. This consumption was happening as a result of sections of the Indian middle class gaining from the policies of reforms and also because cheap credit was available for meeting one's consumption expenditure. Moreover, with the policies of liberalization, newer commodities produced in the advanced capitalist economies were introduced in the market, which the rich wanted to buy and consume. The consumption demand of these commodities having a higher level of technological progress resulted in a higher investment which again propelled the growth rate of the economy, given that G and (X-M) had no discernible change. Now, if interest rate rises, not only is the investment affected but also the consumption demand of the rich gets adversely affected, since credit become costly. If this phenomenon continues over a considerable period, in the absence of any other stimulus to growth, like government expenditure or higher net exports, the growth story of India can falter.

This is again no mere conjecture. If we look at the growth rate of industry in the recent past in India, then it is seen that already the growth rate of industrial output has declined substantially. The growth rate of industrial production in April 2010 was 13.5%, which has now come down to 6.3% in April 2011. This decline in the growth rate of industrial production has taken place across every industry as shown in the following table. Most importantly, the slowdown in the growth rate of capital goods industry, consumer goods industry and infrastructure industry is a matter of worry.

Table 2: Growth Rate of Industry (in %)

Industry	April 2010 Growth Rate	April 2011 Growth Rate
Mining	9.2	2.2
Manufacturing	14.4	6.9
Electricity	6.6	6.4
Basic Goods	6.7	7.3
Capital Goods	35.5	14.5
Intermediate Goods	11.9	3.4
Consumer Goods	13.8	2.9
Core Infrastructure Industries	7.5	5.2

Source: Monthly Economic Report, May 2011, Ministry of Finance, Government of India

It is not the case that we are isolating the month of April to show that there has been a slowdown in the growth rate of industrial output in the economy. Rather, this process of slowdown of industrial output is persisting for sometime now. This is shown in the following table:

Table 3: Quarterly Growth Rate of Industry (in %)

	Q 4 (2009-10)	Q 1 (2010-11)	Q 2 (2010-11)	Q 3 (2010-11)	Q 4 (2010-11)
Industry	12.4	10.2	8.4	7.1	6.1
Mining	8.9	7.1	8.2	6.9	1.7
Manufacturing	15.2	12.7	10	6	5.5
Electricity	7.3	5.6	2.8	6.4	7.8
Construction	9.2	7.7	6.7	9.7	8.2

Source: Monthly Economic Report, May 2011, Ministry of Finance, Government of India

It is seen from the above table that the slowdown in the manufacturing growth rate is continuing over 5 quarters while the other industrial sectors have behaved more or less in the same manner during this time period. In other words, there is a problem of slowdown in manufacturing and industry in India.

Even the service sector growth rate has come down over the last five quarters (Table 4). Within the service sector, the only sub-sector which has shown an increase in the growth rate over the last 5 quarters is finance, real estate and business services. The expansion of this sub-sector of finance, real estate etc essentially shows the effect of a credit demand generated bubble in the real estate and other financial sectors. Moreover, this sector has very little capacity to employ people.

Table 4: Quarterly Growth Rate of Services (in %)

	Q4 (2009-10)	Q1 (2010-11)	Q2 (2010-11)	Q3 (2010-11)	Q4 (2010-11)
Services	10.2	10.7	9.9	8.4	8.7
Trade, Hotel etc	13.7	12.6	10.9	8.6	9.3
Finance, real estate, etc	6.3	9.8	10	10.8	9
Community services etc	8.3	8.2	7.9	5.1	7

Source: Monthly Economic Report, May 2011, Ministry of Finance, Government of India

The above-mentioned discussion therefore shows that the economy of India in the current juncture faces two sets of problems. Firstly, there is a persistent problem of inflation in the economy. Secondly, the growth of the economy and its various sectors are also getting adversely affected. The main reason for both the problems is the pursuance of neo-liberal growth trajectory by successive governments in the centre. With the pursuance of these set of policies, agriculture has been adversely affected leading to a rise in food inflation. On the other hand, with these policies being pursued, the only stimulus for growth can come from the consumption of the rich, since the government is committed to maintaining a low fiscal deficit-GDP ratio, and exports not being able to outcompete other players in the world market. If the demand of the rich gets adversely affected, then so does the growth rate.

However, it must be mentioned that the current problem of the economy does not necessarily mean that the growth story of India is going to plummet in the near future. The growth story of India, is basically a story of a growth led by the consumption of the rich and elite. Therefore, this growth story can be sustained by ensuring that no harm is done to this section of the population. This essentially entails pursuing a policy which favours the rich, in terms of more tax concessions, more incentives to invest in share market and real estate etc. This path however not only bypasses the poor but also harms them, since the demand of the rich entails such concessions from the state which are antithetical to the poor. For example, the demand of the rich for real estate development over vast tracts of land is driving out the poor from their land. The problem however with this growth trajectory is that the problem of inflation will remain unsolved. This ironically will give the neo-liberals even more arguments to attack the poor. For example, the problem of food inflation is being used to open up the retail trade in India to FDI. This will cause unemployment and loss of livelihood for the poor while doing nothing on the inflation issue. But the rich are not bothered about food inflation since their incomes are high enough and rising so that they maintain a high level of consumption. The UPA government in accordance with its class compulsions is also not bothered.

The only alternative available is to throw away the neo-liberal model of growth and adopt a people centric development model. This entails a revitalization of the agricultural sector, undertaking a development strategy aimed at employment generation rather than growth etc. All this can be done only with the presence of pro-people active state intervention. All this however, entails a political struggle to not only defeat this or that government but to mobilize the people on a platform which is explicitly anti-imperialist and anti-neo-liberalism. Only such political struggles can ensure the defeat of neo-liberalism in our country and usher in pro-people development.

CHAPTER-6

STRUCTURE OF THE INDIAN ECONOMY

Independence to 1979

At independence the economy was predominantly agrarian. Most of the population was employed in agriculture, and most of those people were very poor, existing by cropping their own small plots or supplying labor to other farms. Landownership, land rental, and sharecropping rights were complex, involving layers of intermediaries. Moreover, the structural economic problems inherited at independence were exacerbated by the costs associated with the partition of British India, which had resulted in about 12 million to 14 million refugees fleeing past each other across the new borders between India and Pakistan. The settlement of refugees was a considerable financial strain. Partition also divided complementary economic zones. Under the British, jute and cotton were grown in the eastern part of Bengal, the area that became East Pakistan (after 1971, Bangladesh), but processing took place mostly in the western part of Bengal, which became the Indian state of West Bengal in 1947. As a result, after independence India had to employ land previously used for food production to cultivate cotton and jute for its mills.

India's leaders—especially the first prime minister, Jawaharlal Nehru, who introduced the five-year plans—agreed that strong economic growth and measures to increase incomes and consumption among the poorest groups were necessary goals for the new nation. Government was assigned an important role in this process, and since 1951 a series of plans have guided the country's economic development. Although there was considerable growth in the 1950s, the long-term rates of growth were less positive than India's politicians desired and less than those of many other Asian countries. From FY 1951 to FY 1979, the economy grew at an average rate of about 3.1 percent a year in constant prices, or at an annual rate of 1.0 percent per capita. During this period, industry grew at an average rate of 4.5 percent a year, compared with an annual average of 3.0 percent for agriculture. Many factors contributed to the slowdown of the economy after the mid-1960s, but economists differ over the relative importance of those factors. Structural deficiencies, such as the need for institutional changes in agriculture and the inefficiency of much of the industrial sector, also contributed to economic stagnation. Wars with China in 1962 and with Pakistan in 1965 and 1971; a flood of refugees from East Pakistan in 1971; droughts in 1965, 1966, 1971, and 1972; currency devaluation in 1966; and the first world oil crisis, in 1973-74, all jolted the economy.

Growth since 1980

The rate of growth improved in the 1980s. From FY 1980 to FY 1989, the economy grew at an annual rate of 5.5 percent, or 3.3 percent on a per capita basis. Industry grew at an annual rate of 6.6 percent and agriculture at a rate of 3.6 percent. A high rate of investment was a major factor in improved economic growth. Investment went from about 19 percent of GDP in the early 1970s to nearly 25 percent in the early 1980s. India, however, required a higher rate of investment to attain comparable economic growth than did most other low-income developing countries, indicating a lower rate of return on investments. Part of the adverse Indian experience was explained by investment in large, long-gestating, capital-intensive projects, such as electric power, irrigation, and infrastructure. However, delayed completions, cost overruns, and under-use of capacity were contributing factors.

Private savings financed most of India's investment, but by the mid-1980s further growth in private savings was difficult because they were already at quite a high level. As a result, during the late 1980s India relied increasingly on borrowing from foreign sources. This trend led to a balance of payments crisis in 1990; in order to receive new loans, the government had no choice but to agree to further measures of economic liberalization.

This commitment to economic reform was reaffirmed by the government that came to power in June 1991.

India's primary sector, including agriculture, forestry, fishing, mining, and quarrying, accounted for 32.8 percent of GDP in FY 1991. The size of the agricultural sector and its vulnerability to the vagaries of the monsoon cause relatively large fluctuations in the sector's contribution to GDP from one year to another.

In FY 1991, the contribution to GDP of industry, including manufacturing, construction, and utilities, was 27.4 percent; services, including trade, transportation, communications, real estate and finance, and public- and private-sector services, contributed 39.8 percent. The steady increase in the proportion of services in the national economy reflects increased market-determined processes, such as the spread of rural banking, and government activities, such as defense spending.

Despite a sometimes disappointing rate of growth, the Indian economy was transformed between 1947 and the early 1990s. The number of kilowatt-hours of electricity generated, for example, increased more than fiftyfold. Steel production rose from 1.5 million tons a year to 14.7 million tons a year. The country produced space satellites and nuclear-power plants, and its scientists and engineers produced an atomic explosive device. Life expectancy increased from twenty-seven years to fifty-nine years. Although the population increased by 485 million between 1951 and 1991, the availability of food grains per capita rose from 395 grams per day in FY 1950 to 466 grams in FY 1992.

However, considerable dualism remains in the Indian economy. Officials and economists make an important distinction between the formal and informal sectors of the economy. The informal, or unorganized, economy is largely rural and encompasses farming, fishing, forestry, and cottage industries. It also includes petty vendors and some small-scale mechanized industry in both rural and urban areas. The bulk of the population is employed in the informal economy, which contributes more than 50 percent of GDP. The formal economy consists of large units in the modern sector for which statistical data are relatively good. The modern sector includes large-scale manufacturing and mining, major financial and commercial businesses, and such public-sector enterprises as railroads, telecommunications, utilities, and government itself.

The greatest disappointment of economic development is the failure to reduce more substantially India's widespread poverty. Studies have suggested that income distribution changed little between independence and the early 1990s, although it is possible that the poorer half of the population improved its position slightly. Official estimates of the proportion of the population that lives below the poverty line tend to vary sharply from year to year because adverse economic conditions, especially rises in food prices, are capable of lowering the standard of living of many families who normally live just above the subsistence level. The Indian government's poverty line is based on an income sufficient to ensure access to minimum nutritional standards, and even most persons above the poverty line have low levels of consumption compared with much of the world.

Estimates in the late 1970s put the number of people who lived in poverty at 300 million, or nearly 50 percent of the population at the time. Poverty was reduced during the 1980s, and in FY 1989 it was estimated that about 26 percent of the population, or 220 million people, lived below the poverty line. Slower economic growth and higher inflation in FY 1990 and FY 1991 reversed this trend. In FY 1991, it was estimated that 332 million people, or 38 percent of the population, lived below the poverty line.

Farmers and other rural residents make up the large majority of India's poor. Some own very small amounts of land while others are field hands, seminomadic shepherds, or migrant workers. The urban poor include many construction workers and petty vendors. The bulk of the poor work, but low productivity and intermittent employment keep incomes low. Poverty is most prevalent in the states of Orissa, Bihar, Uttar Pradesh, and Madhya Pradesh, and least prevalent in Haryana, Punjab, Himachal Pradesh, and Jammu and Kashmir.

By the early 1990s, economic changes led to the growth in the number of Indians with significant economic resources. About 10 million Indians are considered upper class, and roughly 300 million are part of the rapidly increasing middle class. Typical middle-class occupations include owning a small business or being a corporate executive, lawyer, physician, white-collar worker, or land-owning farmer. In the 1980s, the growth of the middle class was reflected in the increased consumption of consumer durables, such as televisions, refrigerators, motorcycles, and automobiles. In the early 1990s, domestic and foreign businesses hoped to take advantage of India's economic liberalization to increase the range of consumer products offered to this market.

Housing and the ancillary utilities of sewer and water systems lag considerably behind the population's needs. India's cities have large shantytowns built of scrap or readily available natural materials erected on whatever space is available, including sidewalks. Such dwellings lack piped water, sewerage, and electricity. The government has attempted to build housing facilities and utilities for urban development, but the efforts have fallen far short of demand. Administrative controls and other aspects of government policy have discouraged many private investors from constructing housing units.

Liberalization in the Early 1990s

Increased borrowing from foreign sources in the late 1980s, which helped fuel economic growth, led to pressure on the balance of payments. The problem came to a head in August 1990 when Iraq invaded Kuwait, and the price of oil soon doubled. In addition, many Indian workers resident in Persian Gulf states either lost their jobs or returned home out of fear for their safety, thus reducing the flow of remittances. The direct economic impact of the Persian Gulf conflict was exacerbated by domestic social and political developments. In the early 1990s, there was violence over two domestic issues: the reservation of a proportion of public-sector jobs for members of Scheduled Castes and the Hindu-Muslim conflict at Ayodhya. The central government fell in November 1990 and was succeeded by a minority government. The cumulative impact of these events shook international confidence in India's economic viability, and the country found it increasingly difficult to borrow internationally. As a result, India made various agreements with the International Monetary Fund (IMF) and other organizations that included commitments to speed up liberalization.

In the early 1990s, considerable progress was made in loosening government regulations, especially in the area of foreign trade. Many restrictions on private companies were lifted, and new areas were opened to private capital. However, India remains one of the world's most tightly regulated major economies. Many powerful vested interests, including private firms that have benefited from protectionism, labor unions, and much of the bureaucracy, oppose liberalization. There is also considerable concern that liberalization will reinforce class and regional economic disparities.

The balance of payments crisis of 1990 and subsequent policy changes led to a temporary decline in the GDP growth rate, which fell from 6.9 percent in FY 1989 to 4.9 percent in FY 1990 to 1.1 percent in FY 1991. In March 1995, the estimated growth rate for FY 1994 was 5.3 percent. Inflation peaked at 17 percent in FY 1991, fell to 9.5 percent in FY 1993, and then accelerated again, reaching 11 percent in late FY 1994. This increase was attributed to a sharp increase in prices and a shortfall in such critical sectors as sugar, cotton, and oilseeds. Many analysts agree that the poor suffer most from the increased inflation rate and reduced growth rate.

India - The Role of Government in the Economy

Early Policy Developments

Many early post independence leaders, such as Nehru, were influenced by socialist ideas and advocated government intervention to guide the economy, including state ownership of key industries. The objective was to achieve high and balanced economic development in the general interest while particular programs and measures helped the poor. India's leaders also believed that industrialization was the key to economic development. This belief was all the more convincing in India because of the country's large size, substantial natural resources, and desire to develop its own defense industries.

The Industrial Policy Resolution of 1948 gave government a monopoly in armaments, atomic energy, and railroads, and exclusive rights to develop minerals, the iron and steel industries, aircraft manufacturing, shipbuilding, and manufacturing of telephone and telegraph equipment. Private companies operating in those fields were guaranteed at least ten years more of ownership before the government could take them over. Some still operate as private companies.

The Industrial Policy Resolution of 1956 greatly extended the preserve of government. There were seventeen industries exclusively in the public sector. The government took the lead in another twelve industries, but private companies could also engage in production. This resolution covered industries producing capital and intermediate goods. As a result, the private sector was relegated primarily to production of consumer goods. The public sector also expanded into more services. In 1956 the life insurance business was nationalized, and in 1973 the general insurance business was also acquired by the public sector. Most large commercial banks were nationalized in 1969. Over the years, the central and state governments formed agencies, and companies engaged in finance, trading, mineral exploitation, manufacturing, utilities, and transportation. The public sector was extensive and influential throughout the economy, although the value of its assets was small relative to the private sector.

Controls over prices, production, and the use of foreign exchange, which were imposed by the British during World War II, were reinstated soon after independence. The Industries (Development and Regulation) Act of 1951 and the Essential Commodities Act of 1955 (with subsequent additions) provided the legal framework for the government to extend price controls that eventually included steel, cement, drugs, nonferrous metals, chemicals, fertilizer, coal, automobiles, tires and tubes, cotton textiles, food grains, bread, butter, vegetable oils, and other commodities. By the late 1950s, controls were pervasive, regulating investment in industry, prices of many commodities, imports and exports, and the flow of foreign exchange.

Export growth was long ignored. The government's extensive controls and pervasive licensing requirements created imbalances and structural problems in many parts of the economy. Controls were usually imposed to correct specific problems but often without adequate consideration of their effect on other parts of the economy. For example, the government set low prices for basic foods, transportation, and other commodities and services, a policy designed to protect the living standards of the poor. However, the policy proved counterproductive when the government also limited the output of needed goods and services. Price ceilings were implemented during shortages, but the ceiling frequently contributed to black markets in those commodities and to tax evasion by black-market participants. Import controls and tariff policy stimulated local manufacturers toward production of import-substitution goods, but under conditions devoid of sufficient competition or pressure to be efficient.

Private trading and industrial conglomerates (the so-called large houses) existed under the British and continued after independence. The government viewed the conglomerates with suspicion, believing that they often manipulated markets and prices for their own profit. After independence the government instituted licensing controls on new businesses, especially in manufacturing, and on expanding capacity in existing businesses. In the 1960s, when shortages of goods were extensive, considerable criticism was leveled at traders for manipulating markets and prices. The result was the 1970 Monopolies and Restrictive Practices Act, which was designed to provide the government with additional information on the structure and investments of all firms that had assets of more than Rs200 million, to strengthen the licensing system in order to decrease the concentration of private economic power, and to place restraints on certain business practices considered contrary to the public interest. The act emphasized the government's aversion to large companies in the private sector, but critics contended that the act resulted from political motives and not from a strong case against big firms. The act and subsequent enforcement restrained private investment.

The extensive controls, the large public sector, and the many government programs contributed to a substantial growth in the administrative structure of government. The government also sought to take on many of the unemployed. The result was a swollen, inefficient bureaucracy that took inordinate amounts of time to process applications and forms. Business leaders complained that they spent more time getting government approval than running their companies. Many observers also reported extensive corruption in the huge bureaucracy. One consequence was the development of a large underground economy in small-scale enterprises and the services sector.

India's current economic reforms began in 1985 when the government abolished some of its licensing regulations and other competition-inhibiting controls. Since 1991 more "new economic policies" or reforms have been introduced. Reforms include currency devaluations and making currency partially convertible, reduced quantitative restrictions on imports, reduced import duties on capital goods, decreases in subsidies, liberalized interest rates, abolition of licenses for most industries, the sale of shares in selected public enterprises, and tax reforms. Although many observers welcomed these changes and attributed the faster growth rate of the economy in the late 1980s to them, others feared that these changes would create more problems than they solved. The growing dependence of the economy on imports, greater vulnerability of its balance of payments, reliance on debt, and the consequent susceptibility to outside pressures on economic policy directions caused concern. The increase in consumerism and the display of conspicuous wealth by the elite exacerbated these fears.

The pace of liberalization increased after 1991. By the mid-1990s, the number of sectors reserved for public ownership was slashed, and private-sector investment was encouraged in areas such as energy, steel, oil refining and exploration, road building, air transportation, and telecommunications. An area still closed to the private sector in the mid-1990s was defense industry. Foreign-exchange regulations were liberalized, foreign investment was encouraged, and import regulations were simplified. The average import-weighted tariff was reduced from 87 percent in FY 1991 to 33 percent in FY 1994. Despite these changes, the economy remained highly regulated by international standards. The import of many consumer goods was banned, and the production of 838 items, mostly consumer goods, was reserved for companies with total investment of less than Rs6 million. Although the government had sold off minority stakes in public-sector companies, it had not in 1995 given up control of any enterprises, nor had any of the loss-making public companies been closed down. Moreover, although import duties had been lowered substantially, they were still high compared to most other countries.

Political successes in the mid-1990s by nationalist-oriented political parties led to some backlash against foreign investment in some parts of India. In early 1995, official charges of serving adulterated products were made against a KFC outlet in Bangalore, and Pepsi-Cola products were smashed and advertisements defaced in New Delhi. The most serious backlash occurred in Maharashtra in August 1995 when the Bharatiya Janata Party (BJP—Indian People's Party)-led state government halted construction of a US$2.8 million 2,015-megawatt gas-fired electric-power plant being built near Bombay (Mumbai in the Marathi language) by another United States company, Enron Corporation.

Antipoverty Programs

The government has initiated, sustained, and refined many programs since independence to help the poor attain self sufficiency in food production. Probably the most important initiative has been the supply of basic commodities, particularly food at controlled prices, available throughout the country. The poor spend about 80 percent of their income on food while the rest of the population spends more than 60 percent. The price of food is a major determinant of wage scales. Often when food prices rise sharply, rioting and looting follow. Until the late 1970s, the government frequently had difficulty obtaining adequate grain supplies in years of poor harvests. During those times, states with surpluses of grain were cordoned off to force partial sales to public agencies and to keep private traders from shipping grain to deficit areas to secure very high prices; state governments in surplus-grain areas were often less than cooperative. After the late 1970s, the central government, by holding reserve stocks and importing grain adequately and early, maintained sufficient supplies to meet the increased demand during drought years. It also provided more remunerative prices to farmers.

In rural areas, the government has undertaken programs to mitigate the worst effects of adverse monsoon rainfall, which affects not only farmers but village artisans and traders when the price of grain rises. The government has supplied water by financing well digging and, since the early 1980s, by power-assisted well drilling; rescinded land taxes for drought areas; tried to maintain stable food prices; and provided food through a food-for-work program. The actual work accomplished through food-for-work programs is often a secondary consideration, but useful projects sometimes result. Employment is offered at a low daily wage, usually paid in grain, the rationale being that only the truly needy will take jobs at such low pay.

In the 1980s and early 1990s, Indian government programs attempted to provide basic needs at stable, low prices; to increase income through pricing and regulations, such as supplying water from irrigation works, fertilizer, and other inputs; to foster location of industry in backward areas; to increase access to basic social services, such as education, health, and potable water supply; and to help needy groups and deprived areas. The total money spent on such programs for the poor was not discernible from the budget data, but probably exceeded 10 percent of planned budget outlays.

India has had a number of antipoverty programs since the early 1960s. These include, among others, the National Rural Employment Programme and the Rural Landless Employment Guarantee Programme. The National Rural Employment Programme evolved in FY 1980 from the earlier Food for Work Programme to use unemployed and underemployed workers to build productive community assets. The Rural Landless Employment Guarantee Programme was instituted in FY 1983 to address the plight of the hard-core rural poor by expanding employment opportunities and building the rural infrastructure as a means of encouraging rapid economic growth. There were many problems with the implementation of these and otherschemes, but observers credit them with helping reduce poverty. To improve the effectiveness of the National Rural Employment Programme, in 1989 it was combined with the Rural Landless Employment Guarantee Programme and renamed Jawahar Rozgar Yojana, or Jawahar Employment Plan.

State governments are important participants in antipoverty programs. The constitution assigns responsibility to the states in a number of matters, including ownership, redistribution, improvement, and taxation of land. State governments implement most central government programs concerned with land reform and the situation of small landless farmers. The central government tries to establish programs and norms among the states and union territories, but implementation has often remained at the lower bureaucratic levels. In some matters concerning subsoil rights and irrigation projects, the central government exerts political and financial leverage to obtain its objectives, but the states sometimes modify or retard the impact of central government policies and programs.

Development Planning

Planning in India dates back to the 1930s. Even before independence, the colonial government had established a planning board that lasted from 1944 to 1946. Private industrialists and economists published three development plans in 1944. India's leaders adopted the principle of formal economic planning soon after independence as an effective way to intervene in the economy to foster growth and social justice.

The Planning Commission was established in 1950. Responsible only to the prime minister, the commission is independent of the cabinet. The prime minister is chairperson of the commission, and the minister of state with independent charge for planning and program implementation serves as deputy chairperson. A staff drafts national plans under the guidance of the commission; draft plans are presented for approval to the National Development Council, which consists of the Planning Commission and the chief ministers of the states. The council can make changes in the draft plan. After council approval, the draft is presented to the cabinet and subsequently to Parliament, whose approval makes the plan an operating document for central and state governments.

The First Five-Year Plan (FY 1951-55) attempted to stimulate balanced economic development while correcting imbalances caused by World War II and partition. Agriculture, including projects that combined irrigation and power generation, received priority. By contrast, the Second Five-Year Plan (FY 1956-60) emphasized industrialization, particularly basic, heavy industries in the public sector, and improvement of the economic infrastructure. The plan also stressed social goals, such as more equal distribution of income and extension of the benefits of economic development to the large number of disadvantaged people. The Third Five-Year Plan (FY 1961-65) aimed at a substantial rise in national and per capita income while expanding the industrial base and rectifying the neglect of agriculture in the previous plan. The third plan called for national income to grow at a rate of more than 5 percent a year; self-sufficiency in food grains was anticipated in the mid-1960s.

Economic difficulties disrupted the planning process in the mid-1960s. In 1962, when a brief war was fought with China on the Himalayan frontier, agricultural output was stagnating, industrial production was considerably below expectations, and the economy was growing at about half of the planned rate. Defense expenditures increased sharply, and the increased foreign aid needed to maintain development expenditures eventually provided 28 percent of public development spending. Midway through the third plan, it was clear that its goals could not be achieved.

Food prices rose in 1963, causing rioting and looting of grain warehouses in 1964. War with Pakistan in 1965 sharply reduced the foreign aid available. Successive severe droughts in 1965 and 1966 further disrupted the economy and planning. Three annual plans guided development between FY 1966 and FY 1968 while plan policies and strategies were reevaluated. Immediate attention centered on increasing agricultural growth, stimulating exports, and searching for efficient uses of industrial assets. Agriculture was to be expanded, largely through the supply of inputs to take advantage of new high-yield seeds becoming available for food grains. The rupee was substantially devalued in 1966, and export incentives were adjusted to promote exports. Controls affecting industry were simplified, and greater reliance was placed on the price mechanism to achieve industrial efficiency.

The Fourth Five-Year Plan (FY 1969-73) called for a 24 percent increase over the third plan in real terms of public development expenditures. The public sector accounted for 60 percent of plan expenditures, and foreign aid contributed 13 percent of plan financing. Agriculturc, including irrigation, received 23 percent of public outlays; the rest was mostly spent on electric power, industry, and transportation. Although the plan projected national income growth at 5.7 percent a year, the realized rate was only 3.3 percent.

The Fifth Five-Year Plan (FY 1974-78) was drafted in late 1973 when crude oil prices were rising rapidly; the rising prices quickly forced a series of revisions. The plan was subsequently approved in late 1976 but was terminated at the end of FY 1977 because a new government wanted different priorities and programs. The fifth plan was in effect only one year, although it provided some guidance to investments throughout the five-year period. The economy operated under annual plans in FY 1978 and FY 1979.

The Sixth Five-Year Plan (FY 1980-84) was intended to be flexible and was based on the principle of annual "rolling" plans. It called for development expenditures of nearly Rs1.9 trillion (in FY 1979 prices), of which 90 percent would be financed from domestic sources, 57 percent of which would come from the public sector. Public-sector development spending would be concentrated in energy (29 percent); agriculture and irrigation (24 percent); industry including mining (16 percent); transportation (16 percent); and social services (14 percent). In practice, slightly more was spent on social services at the expense of transportation and energy. The plan called for GDP growth to increase by 5.1 percent a year, a target that was surpassed by 0.3 percent. A major objective of the plan was to increase employment, especially in rural areas, in order to reduce the level of poverty. Poor people were given cows, bullock carts, and handlooms;

however, subsequent studies indicated that the income of only about 10 percent of the poor rose above the poverty level.

The Seventh Five-Year Plan (FY 1985-89) envisioned a greater emphasis on the allocation of resources to energy and social spending at the expense of industry and agriculture. In practice, the main increase was in transportation and communications, which took up 17 percent of public-sector expenditure during this period. Total spending was targeted at nearly Rs3.9 trillion, of which 94 percent would be financed from domestic resources, including 48 percent from the public sector. The planners assumed that public savings would increase and help finance government spending. In practice that increase did not occur; instead, the government relied on foreign borrowing for a greater share of resources than expected.

The schedule for the Eighth Five-Year Plan (FY 1992-96) was affected by changes of government and by growing uncertainty over what role planning could usefully perform in a more liberal economy. Two annual plans were in effect in FY 1990 and FY 1991. The eighth plan was finally launched in April 1992 and emphasized market-based policy reform rather than quantitative targets. Total spending was planned at Rs8.7 trillion, of which 94 percent would be financed from domestic resources, 45 percent of which would come from the public sector. The eighth plan included three general goals. First, it sought to cut back the public sector by selling off failing and inessential industries while encouraging private investment in such sectors as power, steel, and transport. Second, it proposed that agriculture and rural development have priority. Third, it sought to renew the assault on illiteracy and improve other aspects of social infrastructure, such as the provision of fresh drinking water. Government documents issued in 1992 indicated that GDP growth was expected to increase from around 5 percent a year during the seventh plan to 5.6 percent a year during the eighth plan. However, in 1994 economists expected annual growth to be around 4 percent during the period of the eighth plan.

Four decades of planning show that India's economy, a mix of public and private enterprise, is too large and diverse to be wholly predictable or responsive to directions of the planning authorities. Actual results usually differ in important respects from plan targets. Major shortcomings include insufficient improvement in income distribution and alleviation of poverty, delayed completions and cost overruns on many public-sector projects, and far too small a return on many public-sector investments. Even though the plans have turned out to be less effective than expected, they help guide investment priorities, policy recommendations, and financial mobilization.

India - Labor

Size and Composition of the Work Force

Based on the 1991 census, the government estimated that the labor force had grown by more than 65 million since 1981 and that the total number of "main workers"—the "economically active population"—had reached 285.9 million people. This total did not include Jammu and Kashmir, which was not enumerated in the 1991 census. Labor force statistics for 1991 covered nine main-worker "industrial" categories: cultivators (39 percent of the main-worker force); agricultural laborers (26 percent); livestock, forestry, fishing, hunting, plantations, orchards, and allied activities (2 percent); mining and quarrying (1 percent); manufacturing (household 2 percent, other than household 7 percent); construction (2 percent); trade and commerce (8 percent); transportation, storage, and communications (3 percent); and "other services" (10 percent). Another 28.2 million "marginal workers" were also counted in the census but not tabulated among the nine categories even though unpaid farm and family enterprise workers were counted among the nine categories. Of the total work force—both main and marginal workers—29 percent were women, and nearly 78 percent worked in rural areas.

Included in the labor force are some 55 million children, other than those working directly for their parents. The Ministry of Labour and nongovernmental organizations estimate that there are 25 million children employed in the agricultural sector, 20 million in service jobs (hotels, shops, and as servants in homes), and 5 million in the handloom, carpet-making, gem-cutting, and match-making industries. With mixed success, nongovernmental organizations monitor the child labor market for abuse and conformity to child labor laws.

In government organizations throughout the nation and in nonagricultural enterprises with twenty-five persons or more in 1991, the public sector employed nearly 19 million people compared with about 8 million people employed in the private sector. Most of the growth in the organized work force between 1970 and 1990 was in the public sector. Observers expected that this trend might be reversed if the government's policy of economic liberalization continued. Labor law makes it very difficult for companies to lay off workers. Some observers feel that this restriction deters companies from hiring because they fear carrying a bloated workforce in case of an economic turndown.

A new source of employment appeared after OPEC sharply increased crude oil prices in 1974. The Middle East oil-exporting countries quickly undertook massive development programs based on their large oil revenues. Most of these countries required the importation of labor, both skilled and unskilled, and India became one of many nations supplying the labor. Because some labor agents and employers took advantage of expatriate workers, especially those with little education or few skills, in 1983 India enacted a law governing workers going abroad. In general, the new legislation provided more protection and required fairer treatment of Indians employed outside the country. By 1983 some 900,000 Indian workers were registered as temporary residents in the Middle East. In the mid-1980s, there was a shift in the kinds of skills needed. Fewer laborers, metalworkers, and engineers, for example, were required for construction projects, but the need for maintenance workers and operating staff in power plants, hospitals, and offices increased. In 1990 it was estimated that more than 1 million Indians were resident in the Middle East. India benefited not only from the opening of job opportunities but also from the remittances the workers sent back, which amounted to around US$4.3 billion of foreign exchange in FY 1988. Both employment and remittances suffered as a result of the 1991 Persian Gulf War, when about 180,000 Indian workers were displaced. In the mid-1990s, the outlook for Indian employment in the Middle East was only fair.

India's labor force exhibits extremes ranging from large numbers of illiterate workers unaccustomed to machinery or routine, to a sizable pool of highly educated scientists, technicians, and engineers, capable of working anywhere in the world. A substantial number of skilled people have left India to work abroad; the country has suffered a brain drain since independence. Nonetheless, many remain in India working alongside a trained industrial and commercial work force. Administrative skills, particularly necessary in large projects or programs, are in short supply, however. In the mid-1990s, salaries for top administrators and technical staff rose sharply, partly in response to the arrival of foreign companies in India.

Labor Relations

The Trade Unions Act of 1926 provided recognition and protection for a nascent Indian labor union movement. The number of unions grew considerably after independence, but most unions are small and usually active in only one firm. Union membership is concentrated in the organized sector, and in the early 1990s total membership was about 9 million. Many unions are affiliated with regional or national federations, the most important of which are the Indian National Trade Union Congress, the All-India Trade Union Congress, the Centre of Indian Trade Unions, the Indian Workers' Association, and the United Trade Union Congress. Politicians have often been union leaders, and some analysts believe that strikes and other labor protests are called primarily to further the interests of political parties rather than to promote the interests of the work force.

The government recorded 1,825 strikes and lockouts in 1990. As a result, 24.1 million workdays were lost, 10.6 million to strikes and 13.5 million to lockouts. More than 1.3 million workers were involved in these labor disputes. The number and seriousness of strikes and lockouts have varied from year to year. However, the figures for 1990 and preliminary data from 1991 indicate declines from levels reached in the 1980s, when in some years as many as 35 million workdays were lost because of labor disputes.

The isolated, insecure, and exploited laborers in rural areas and in the urban unorganized sectors present a stark contrast to the position of unionized workers in many modern enterprises. In the early 1990s, there were estimates that between 10 percent and 20 percent of agricultural workers were bonded laborers. The International Commission of Jurists, studying India's bonded labor, defines such a person as one who works for a creditor or someone in the creditor's family against nominal wages in cash or kind until the creditor, who keeps the books and sets the prices, declares the loan repaid, often with usurious rates of interest. The system sometimes extends to a debtor's wife and children, who are employed in appalling working conditions and exposed to sexual abuse. The constitution, as interpreted by India's Supreme Court, and a 1976 law prohibit bonded labor. Implementation of the prohibition, however, has been inconsistent in many rural areas.

Many in the urban unorganized sector are self-employed laborers, street vendors, petty traders, and other services providers who receive little income. Along with the unemployed, they have no unemployment insurance or other benefits.

India - Industry

At independence, industrialization was viewed as the engine of growth for the rest of the economy and the supplier of jobs to reduce poverty. By the early 1990s, substantial progress had been made, but industrial growth had failed to live up to expectations. Industrial production rose an average of 6.1 percent in the 1950s, 5.3 percent in the 1960s, and 4.2 percent in the 1970s. Although this increase was respectable, it was less than the rate achieved by some other developing countries and less than what the planners expected and the economy needed to bring about a large reduction in poverty. The emphasis on large-scale, capital-intensive industries created far fewer jobs than the estimated 10 million annual entrants into the labor force required. Hence unemployment and underemployment remained growing problems. In the 1980s, however, industrial production rose at an average rate of 6.6 percent. Observers believed that this increase was largely a response to economic liberalization, which led to increased investment and competition.

Government Policies

Government has played an important role in industry since independence. The government has both owned a large proportion of industrial establishments and has tightly regulated the private sector. From the late 1970s, the government sought to reduce its role, but progress remained slow throughout the 1980s. The Congress (I) government that came to power in June 1991 had a renewed commitment to cutting back the role of government, and in the mid-1990s the liberalization program made progress, although many uncertainties remained about its implementation.

The Industrial Policy Resolution of 1948 gave the government the go-ahead to build and operate key industries, which largely meant those producing capital and intermediate goods. This policy partly reflected socialist ideas then current in India. It was believed that public ownership of basic industry was necessary to ensure development in the interest of the whole population. The decision also reflected the belief that private industrialists would find establishment of many of the basic industries on the scale that the country needed either unattractive or beyond their financial capabilities. Moreover, there was concern that private industrialists could enlarge their profits by dominating markets in key commodities. The industrial policy resolutions of 1948 and 1956 delineated the lines between the public and private sectors and stressed the need for a large degree of self-sufficiency in manufacturing, the basic strategy that guided industrialization until the mid-1980s.

Another early decision on industrial policy mandated that defense industries would be developed by the public sector. Building defense industries for a modern military force required the concomitant development of heavy industries, including metallurgy and machine tools.

Production often started under foreign licensing, but as much as possible, design and production became Indianized. India was one of only a few developing countries to produce a variety of high-technology military equipment to supply its own needs.

Before independence there was a strong tendency for ownership or control of much of the large-scale private industrial economy to be concentrated in managing agencies, which became powerful under the British because they had access to London money markets. Through diversified investments and interlocking directorates, the individuals who controlled the managing agencies controlled much of the preindependence economy. After independence Parliament passed legislation to restrain further concentration, used the development of the stock market to induce the sale of stock in tightly held companies to the public, and applied high corporate tax rates to such companies. It also attempted to offset the monopoly effects of the managing agencies by fixing prices on a number of basic commodities, including cement, steel, and coal, and assumed considerable control of their distribution. The government eventually abolished some of the managing agencies in 1969 and the remainder in 1971. In 1970 the Monopolies and Restrictive Practices Act supplied the government with additional authority to diminish concentrations of private economic power and to restrict business practices contrary to the public interest. This act was strengthened in 1984.

Industrialization occurred in a protected environment, which led to distortions that, after the mid-1960s, contributed to the sagging industrial growth rate. Tariffs and quantitative controls largely kept foreign competition out of the domestic market, and most Indian manufacturers looked on exports only as a residual possibility. Industry paid insufficient attention to the quality of products, technological development elsewhere, and economies of scale. Management was weak in many private and public plants. Shortfalls in reaching plan goals in public enterprises, moreover, denied the rest of the industrial sector key inputs, such as coal and electricity.

In the 1980s and early 1990s, India began increasingly to remove some of the controls on industry. Nevertheless, in the mid-1990s, there were state monopolies for most energy and communications production and services, and the state dominated the steel, nonferrous metal, machine tool, shipbuilding, chemical, fertilizer, paper, and coal industries. In FY 1992, public enterprises had a turnover of Rs1.7 trillion. Well over 50 percent of this total was accounted for by ten enterprises, the most important of which were the oil, steel, and coal companies. Public enterprises in aggregate made a net profit after tax of 2.4 percent on capital in FY 1992, but the three oil companies earned 95 percent of these net profits. In fact, 106 of the 233 public companies sustained losses. Some analysts believed that the inefficiency of the public sector was concealed by passing on to consumers the high costs of monopoly products.

India - Manufacturing

Textiles

Cotton textiles is a well-established manufacturing industry and employs more workers than any other sector. Production in FY 1992 was 19 billion square meters of cloth. In Indian textile mills, yarn is spun, woven into fabrics, and processed under one roof. Production as a share of the manufacturing industry fell from 79 percent in 1951 to under 30 percent in the early 1990s as a result of curbs on capacity expansion and new equipment and differential excise duties. The main export market is Russia and other former Soviet republics. The power-loom sector forms the largest portion of the decentralized part of the textile industry. It expanded from 24,000 units in 1951 to 800,000 units in 1989. Power-loom fabric dominates India's garment export industry. There is also a substantial handloom sector, which provides employment in rural areas.

Steel and Aluminum

After independence, successive governments placed great emphasis on the development of a steel industry. In FY 1991, the six major plants, of which five were in the public sector, produced 10 million tons. The rest of the steel production, 4.7 million tons, came from 180 small plants, almost all of which were in the private sector. Steel production more than doubled during the 1980s but still did not meet demand in FY 1991, when 2.7 million tons were imported. In the mid-1990s, the government is seeking private-sector investment in new steel plants. Production is projected to increase substantially as the result of plans to set up a 1 million ton steel plant and three pig-iron plants totalling 600,000 tons capacity in West Bengal, with Chinese technical assistance and financial investment.

The aluminum industry grew from 5,000 tons a year at independence to 483,000 tons in FY 1992, of which 113,000 tons were exported. Analysts believe the industry has a good long-term future because of India's abundant supply of bauxite.

Fertilizer and Petrochemicals

The fertilizer industry is another major industrial sector. In FY 1991, production reached 7.4 million tons of nitrogen and 2.6 million tons of phosphate. In the early 1990s, an increasing share of fertilizer production came from private-sector plants. Substantial imports were necessary in FY 1990, but the prospects for expansion of domestic production are good.

In the early 1990s, the petrochemical industry was expanding rapidly. It produces a wide variety of thermoplastics, elastomers, synthetic fibers, and chemicals. Substantial imports, however, are required to meet domestic demand. Analysts forecast a major expansion in production during the 1990s.

Electronics and Motor Vehicles

The engineering sector is large and varied and provides around 12 percent of India's exports in the mid-1990s. Two subsectors, electronics and motor vehicles, are the most dynamic.

Electronics companies benefited from the economic liberalization policies of the 1980s, including the loosening of restrictions on technology and component imports, delicensing, foreign investment, and reduction of excise duties. Output from electronics plants grew from Rs1.8 billion in FY 1970 to Rs8.1 billion in FY 1980 and to Rs123 billion in FY 1992. Most of the expansion took place in the production of computers and consumer electronics.

Computer production rose from 7,500 units in 1985 to 60,000 units in 1988 and to an estimated 200,000 units in 1992. During this period, major advances were made in the domestic computer industry that led to further sales.

Consumer electronics account for about 30 percent of total electronics production. In FY 1990, production included 5 million television sets, 6 million radios, 5 million tape recorders, 5 million electronic watches, and 140,000 video cassette recorders.

A similar expansion occurred in the motor vehicle industry. Until the 1980s, the government considered automobiles an unnecessary luxury and discouraged their production and use. Production rose from 30,000 cars in FY 1980 to 181,000 cars in FY 1990.

The largest company, Maruti, which is publicly owned, exports some automobiles to Eastern Europe and to France and became a net foreign-exchange earner in FY 1991. The production of other motor vehicles is also expanding. In FY 1990, India produced 176,000 commercial vehicles, such as trucks and buses, and 1.8 million two-wheeled motor vehicles. Following the government's abolition of the manufacturing licensing system in March 1993, British, French, German, Italian, and United States manufacturers and firms in the Republic of Korea (South Korea) announced they would join Japanese and other South Korean companies already operating in India in joint-venture passenger car production in 1995. The growth of the Indian middle class sustains such industrial expansion and is forcing old-line domestic companies, such as Hindustan Motors, to become more competitive.

Construction

Construction contributes 5 to 6 percent of GDP and employs a similar proportion of the organized labor force plus large numbers of people in the informal sector. In the early 1990s, construction absorbed around 40 percent of public-sector plan outlays, and more than 1 million workers were engaged in public-sector construction projects. Indian firms also won many construction contracts in the Middle East during the 1980s and early 1990s. Most companies are small and lack access to modern equipment.

House building has not been a priority of the government, and a housing shortage persists in both urban and rural areas. Analysts believe that one-third of the population of big cities live in areas officially regarded as slums.

India - Energy

India produces nearly 90 percent of its energy requirements, 65 percent of which are met by coal. Although commercial energy production has expanded substantially since independence, an inadequate supply of energy remains a constraint on industrial growth. Overall growth in the demand for energy was rapid in the early 1990s, but commercial energy consumption was among the lowest in the world. Much energy use in the subsistence sector, such as the use of firewood and cattle dung, is unrecorded. Analysts believe that the share of noncommercial energy fell from around 65 percent in the early 1950s to 23 percent in 1991, and they expect this proportion to fall further during the 1990s. Most commercial energy production and distribution are in the public sector, but in the mid-1990s, the government was moving slowly to encourage the entry of private capital.

Coal

The coal industry is a key segment of the economy. Reserves are estimated at 192 billion tons, 78 billion tons of which are proven reserves.

Additional coal exists in small seams, at great depths, and in undiscovered locations. The bulk of the coal found has been in Bihar, Madhya Pradesh, Orissa, and West Bengal. Known reserves should last well into the twenty-first century. In the 1980s, development of strip mines was stressed over underground mines because of the speed with which they could be exploited. Most of the industry was nationalized in the early 1970s. Coal India Limited was established in 1975 as the government's holding company for several operating subsidiaries. Production stagnated in the second half of the 1970s at around 105 million tons after an initial surge in production following nationalization. In the late 1970s and throughout the 1980s, the industry was plagued by the flooding of mines, serious power outages, delays in commissioning new mines, labor unrest, lack of explosives, poor transportation, and environmental problems. Government-set coal prices did not cover operating expenses of the more technically difficult mines. The central government was the main source of investment funds.

Throughout the late 1970s and 1980s, the coal industry—along with the electric power and transportation sectors—was a critical bottleneck in the economy and particularly handicapped industrial growth. The Seventh Five-Year Plan (1985-89) set a target of 226 million tons for coal production in FY 1989, but actual production reached only 214 million tons. Production rose to 241 million tons in FY 1991 and to 251 million tons in FY 1992. The annual demand for coal in the mid-1990s was around 320 million tons, a level that appeared to be out of reach without a significant leap in efficiency and large-scale investment. Subsurface mine fires in Bihar, some of which have been burning since 1916, have consumed some 37 million tons of coal and make another 2 billion tons inaccessible.

Oil and Natural Gas

India has significant amounts of oil and natural gas, and four of India's top six revenue-generating companies are in the oil and natural gas business. India has indigenous sources for around 60 percent of its oil needs and has worked diligently to use substitute forms of energy to fulfill the other 40 percent. Oil in commercial quantities was first discovered in Assam in 1889. The Oil and Natural Gas Commission was established in 1954 as a department of the Geological Survey of India, but a 1959 act of Parliament made it, in effect, the country's national oil company. Oil India Limited, at one time one-third government owned, was also established in 1959 and developed an oil field that had been discovered by the Burmah Oil Company. By 1981 the government had purchased all of the Burmah Oil

Company's assets in India and completely owned Oil India Limited. The Oil and Natural Gas Commission discovered oil in Gujarat in 1959 and opened other fields in the 1960s and 1970s.

The early oil fields discovered in India were of modest size. Oil production amounted to 200,000 tons in 1950 and 400,000 tons in 1960. By the early 1970s, production had increased to more than 8 million tons. In 1974 the Oil and Natural Gas Commission discovered a large field—called the Bombay High—offshore from Bombay. Production from that field was responsible for the rapid growth of the country's total crude oil production in the late 1970s and throughout the 1980s. In FY 1989, oil production peaked at 34 million tons, of which Bombay High accounted for 22 million tons. In the early 1990s, wells were shut in offshore fields that had been inefficiently exploited, and production fell to 27 million tons in FY 1993. That amount did not meet India's needs, and 30.7 million tons of crude oil were imported in FY 1993.

India has thirty-five major fields onshore (primarily in Assam and Gujarat) and four major offshore oil fields (near Bombay, south of Pondicherry, and in the Palk Strait). Of the 4,828 wells, in 1990 2,514 were producing at a rate of 664,582 barrels per day. The oil field with the greatest output is Bombay High, with 402,797 barrels per day production in 1990, about fifteen times the amount produced by the next largest fields. Total reserves are estimated at 6.1 billion barrels.

The government has sanctioned ambitious exploration plans to raise production in line with demand and to exploit new discoveries as rapidly as possible. In the late 1980s and early 1990s, there were encouraging finds in Tamil Nadu, Gujarat, Andhra Pradesh, and Assam; many of these discoveries were made offshore. Officials estimated that by the mid-1990s these new fields could contribute as much as 15 million to 20 million tons in new production and that total crude oil production could increase to 51 million tons in FY 1994. In the early 1990s, the government renewed attempts, which had begun in the early 1980s, to interest foreign oil companies in purchasing exploration and production leases. These efforts drew only a modest response because the terms offered were difficult, and foreign companies remained suspicious of India's investment climate. One response, agreed on in January 1995, was an Indian-Kuwaiti joint venture to invest in a new oil refinery to be built on the east coast of India.

Substantial quantities of natural gas are produced in association with crude oil production. Until the 1980s, most of this gas was flared off because there were no pipelines or processing facilities to bring it to customers. In the early 1980s, large investments were made to bring gases from Bombay High and other offshore fields ashore for use as fuel and to supply feedstock to fertilizer and petrochemical plants, which also had to be constructed or converted to use gas. By the mid-1980s, natural gas could be delivered to facilities near Bombay and near Kandla in Gujarat. In the mid-1990s, a 1,700-kilometer trans-India pipeline was being built; the pipeline will link the facilities near Bombay and Kandla to a series of gas-based fertilizer plants and power stations. Officials envisage a grid system covering 11,500 kilometers by FY 2004, which will supply 120 million cubic meters of gas a day. Total production in FY 1992 was 18.1 billion cubic meters.

India's need for oil and petroleum-based products—about 40 million tons per year—far exceeded its domestic production capabilities of 28 million tons per year in the early 1990s. Given India's dependency on Persian Gulf resources, proposals were made in the early 1990s to develop natural gas pipelines from Iran, Qatar, and Oman that would run under the Arabian Sea to one or more west coast terminals. To assist with oil and natural gas production, in 1992 the government decided to open reserves to private offshore developers. In February 1994, contracts were awarded for three offshore fields in the Arabian Sea to an Indian-United States consortium and one in the Bay of Bengal to an Indian-Australian-Japanese consortium. In June 1995, an agreement was reached to set a joint-venture company to construct the first leg of the pipeline, from Iran to Pakistan.

Electric Power

The electric power industry is both a supplier and a consumer of primary energy, depending on the kind of energy used to turn the generators. Hydroelectric and nuclear power plants add to the country's supply of primary energy. The total installed electricity capacity in public utilities in 1992 was 69,100 megawatts, of which 70 percent was thermal, 27 percent hydropower, and 3 percent nuclear. The total installed capacity was programmed to reach around 100,000 megawatts by FY 1996 through a package of government-supported incentives to the private sector.

Because they cannot always depend on public utilities, many larger industrial enterprises have developed their own power generation systems. In 1992 there was a capacity of 9,000 megawatts outside the public utility system. Overall, the generation and transmission of power—with an average 57 percent plant load factor in FY 1992 in thermal plants and transmission losses of 22 percent—were inefficient. About 322 billion kilowatt- hours of power were generated by utilities in FY 1992, approximately 8.5 percent shy of demand. The resulting deficit led to acute shortages in some states. This trend continued the next year when 315 billion kilowatt-hours were produced. Many factors contributed to the shortfall of electric power, including slow completion of new installations, low use of installed capacity because of insufficient maintenance and coal, and poor management. In FY 1990, industry accounted for 45 percent of electricity consumed, agriculture 26 percent, and domestic use 16.5 percent. Other sectors, including commerce and railroads, accounted for the remaining 12.5 percent.

Rural electrification made great progress in the 1980s; more than 200,000 villages received electricity for the first time. In 1990 around 84 percent of India's villages had access to electricity. Most of the villages without electricity were in Bihar, Orissa, Rajasthan, Uttar Pradesh, and West Bengal. Villagers complain that government figures on electrification of villages are artificially inflated. Actually, although lines have been run to most villages, electricity is provided only sporadically (for example, only nine to twelve hours per day), and villagers feel they cannot depend on electricity to operate pumps and other equipment. Electricity to cities also is sporadic; blackouts occur every day in most cities.

India's first hydroelectric station was constructed in 1897 in Darjiling (then Darjeeling). In FY 1990, installed capacity for hydroelectric power was 18,000 megawatts. The country has a large economically exploitable hydroelectric potential, especially in the foothills of the Himalayas, but no large increase in capacity is predicted for the mid-1990s. Hydroelectric facilities have to be coordinated with other sources of electricity because seasonal and annual variations in rainfall affect the amount of water needed to turn the generators and consequently the amount of electricity that can be produced.

Hydroelectric power projects have not been without controversy. Dams for irrigation and power generation have displaced people and raised the specter of ecological problems.

Nuclear Power

Nuclear-power developments are under the purview of the Nuclear Power Corporation of India, a government-owned entity under the Department of Atomic Energy. The corporation is responsible for designing, constructing, and operating nuclear-power plants. In 1995 there were nine operational plants with a potential total capacity of 1,800 megawatts, about 3 percent of India's total power generation. There are two units each in Tarapur, north of Bombay in Maharashtra; in Rawatbhata in Rajasthan; in Kalpakkam near Madras in Tamil Nadu; and in Narora in Uttar Pradesh;

and one unit in Kakrapur in southeastern Gujarat. However, of the nine plants, all have been faced with safety problems that have shut down reactors for periods ranging from months to years. The Rajasthan Atomic Power Station in Rawatbhata was closed indefinitely, as of February 1995. Moreover, environmental problems, caused by radiation leaks, have cropped up in communities near Rawatbhata. Other plants operate at only a fraction of their capacity, and some foreign experts consider them the most inefficient nuclear-power plants in the world.

In addition to the nine established plants, seven reactors are under construction in the mid-1990s: one at Kakrapur and two each at Kaiga, on the coast of Karnataka, Rawatbhata, and Tarapur, which, when finished, will bring an additional 2,320 megawatts of energy online. Construction of ten additional reactors is in the planning stage for Kaiga, Rawatbhata, and Kudangulam in Tamil Nadu, which, when combined, will supply 4,800 megawatts capacity. The overall plan is to increase nuclear-generation capacity to 10,000 megawatts by FY 2000, but work has been slowed because of financial shortages. India partially overcame its shortage of enriched uranium—needed to fuel the Tarapur units—by imports from China, starting in 1995.

India - Mining and Quarrying

For a country of its size, India does not have a great deal of mineral wealth. Mining accounted for less than 2 percent of GDP in FY 1990. Nonetheless, iron and bauxite are found in sufficient quantities to base industries on their extraction and processing. Assessment of the country's resources by the Geological Survey of India is still far from complete in the mid-1990s, and observers do not rule out the possibility of important new finds.

In 1992 reserves of iron ore were estimated at among the world's largest—at 19.2 billion tons. Extraction capacity is 67 million tons of ore per year, but only 53 million tons were produced in FY 1992. About 60 percent of output is exported, mainly to the South Korea and Japan. The largest iron ore mining project is at Kudremukh, Chikmagalore District, Karnataka. India also has abundant bauxite, the main mineral source for aluminum. Reserves are estimated at about 2.7 billion tons, or 8 percent of the world total. In FY 1991, 512,000 tons of aluminum were produced, of which 61,000 tons were exported. Most bauxite mines are in Bihar and Karnataka. India is the world's third largest producer of manganese, and its mines extracted around 1.4 million tons of manganese ore per year in the early 1990s from a total estimated reserve of 180 million tons. India also has significant reserves of copper, estimated at 422 million tons. However, the production of copper, at 46,000 tons in FY 1991, fell well short of domestic demand. Most copper mines are in Bihar and Rajasthan. Smaller amounts of lead, zinc, and mica are also produced.

Ownership and the power to grant mineral concessions generally have rested with the state governments. The central government, however, has exerted considerable influence over such leases, particularly in cases of important and strategic minerals. In fact, most mining of important and strategic minerals is undertaken by central government enterprises in which states sometimes hold part ownership. In the early 1990s, uranium ore was mined, milled, and processed only in Bihar; rare earths—including mineral sands, monazite, ilmenite, rutile, zircon, rare earths chloride, and others—were mined in Tamil Nadu, Kerala, and Orissa. During this period, the central government was attempting to increase the private sector's share of this industry.

India - Tourism

Tourism has not been a government priority, but it nonetheless provides around 6 percent of foreign-exchange earnings. The total number of visitors to India was estimated at nearly 1.8 million in FY 1992. The Eighth Five-Year Plan estimated an annual increase of 6 to 7 percent in visitor arrivals; tourists from Europe and North America were targeted. In the mid-1990s, the government offered special tax incentives to the industry to help alleviate a shortage of hotel rooms. Estimated gross export earnings from tourism were Rs24 billion and net earnings Rs17 billion, making the industry an important foreign-exchange earner. With under 0.3 percent of the world's tourists and around 1 percent of world tourism spending, India, however, has barely tapped its tourism potential.

India - Science and Technology

Origin and Development

Indian scientific research and technological developments since independence in 1947 have received substantial political support and most of their funding from the government. Science and technology initiatives have been important aspects of the government's five-year plans and usually are based on fulfilling short-term needs, while aiming to provide the institutional base needed to achieve long-term goals. As India has striven to develop leading scientists and world-class research institutes, government-sponsored scientific and technical developments have aided diverse areas such as agriculture, biotechnology, cold regions research, communications, environment, industry, mining, nuclear power, space, and transportation. As a result, India has experts in such fields as astronomy and astrophysics, liquid crystals, condensed matter physics, molecular biology, virology, and crystallography. Observers have pointed out, however, that India's emphasis on basic and theoretical research rather than on applied research and technical applications has diminished the social and economic effects of the government's investments. In the mid-1990s, government funds supported nearly 80 percent of India's research and development activities, but, as elsewhere in the economic sector, emphasis increasingly was being put on independent, nongovernmental sources of support.

India has a long and proud scientific tradition. Nehru, in his *Discovery of India* published in 1946, praised the mathematical achievements of Indian scholars, who are said to have developed geometric theorems before Pythagoras did in the sixth century B.C. and were using advanced methods of determining the number of mathematical combinations by the second century B.C. By the fifth century A.D., Indian mathematicians were using ten numerals and by the seventh century were treating zero as a number. These breakthroughs, Nehru said, "liberated the human mind . . . and threw a flood of light on the behavior of numbers." The conceptualization of squares, rectangles, circles, triangles, fractions, the ability to express the number ten to the twelfth power, algebraic formulas, and astronomy had even more ancient origins in Vedic literature, some of which was compiled as early as 1500 B.C. The concepts of astronomy, metaphysics, and perennial movement are all embodied in the Rig Veda. Although such abstract concepts were further developed by the ancient Greeks and the Indian numeral system was popularized in the first millennium A.D. by the Arabs (the Arabic word for number, Nehru pointed out, is *hindsah* , meaning "from Hind (India)"), their Indian origins are a source of national pride.

Technological discoveries have been made relating to pharmacology, brain surgery, medicine, artificial colors and glazes, metallurgy, recrystalization, chemistry, the decimal system, geometry, astronomy, and language and linguistics (systematic linguistic analysis having originated in India with Panini's fourth-century B.C. Sanskrit grammar, the *Ashtadhyayi*). These discoveries have led to practical applications in brick and pottery making, metal casting, distillation, surveying, town planning, hydraulics, the development of a lunar calendar, and the means of recording these discoveries as early as the era of Harappan culture (ca. 2500-1500 B.C.; see Harappan Culture, ch. 1).

Written information on scientific developments from the Harrapan period to the eleventh century A.D. (when the first permanent Muslim settlements were established in India) is found in Sanskrit, Pali, Arabic, Persian, Tamil, Malayalam, and other classical languages that were intimately connected to Indian religious and philosophical traditions. Archaeological evidence and written accounts from other cultures with which India has had contact have also been used to corroborate the evidence of Indian scientific and technological developments. The technology of textile production, hydraulic engineering, water-powered devices, medicine, and other innovations, as well as mathematics and other theoretical sciences, continued to develop and be influenced by techniques brought in from the Muslim world by the Mughals after the fifteenth century.

The practical applications of scientific and technical developments are witnessed, for example, by the proliferation of hundreds of thousands of water tanks for irrigation in South India by the eighteenth and nineteenth centuries. Although each tank was built through local efforts, together, in effect, they created a closely integrated network supplying water throughout the region. The science of metallurgy led to the construction of numerous small but sophisticated furnaces for producing iron and steel. By the late eighteenth century, it is estimated that production capability may have reached 200,000 tons per year. High levels of textile production—making India the world's leading producer and exporter of textiles before 1800—were the result of refinements in spinning technology.

Several millennia of interest in astronomy in India eventually resulted in the invention and construction of a network of sophisticated, large-scale astronomical observatories—the Jantar Mantars (meaning "house of instruments")—in the early eighteenth century. Constructed of stone, brick, stucco, and marble, the Jantar Mantar complexes were used to determine the seasons, phases of the moon and sun, and locations of stars and planets from points in Delhi, Mathura, Jaipur, Varanasi, and Ujjain. The Jantar Mantars were designed and built by a renowned astronomer and city planner, Sawai Jai Singh II, the Hindu maharajah of Amber, between 1725 and 1734, after he been asked by Mohammad Shah, the tenth Mughal emperor, to reform the calendar. These complexes had the patronage of the Mughal emperors and have long attracted the attention of Western scholars and travelers, some of whom have found them anachronistic in light of the use of telescopes in Europe and China more than a century before Jai Singh's projects. As United States scientist William A. Blanpied has pointed out, Jai Singh, who subscribed to Hindu cosmology, was aware of Western developments but preferred to perfect his naked-eye observations rather than concentrate on precise calculational astronomy.

The arrival of the British in India in the early seventeenth century—the Portuguese, Dutch, and French also had a presence, although it was much less pervasive—led eventually to new scientific developments that added to the indigenous achievements of the previous millennia. Although colonization subverted much of Indian culture, turning the region into a source of raw materials for the factories of England and France and leaving only low-technology production to local entrepreneurs, a new organization was brought to science in the form of the British education system. Science education under British rule (by the East India Company from 1757 to 1857 and by the British government from 1858 to 1947) initially involved only rudimentary mathematics, but as greater exploitation of India took place, there was more need for surveying and medical schools to train indigenous people to assist Europeans in their explorations and research. What new technologies were implemented were imported rather than developed indigenously, however, and it was only during the immediate preindependence period that Indian scientists came to enjoy political patronage and support for their work.

Western education and techniques of scientific inquiry were added to the already established Indian base, making way for later developments. The major result of these developments was the establishment of a large and sophisticated educational infrastructure that placed India as the leader in science and technology in Asia at the time of independence in 1947. Thereafter, as other Asian nations emerged, India lost its primacy in science, a situation much lamented by India's leaders and scientists. However, the infrastructure was in place and has continued to produce generations of top scientists.

One of the most famous scientists of the pre- and postindependence era was Indian-trained Chandrasekhara Venkata (C.V.) Raman, an ardent nationalist, prolific researcher, and writer of scientific treatises on the molecular scattering of light and other subjects of quantum mechanics. In 1930 Raman was awarded the Nobel prize in physics for his 1928 discovery of the Raman Effect, which demonstrates that the energy of a photon can undergo partial transformation within matter. In 1934-36, with his colleague Nagendra Nath, Raman propounded the Raman-Nath Theory on the diffraction of light by ultrasonic waves. He was a director of the Indian Institute of Science and founded the Indian Academy of Sciences in 1934 and the Raman Research Institute in 1948.

Another leading scientist was Homi Jehangir Bhabha, an eminent physicist internationally recognized for his contributions to the fields of positron theory, cosmic rays, and muon physics at the University of Cambridge in Britain. In 1945, with financial assistance from the Sir Dorabji Tata Trust, Bhabha established the Tata Institute of Fundamental Research in Bombay.

Other eminent preindependence scientists include Sir Jagadish Chandra (J.C.) Bose, a Cambridge-educated Bengali physicist who discovered the application of electromagnetic waves to wireless telegraphy in 1895 and then went on to a second notable career in biophysical research. Meghnad Saha, also from Bengal, was trained in India, Britain, and Germany and became an internationally recognized nuclear physicist whose mathematical equations and ionization theory gave new insight into the functions of stellar spectra. In the late 1930s, Saha began promoting the importance of science to national economic modernization, a concept fully embraced by Nehru and several generations of government planners. The Bose-Einstein Statistics, used in quantum physics, and Boson particles are named after another leading scientist, mathematician Satyendranath (S.N.) Bose. S.N. Bose was trained in India, and his research discoveries gave him international fame and an opportunity for advanced studies in France and Germany. In 1924 he sent the results of his research on radiation as a form of gas to Albert Einstein. Einstein extended Bose's statistical methods to ordinary atoms, which led him to predict a new state of matter—called the Bose-Einstein Condensation—that was scientifically proved in United States laboratory experiments in 1995. Prafulla Chandra Ray, another Bengali, earned a doctorate in inorganic chemistry from the University of Edinburgh in 1887 and went on to a devoted career of teaching and research. His work was instrumental in establishing the chemical industry in Bengal in the early twentieth century.

At the onset of independence, Nehru called science "the very texture of life" and optimistically declared that "science alone . . . can solve problems of hunger and poverty, of insanitation and illiteracy, of superstition and deadening customs." Under his leadership, the government set out to cure numerous societal problems. The Green Revolution, educational improvement, establishment of hundreds of scientific laboratories, industrial and military research, massive hydraulic projects, and entry into the frontiers of space all evolved from this early decision to embrace high technology.

One of the early planning documents was the Scientific Policy Resolution of 1958, which called for embracing "by all appropriate means, the cultivation of science and scientific research in all its aspects—pure, applied, and educational" and encouraged individual initiatives. In 1983 the government issued a similar statement, which, while stressing the importance of international cooperation and the diffusion of scientific knowledge, put considerable emphasis on self-reliance and the development of indigenous technology. This goal is still in place in the mid-1990s.

Infrastructure and Government Role

Science and technology policy and research have largely been the domains of government since 1947 and are largely patterned after the structure left behind by the British. Within the central government, there are a top-down apparatus and a plethora of ministries, departments, lower-level agencies, and institutions involved in the science and technology infrastructure.

Government-administered science and technology emanate from the Office of the Prime Minister, to which a chief science adviser and the Science Advisory Council, when they are appointed, have direct input. The prime minister de jure controls the science and technology sector through the National Council on Science and Technology, the minister of state for science and technology (who has control over day-to-day operations of the science and technology infrastructure), and ministers responsible for ocean development, atomic energy, electronics, and space. Other ministries and departments also have significant science and technology components and answer to the prime minister through their respective ministers. Among them are agriculture, chemicals and fertilizers, civil aviation and tourism, coal, defence, environment, food, civil supplies, forests and wildlife, health and family welfare, home affairs, human resource development, nonconventional energy sources, petrochemicals, and petroleum and natural gas, as well as other governmental entities.

The Ministry of Science and Technology was established in 1971 to formulate science and technology policies and implement, identify, and promote "frontline" research throughout the science and technology infrastructure. The ministry, through its subordinate Department of Science and Technology, also coordinates intragovernmental and international cooperation and provides funding for domestic institutions and research programs. The Department of Scientific and Industrial Research, a technology transfer organization, and the Department of Biotechnology, which runs a number of developmental laboratories, are the ministry's other administrative elements. Indicative of the level of importance placed on science and technology is the fact that Prime Minister P.V. Narasimha Rao held the portfolio for this ministry in the early and mid-1990s. Some argued, however, that Rao could truly strengthen the sector by appointing, as his predecessors did, a chief science adviser and a committee of leading scientists to provide high-level advice and delegate the running of these ministries to others.

The National Council on Science and Technology is at the apex of the science and technology infrastructure and is chaired by the prime minister. The integration of science and technology planning with national socioeconomic planning is carried out by the Planning Commission. Scientific advisory committees in individual socioeconomic ministries formulate long-term programs and identify applicable technologies for their particular area of responsibility. The rest of the infrastructure has seven major components. The national-level component includes government organizations that provide hands-on research and development, such as the ministries of atomic energy and space, the Council of Scientific and Industrial Research (CSIR—a component of the Ministry of Science and Technology), and the Indian Council of Agricultural Research. The second component, organizations that support research and development, includes the departments or ministries of biotechnology, nonconventional energy sources, ocean development, and science and technology. The third-echelon component includes state government research and development agencies, which are usually involved with agriculture, animal husbandry, irrigation, public health, and the like and that also are part of the national infrastructure. The four other major components are the university system, private research organizations, public-sector research and development establishments, and research and development centers within private industries. Almost all internationally recognized university-level research is carried out in government-controlled or government-supported institutions. The results of government-sponsored research are transferred to public- and private-sector industries through the National Research and Development Corporation. This corporation is part of the Ministry of Science and Technology and has as its purpose the commercialization of scientific and technical know-how, the promotion of research through grants and loans, promotion of government and industry joint projects, and the export of Indian technology.

Resource Allocation

Central government financial support of research and development—including subsidies to public-sector industries—was 75.7 percent of total financial support in FY 1992. State governments provided an additional 9.3 percent. However, even when combined with the private-sector contribution (15.0 percent), research and development expenditures were only just over 0.8 percent of the GDP in FY 1992. Although there was growth in research and development expenditures during the 1980s and early 1990s, the rate of growth was less than the GNP rate of growth during the same period and was a cause of concern for government planners. Moreover, the bulk of government research and development expenditures (80 percent in FY 1992) goes to only five agencies: the Defence Research and Development Organisation (DRDO), the Ministry of Space, the Indian Council of Agricultural Research, the Ministry of Atomic Energy, and CSIR, and to their constituent organizations.

Despite long-term government commitment to research and development, India compares poorly with other major Asian countries. In Japan, for example, nearly 3 percent of GDP goes to research and development; in South Korea and Taiwan, the figure is nearly 2 percent. In India, research and development receives only 0.8 percent of GDP; only China among the major players spends less (0.7 percent). However, India's share of GDP expenditure on research and development has increased slightly: in 1975 it stood at 0.5 percent, in 1980 at 0.6 percent, and in 1985 at 0.8, where it has become static.

Because of the allocation of financial inputs, India has been more successful at promoting security-oriented and large-scale scientific endeavors, such as space and nuclear science programs, than at promoting industrial technology. Part of the latter lack of achievement has been attributed to the limited role of universities in the research and development system. Instead, India has concentrated on government-sponsored specialized institutes and provided minimal funding to university research programs. The low funding level has encouraged university scientists to find jobs in the more liberally funded public-sector national laboratories. Moreover, private industry in India plays a relatively minor role in the science and technology system (15 percent of the total investment compared with Japan's 80 percent and slightly more than 50 percent in the United States). This low level of private-sector investment has been attributed to a number of factors, including the preponderance of trade-oriented rather than technology-oriented industries, protectionist tariffs, and rigid regulation of foreign investment. The largest private-sector research and development expenditures during the FY 1990-FY 1992 period were in the areas of engineering and technology, particularly in the industrial development, transportation, communications, and health services sectors. Nonetheless, they were relatively small expenditures when compared with government and public-sector inputs in the same fields. The key element for Indian industry to benefit from the greater government and public-sector efforts in the 1990s is the ability of the government and public-sector laboratories to develop technologies with broad applications and to transfer these technologies—as is done by the National Research and Development Corporation—to private-sector industries able to apply them with maximum efficiency.

India ranks eleventh in the world in its number of active scientific and technical personnel. Including medical personnel, they were estimated at around 188,000 in 1950, 450,000 in 1960, 1.2 million in 1970, 1.8 million in 1980, and 3.8 million in 1990. India's universities, university-level institutions, and colleges have produced more than 200,000 science and technology graduates per year since 1985. Doctorates are awarded each year to about 3,000 people in science, between 500 and 600 in engineering, around 800 in agricultural sciences, and close to 6,000 in medicine. However, in 1990 India had the lowest number of scientific and engineering personnel (3.3) per 10,000 persons in the national labor force of the major Asian nations. For example, Japan, had nearly seventy-five per 10,000, South Korea had more than thirty-seven per 10,000, and China had 5.6 per 10,000.

The quality of higher education in the sciences has not improved as quickly as desired since independence because of the flight of many top scientists from academia to higher-paying jobs in government-funded research laboratories. Foreign aid, aimed at counteracting university faculty shortages, has produced top-rate graduates as intended. However, because of limited job prospects at home, many of the brightest physicians, scientists, and engineers have been attracted by opportunities abroad, particularly in Western nations. Since the early 1990s, this trend has appeared to be changing as more high-technology jobs, especially in fields requiring computer science skills, have begun to open in India as a result of economic liberalization. The "brain bank" network of Indian scientists abroad that was seen as a potential source of talent by some observers in the 1980s has proven to be a valuable resource in the 1990s.

Using imported technology, scientists made major advances in microprocessors during the 1980s that brought the country to only one generation (three to four years) behind international leaders. A sign of how much microcomputer use has developed could be seen in sales: from

US$93 million in FY 1983 to US$488 million in FY 1988. Facilitating the use of automation has been a counterpart to the expansion of the data communication field. The development of the "Param 9000" supercomputer prototype, reportedly capable of billions of floating point operations per second, was completed in December 1994 and was announced by the state-owned Centre for Development of Advanced Computing as ready for sale to operational users in March 1995. Earlier Param models, using parallel processing technologies to achieve near-supercomputer performance, were produced in sufficient quantity for export in the early 1990s.

DRDO developed its own parallel processing computer, which was unveiled by Prime Minister Rao in April 1995. Developed by DRDO's Advanced Numerical Research and Analysis Group in Hyderabad, the supercomputer is capable of 1 billion points per second speed and can be used for geophysics, image processing, and molecular modeling.

India - Agriculture

AGRICULTURE HAS ALWAYS BEEN INDIA'S most important economic sector. In the mid-1990s, it provides approximately one-third of the gross domestic product (GDP—see Glossary) and employs roughly two-thirds of the population. Since independence in 1947, the share of agriculture in the GDP has declined in comparison to the growth of the industrial and services sectors. However, agriculture still provides the bulk of wage goods required by the nonagricultural sector as well as numerous raw materials for industry. Moreover, the direct share of agricultural and allied sectors in total exports is around 18 percent. When the indirect share of agricultural products in total exports, such as cotton textiles and jute goods, is taken into account, the percentage is much higher.

Dependence on agricultural imports in the early 1960s convinced planners that India's growing population, as well as concerns about national independence, security, and political stability, required self-sufficiency in food production. This perception led to a program of agricultural improvement called the Green Revolution, to a public distribution system, and to price supports for farmers. In the 1980s, despite three years of meager rainfall and a drought in the middle of the decade, India managed to get along with very few food imports because of the growth in food-grain production and the development of a large buffer stock against potential agricultural shortfalls. By the early 1990s, India was self-sufficient in food-grain production. Agricultural production has kept pace with the food needs of the growing population as the result of increased yields in almost all crops, but especially in cereals. Food grains and pulses account for two-thirds of agricultural production in the mid-1990s. The growth in food-grain production is a result of concentrated efforts to increase all the Green Revolution inputs needed for higher yields: better seed, more fertilizer, improved irrigation, and education of farmers. Although increased irrigation has helped to lessen year-to-year fluctuations in farm production resulting from the vagaries of the monsoons, it has not eliminated those fluctuations.

Food-grain production increased from 50.8 million tons in fiscal year (FY—see Glossary) 1950 to 176.3 million tons in FY 1990. The compound growth rate from FY 1949 to FY 1987 was 2.7 percent per annum. Overall, wheat was the best performer, with production increasing more than eightfold in forty years. Wheat was followed by rice, which had a production increase of more than 350 percent. Coarse grains had a poorer rate of increase but still doubled in output during those years; production of pulses went up by less than 70 percent. The increase in oilseed production, however, was not enough to fill consumer demands, and India went from being an exporter of oilseeds in the 1950s to a major importer in the 1970s and the early 1980s. The agricultural sector attempted to increase oilseed production in the 1980s and early 1990s. These efforts were successful: oilseed production doubled and the need for imports was reduced. In the early 1990s, India was on the verge of self-sufficiency in oilseed production.After independence in 1947, the cropping pattern became more diversified, and cultivation of commercial crops received a new impetus in line with domestic demands and export requirements. Nontraditional crops, such as summer mung (a variety of lentil, part of the pulse family), soybeans, peanuts, and sunflowers, were gradually gaining importance.

The per capita availability of a number of food items increased significantly in the postindependence period despite a population increase from 361 million in 1951 to 846 million in 1991. Per capita availability of cereals went up from 334 grams per day in 1951 to 470 grams per day in 1990. Availability of edible oils increased significantly, from 3.2 kilograms per year per capita in FY 1960 to 5.4 kilograms in FY 1990. Similarly, the availability of sugar per capita increased from 4.7 to 12.5 kilograms per year during the same period. The one area in which availability decreased was pulses, which went from 60.7 grams per day to 39.4 grams per day. This shortfall presents a serious problem in a country where a large part of the population is vegetarian and pulses are the main source of protein.

There are large disparities among India's states and territories in agricultural performance, only some of which can be attributed to differences in climate or initial endowments of infrastructure such as irrigation. Realizing the importance of agricultural production for economic development, the central government has played an active role in all aspects of agricultural development. Planning is centralized, and plan priorities, policies, and resource allocations are decided at the central level. Food and price policy also are decided by the central government. Thus, although agriculture is constitutionally the responsibility of the states rather than the central government, the latter plays a key role in formulating policy and providing financial resources for agriculture.

Land Use

In FY 1987, field crops were planted on about 45 percent of the total land mass of India. Of this cultivated land, almost 37 million hectares were double-cropped, making the gross sown area equivalent to almost 173 million hectares. About 15 million hectares were permanent pastureland or were planted in various tree crops and groves. Approximately 108 million hectares were either developed for nonagricultural uses, forested, or unsuited for agriculture because of topography. About 29.6 million hectares of the remaining land were classified as cultivable but fallow, and 15.6 million hectares were classified as cultivable wasteland. These 45 million hectares constitute all the land left for expanding the sown area; for various reasons, however, much of it is unsuited for immediate cropping. Expansion in crop production, therefore, has to come almost entirely from increasing yields on lands already in some kind of agricultural use.

Topography, soils, rainfall, and the availability of water for irrigation have been major determinants of the crop and livestock patterns characteristic of the three major geographic regions of India—the Himalayas, the Indo-Gangetic Plain, and the Peninsula—and their agro-ecological subregions. Government policy as regards irrigation, the introduction of new crops, research and education, and incentives has had some impact on changing the traditional crop and livestock patterns in these subregions. The monsoons, however, play a critical role in determining whether the harvest will be bountiful, average, or poor in any given year. One of the objectives of government policy in the early 1990s was to find methods of reducing this dependence on the monsoons.

Landholding Categories

India is a land of small farms, of peasants cultivating their ancestral lands mainly by family labor and, despite the spread of tractors in the 1980s, by pairs of bullocks. About 50 percent of all operational holdings in 1980 were less than one hectare in size. About 19 percent fell in the one-to-two hectare range, 16 percent in the two-to-four hectare range, and 11 percent in the four-to-ten hectare range. Only 4 percent of the working farms encompassed ten or more hectares.

Although farms are typically small throughout the country, the average size holding by state ranges from about 0.5 hectare in Kerala and 0.75 hectare in Tamil Nadu to three hectares in Maharashtra and five hectares in Rajasthan. Factors influencing this range include soils, topography, rainfall, rural population density, and thoroughness of land redistribution programs.

Many factors—historical, political, economic, and demographic—have affected the development of the prevailing land-tenure status. The operators of most agricultural holdings possess vested rights in the land they till, whether as full owners or as protected tenants. By the early 1990s, there were tenancy laws in all the states and union territories except Nagaland, Meghalaya, and Mizoram. The laws provide for states to confer ownership on tenants, who can buy the land they farm in return for fair payment; states also oversee provision of security of tenure and the establishing of fair rents. The implementation of these laws has varied among the states. West Bengal, Karnataka, and Kerala, for example, have achieved more success than other states. The land tenure situation is complicated, and it has varied widely from state to state. There is, however, much less variation in the mid-1990s than in the postindependence period.

Independent India inherited a structure of landholding that was characterized by heavy concentration of cultivable areas in the hands of relatively large absentee landowners (zamindars—see Glossary), the excessive fragmentation of small landholdings, an already growing class of landless agricultural workers, and the lack of any generalized system of documentary evidence of landownership or tenancy. Land was important as a status symbol; from one generation to the next, there was a tendency for an original family holding to be progressively subdivided, a situation that continued in the early 1990s. This phenomenon resulted in many landholdings that were too small to provide a livelihood for a family. Borrowing money against land was almost inevitable and frequently resulted in the loss of land to a local moneylender or large landowner, further widening the gap between large and small landholders. Moreover, inasmuch as landowners and moneylenders tended to belong to higher castes and petty owners and tenants to lower castes, land tenure had strong social as well as economic impact.

By the early 1970s, after extensive legislation, large absentee landowners had, for all practical purposes, been eliminated; their rights had been acquired by the state in exchange for compensation in cash and government bonds. More than 20 million former zamindar-system tenants had acquired occupancy rights to the land they tilled. Whereas previously the landlord collected rent from his tenants and passed on a portion of it as land revenue to the government, starting in the early 1970s, the state collected the rent directly from cultivators who, in effect, had become renters from the state. Most former tenants acquired the right to purchase the land they tilled, and payments to the state were spread out over ten to twenty years. Large landowners were divested not only of their cultivated land but also of ownership of forests, lakes, and barren lands. They were also stripped of various other economic rights, such as collection of taxes on sales of immovable property within their jurisdiction and collection of money for grazing privileges on uncultivated lands and use of river water. These rights also were taken over by state governments in return for compensation. By 1980 more than 6 million hectares of waste, fallow, and other categories of unused land had been vested in state governments and, in turn, distributed to landless agricultural workers.

Land Reform

A major concern in rural India is the huge number of landless or near-landless families, many of whom are wholly dependent on a few weeks of work at the peak planting and harvesting seasons. The number of landless rural families has grown steadily since independence, both in absolute terms and as a proportion of the population. In 1981 there were 195.1 million rural workers: 55.4 million were agricultural laborers who depended primarily on casual farm work for a livelihood. In the early 1990s, the rural work force had grown to 242 million, of whom 73.7 million were classified as agricultural laborers. Approximately 33 percent of the employed rural workers were classified as casual wage laborers.

Because of the large number of landless farmers and the frequent neglect of land by absentee landlords in the early years of independence, the principle that there should be a ceiling on the size of landholdings, depending on the crop planted and the quality of the land, was embodied in the First Five-Year Plan (FY 1951-55). An agricultural census was conducted to provide guidance in setting such ceilings. During the Second Five-Year Plan (FY 1956-60), most states legislated fixed ceilings, but there was little uniformity among the states; ceilings ranged from six to 132 hectares. Certain specialized branches of agriculture, such as horticulture, cattle breeding, and dairy farming, were usually exempted from ceilings.

All the states instituted programs to force landowners to sell their over-the-ceiling holdings to the government at fixed prices; the states, in turn, were to redistribute the land to the landless. But adamant resistance, high costs, sloppy record keeping, and poor administration in general combined to weaken and delay this aspect of land reform. The delays in legislation allowed large landowners to circumvent the intent of the laws by spurious partitioning, sales, gifts to family members, and other methods of evading ceilings. Many exemptions were granted so that there was little surplus land.

To ensure more uniformity in income, to combat evasion of the intent of the laws, and to secure more land for distribution to the landless, the central government in the 1970s pushed for greatly reduced ceilings. For a family of five, the central government guidelines called for not more than 10.9 hectares of good, irrigated land suitable for double-cropping, not more than 10.9 hectares of land suited for one crop annually, and not more than 21.9 hectares for orchards. Exemptions were continued for land used as cocoa, coffee, tea, and rubber plantations; land held by official banks and other government units; and land held by agricultural schools and research organizations. At the option of the states, land held by religious, educational, and charitable trusts also could be exempted. To protect the states from legal challenges to their land reform laws, the constitution was amended in 1974 to include in its Ninth Schedule the state laws that had been enacted in conformance with national guidelines. Land reform laws enacted after 1974 also were included in the amendment.

By the beginning of the 1990s, all states and union territories, except Goa, Arunachal Pradesh, Nagaland, Manipur, Mizoram, and Tripura, had passed ceiling laws to conform to central government guidelines. In Maharashtra, for example, the revised ceiling law that became effective in 1975 set upper limits at perennially irrigated land, 7.2 hectares; seasonally irrigated land, 10.8 hectares; paddy land in an assured rainfall area, 14.6 hectares; and other dry land, 21.9 hectares. By the early 1980s, about 150,000 hectares had been declared surplus under this act, about 100,000 of which had been distributed to 6,500 landless persons. A 1973 land reform amendment in Bihar set a range of ceilings on holdings for a family of five, from six to eighteen hectares depending on land quality, and offered an allowance for each additional family member, subject to a maximum of one-and-one-half times the holding. Within five years, the Bihar government had acquired 94,000 hectares of surplus land and had distributed 53,000 hectares to 138,000 landless families. Success nationwide was limited. Of the 2.9 million hectares of land declared surplus, nearly 1.9 million hectares had been distributed by the end of the seventh plan, leaving 1 million hectares still to be distributed as of early 1993.

By the early 1990s, nearly all the states had enacted legislation aimed at the consolidation of each tiller's landholdings into one contiguous plot. Implementation was patchy and sporadic, however. By the early 1980s, the work had been completed only in Punjab, Haryana, and western Uttar Pradesh and had begun in Orissa and Bihar. In most of the other states, nothing had been accomplished by the early 1990s. The Sixth Five-Year Plan (FY 1980-84) set a goal for the completion of the consolidation of holdings within ten years, which was not achieved.

In order to protect tenants from exorbitant rents (often up to 50 percent of their produce), the states passed legislation to regulate rents. The maximum rate was fixed at levels not exceeding 20 to 25 percent of the gross produce in all states except Andhra Pradesh, Haryana, and Punjab. The states also adopted various other measures for the protection of tenants, including moratoriums on evictions, minimum periods of tenure, and security of tenure subject to eviction on prescribed grounds only.

By the early 1980s, most of the cultivated area had been surveyed and records of rights prepared. In most states, revenue assessment—the tax on land—against farmland had been revised upward in keeping with a rise in farm prices. In several states, steps were taken to associate village assemblies, or *panchayat*, with the maintenance of land records, the collection of land revenue, and the management of lands belonging to government; the results of these efforts have frequently been unsatisfactory.

India - Crops

The average rate of output growth since the 1950s has been more than 2.5 percent per year and was greater than 3 percent during the 1980s, compared with less than 1 percent per annum during the period from 1900 to 1950. Most of the growth in aggregate crop output was the result of an increase in yields, rather than an increase in the area under crops. The yield performance of crops has varied widely.

The national growth rates mask variability in the performance of different states, but in the regions with the greatest increases three categories are discernible. The first category includes states or areas that have an exceptionally high agricultural growth rate—Punjab, Haryana, and western Uttar Pradesh. The second is states or areas that have high growth rates, but not as high as the first category—Andhra Pradesh, Maharashtra, and Jammu and Kashmir. A third category has a lesser growth rate and includes Bihar, Gujarat, Karnataka, Orissa, Rajasthan, Tamil Nadu, eastern Uttar Pradesh, and West Bengal. These eight states, however, comprise 55 percent of the total food-grains area.

Some observers believe that the increase in productivity has been an important factor explaining the satisfactory growth of food-grain production since the mid-1960s. However, the gains in productivity remain confined to select areas. Between FY 1960 and FY 1980, yields increased by 125.6 percent in North India (Punjab, Haryana, and western Uttar Pradesh). The increase in the other regions was much less: central India, 36 percent; eastern, 22.7 percent; southern, 58.3 percent; and western India, 31.6 percent. The national average was nearly 40.9 percent. Part of this disparity can be explained by the fact that during this period Punjab and Haryana were way ahead of other states in terms of irrigated area, intensity of irrigation, and intensity of cropping. Availability of irrigation is one of the crucial factors governing regional variations.

As a result of a good monsoon during FY 1990, food grain production reached 176 million tons, 3 percent more than in FY 1989. The production of rice and wheat was 74.6 million and 54.5 million tons, respectively. Among the commercial crops, sugarcane and oilseeds reached production levels of 240.3 million tons and 21.8 million tons, respectively. The increased production in FY 1990 was mainly the result of continuing increases in yields for all the main crops—rice, wheat, pulses, and oilseeds. In the case of oilseeds and sugarcane, higher production was also the result of the increased number of hectares planted.

The growth in food-grain production did not occur in a linear trend, but as a series of spurts depending mostly on the weather, input availability, and price policy. Aggregate growth was composed of an even split between area expansion and yield growth before FY 1964. Since FY 1967, the contribution of growth in yields has become dominant and attests to the vigor with which agriculture has responded to the opportunities opened up by new seed, water, and fertilizer technology.

Food-Grain Production

Food grains include rice, wheat, corn (maize), coarse grains (sorghum and millet), and pulses (beans, dried peas, and lentils). In FY 1990, approximately 127.5 million hectares were sown with food grains, about 75 percent of the total planted area. The total number of hectares increased by 31 percent over the forty-year period from FY 1950 to FY 1990. Most of this increase occurred in the 1950s; there was almost no change in the sown number of hectares through the 1980s. Around 33 percent of cropland was given over to rice, about 29 percent to coarse grains, and the rest evenly divided between wheat and pulses.

Rice, India's preeminent crop, is the staple food of the people of the eastern and southern parts of the country. Production increased from 53.6 million tons in FY 1980 to 74.6 million tons in FY 1990, a 39 percent increase over the decade. By FY 1992, rice production had reached 111 million tons, second in the world only to China with its 182 million tons. Since 1950 the increase has been more than 350 percent. Most of this increase was the result of an increase in yields; the number of hectares increased only 40 percent during this period. Yields increased from 1,336 kilograms per hectare in FY 1980 to 1,751 kilograms per hectare in FY 1990. The per-hectare yield increased more than 262 percent between 1950 and 1992.

Wheat production showed an 843 percent increase, from nearly 6.5 million tons in FY 1950 to 54.5 million tons in FY 1990 to 56.7 million tons in FY 1992. Most of this greater production was the result of an increase in yields that went from 663 kilograms per hectare in FY 1950 to 2,274 kilograms in FY 1990. Along with the excellent performance in yields, improved wheat production resulted from an increase in the area planted from nearly 9.8 million hectares in FY 1950 to 24.0 million hectares in FY 1990.

Sorghum and millet, the principal coarse grains, are dryland crops most frequently grown as staples in central and western India. Corn and barley are staple foods grown mainly near and in the Himalayan region. As the result of increased yields, the production of coarse grains has doubled since 1950; there was hardly any change in the area sown for these grains. The production of pulses did not fare well, increasing by only 68 percent over the four decades. Land devoted to pulses increased by 28 percent, and yields were up by 30 percent. Pulses are an important source of protein in the vegetarian diet; the small improvement in production along with the increase in population meant a reduced availability of pulses per capita.

Before the Green Revolution, coarse grains showed satisfactory rates of growth but afterward lost cultivated areas to wheat and rice, and their growth declined. The area sown with coarse grains increased from FY 1950 to FY 1970 by roughly 20 percent but declined subsequently up to the early 1990s. In FY 1990 the area sown was 3 percent less than in FY 1950 and 20 percent less than in FY 1970. The area sown with two coarse grains, *jowar* (barley) and *bajra* (millet), increased from FY 1950 to FY 1970 and then declined during the 1970s and the 1980s. The area sown with *jowar* increased from 15.6 million hectares in FY 1950 to 17.4 million hectares in FY 1970 and then decreased to 14.5 million hectares in FY 1990. The area sown with *bajra* increased from 9.0 million hectares in FY 1950 to 12.9 million hectares in FY 1970 and stood at 10.4 million hectares in FY 1990. A similar pattern existed for other coarse grains. Overall, India's coarse-grain production increased from 15.4 million tons in 1950 to 29 million tons in 1980 to 33.1 million tons in 1990 and 33.7 million tons in 1993.

Oilseeds

India in the mid-1990s has almost attained self-sufficiency in the production of oilseeds to extract vegetable oil, essential in the Indian diet. Peanuts, grown mainly as a rain-fed crop on part of the semiarid areas of western and southern India, account for the largest source of the nation's production of vegetable oils. The second-ranking source of vegetable oils in the early 1990s was rapeseed. Cottonseed, an important by-product of cotton fiber and once mostly fed to cattle, was another source of vegetable oils. Soybeans and sunflower seeds were relatively new as significant oilseeds, but their production increased rapidly in the 1980s.

The production of oilseeds increased from 5.2 million tons in FY 1950 to 21.8 million tons in FY 1990. Specific information regarding area planted is not available for all oilseeds, but it increased in the 1980s, as did the yields. The growth of production before the mid-1970s was not adequate to meet the needs of the increasing population, and large quantities had to be imported from the 1970s to the mid-1980s, using scarce foreign exchange.

Commercial Crops

India is the largest producer of sugar in the world, harvesting 12 million tons in 1993, followed by Brazil's 9 million tons and China's 7 million tons. Sugar availability per capita increased from 4.7 kilograms per year in FY 1960 to 12.5 kilograms per year in FY 1990, following the more than fourfold increase in production from 57 million tons in FY 1950 to 240 million tons in FY 1990. This increase in production was a result of the doubling of the yield per hectare and a doubling of the area sown with sugar. Imports of sugar were negligible in FY 1992 and FY 1993. However, in the FY 1995 budget presentation to the Lok Sabha in March 1995, Minister of Finance Manmohan Singh said it was necessary to supplement the public distribution system with "necessary imports of sugar."

Raw cotton is the most important nonfood commodity produced on India's farms. Cotton was an important export crop in the 1950s, but thereafter it provided the raw material for India's textile industry, which grew greatly to meet the needs of an expanding population. Cotton fabrics found an expanding international market in the 1980s and earned valuable foreign exchange. The foreign exchange earned from raw cotton, cotton yarn, and fabrics of all textile materials increased from US$163 million in FY 1960 to US$1.4 billion in FY 1980 to nearly US$3.9 billion in FY 1990 and US$3.8 billion by FY 1992. Cotton production increased from 600,000 tons in FY 1950 to nearly 1.7 million tons in FY 1990. These improvements largely resulted from increased yields, as there was little increase in the sown area devoted to cotton.

Raw jute is second only to cotton as a farm-produced industrial raw material. Before partition in 1947, India was the world's main supplier of jute and jute goods used as packaging material. As a result of the partition of India and Pakistan, the main jute growing area was in East Pakistan (eastern Bengal, after 1971 the independent nation of Bangladesh), and the factories manufacturing jute goods were in West Bengal, which remained part of India after partition. Jute also had been India's main source of export earnings. As a result, there was a concerted effort to increase raw jute production. The area sown with jute increased from 571,000 hectares in FY 1950 to nearly 1.2 million hectares in FY 1985 but then decreased to 692,000 hectares in FY 1988. Yields increased steadily from 1,040 kilograms per hectare in FY 1950 to 1,803 kilograms per hectare in FY 1990. These two factors combined to more than double jute production from 595 million tons in FY 1950 to 1.4 billion tons in FY 1990, with a maximum production of nearly 2 billion tons in FY 1985. Because technological changes in packaging reduced the worldwide demand for jute, production in the early 1990s was mainly for the domestic market. In FY 1990, jute provided less than 1 percent of export earnings.

India - The Green Revolution

The introduction of high-yielding varieties of seeds after 1965 and the increased use of fertilizers and irrigation are known collectively as the Green Revolution, which provided the increase in production needed to make India self-sufficient in food grains. The program was started with the help of the United States-based Rockefeller Foundation and was based on high-yielding varieties of wheat, rice, and other grains that had been developed in Mexico and in the Philippines. Of the high-yielding seeds, wheat produced the best results. Production of coarse grains—the staple diet of the poor—and pulses—the main source of protein—lagged behind, resulting in reduced per capita availability.

The total area under the high-yielding-varieties program was a negligible 1.9 million hectares in FY 1960. Since then growth has been spectacular, increasing to nearly 15.4 million hectares by FY 1970, 43.1 million hectares by FY 1980, and 63.9 million hectares by FY 1990. The rate of growth decreased significantly in the late 1980s, however, as additional suitable land was not available.

The major benefits of the Green Revolution were experienced mainly in northern and northwestern India between 1965 and the early 1980s; the program resulted in a substantial increase in the production of food grains, mainly wheat and rice. Food-grain yields continued to increase throughout the 1980s, but the dramatic changes in the years between 1965 and 1980 were not duplicated. By FY 1980, almost 75 percent of the total cropped area under wheat was sown with high-yielding varieties. For rice the comparable figure was 45 percent. In the 1980s, the area under high-yielding varieties continued to increase, but the rate of growth overall was slower. The eighth plan aimed at making high-yielding varieties available to the whole country and developing more productive strains of other crops.

The Green Revolution created wide regional and interstate disparities. The plan was implemented only in areas with assured supplies of water and the means to control it, large inputs of fertilizers, and adequate farm credit. These inputs were easily available in at least parts of the states of Punjab, Haryana, and western Uttar Pradesh; thus, yields increased most in these states. In other states, such as Andhra Pradesh and Tamil Nadu, in areas where these inputs were not assured, the results were limited or negligible, leading to considerable variation in crop yields within these states. The Green Revolution also increased income disparities: higher income growth and reduced incidence of poverty were found in the states where yields increased the most and lower income growth and little change in the incidence of poverty in other states.

India - Livestock and Poultry

A large number of farmers depend on livestock for their livelihood. In addition to supplying milk, meat, eggs, and hides, animals, mainly bullocks, are the major source of power for both farmers and drayers. Thus, animal husbandry plays an important role in the rural economy. The gross value of output from this sector was Rs358 billion in FY 1989, an amount that constituted about 25 percent of the total agricultural output of Rs1.4 trillion.

In FY 1992, India had approximately 25 percent of the world's cattle, with a collective herd of 193 million head. India also had 110 million goats, 75 million water buffalo, 44 million sheep, and 10 million pigs. Milk production in FY 1990 was estimated to have reached 53.5 million tons, and egg production had reached a level of 23.3 billion eggs. Dairy farming provided supplementary employment and an additional source of income to many small and marginal farmers. The National Dairy Development Board was established in 1965 under the auspices of Operation Flood at Anand, in Gujarat, to promote, plan, and organize dairy development through cooperatives; to provide consultations; and to set up dairy plants, which were then turned over to the cooperatives. There were more than 63,000 Anand-style dairy cooperative societies with some 7.5 million members in the early 1990s. The milk produced and sold by these farmers brought Rs320 million a day, or more than Rs10 trillion a year. The increase in milk production permitted India to end imports of powdered milk and milk-related products. In addition, 30,000 tons of powdered milk were exported annually to neighboring countries.

Operation Flood, the world's largest integrated dairy development program, attempted to establish linkages between rural milk producers and urban consumers by organizing farmer-owned and -managed dairy cooperative societies. In the early 1990s, the program was in its third phase and was receiving financial assistance from the World Bank and commodity assistance from the European Economic Community. At that time, India had more than 64,000 dairy cooperative societies, with close to 7.7 million members. These cooperatives established a daily processing capacity of 15.5 million liters of whole milk and 727 tons of milk powder.

India - Forestry

Some 50 million hectares, about 17 percent of India's land area, were regarded as forestland in the early 1990s. In FY 1987, however, actual forest cover was 64 million hectares. However, because more than 50 percent of this land was barren or brushland, the area under productive forest was actually less than 35 million hectares, or approximately 10 percent of the country's land area. The growing population's high demand for forest resources continued the destruction and degradation of forests through the 1980s, taking a heavy toll on the soil. An estimated 6 billion tons of topsoil were lost annually. However, India's 0.6 percent average annual rate of deforestation for agricultural and nonlumbering land uses in the decade beginning in 1981 was one of the lowest in the world and on a par with Brazil.

Many forests in the mid-1990s are found in high-rainfall, high-altitude regions, areas to which access is difficult. About 20 percent of total forestland is in Madhya Pradesh; other states with significant forests are Orissa, Maharashtra, and Andhra Pradesh (each with about 9 percent of the national total); Arunachal Pradesh (7 percent); and Uttar Pradesh (6 percent). The variety of forest vegetation is large: there are 600 species of hardwoods, *sal* (*Shorea robusta*) and teak being the principal economic species.

Conservation has been an avowed goal of government policy since independence. Afforestation increased from a negligible amount in the first plan to nearly 8.9 million hectares in the seventh plan. The cumulative area afforested during the 1951-91 period was nearly 17.9 million hectares. However, despite large-scale tree planting programs, forestry is one arena in which India has actually regressed since independence. Annual fellings at about four times the growth rate are a major cause. Widespread pilfering by villagers for firewood and fodder also represents a major decrement. In addition, the forested area has been shrinking as a result of land cleared for farming, inundations for irrigation and hydroelectric power projects, and construction of new urban areas, industrial plants, roads, power lines, and schools.

India's long-term strategy for forestry development reflects three major objectives: to reduce soil erosion and flooding; to supply the growing needs of the domestic wood products industries; and to supply the needs of the rural population for fuelwood, fodder, small timber, and miscellaneous forest produce. To achieve these objectives, the National Commission on Agriculture in 1976 recommended the reorganization of state forestry departments and advocated the concept of social forestry. The commission itself worked on the first two objectives, emphasizing traditional forestry and wildlife activities; in pursuit of the third objective, the commission recommended the establishment of a new kind of unit to develop community forests. Following the leads of Gujarat and Uttar Pradesh, a number of other states also established community-based forestry agencies that emphasized programs on farm forestry, timber management, extension forestry, reforestation of degraded forests, and use of forests for recreational purposes.

Such socially responsible forestry was encouraged by state community forestry agencies. They emphasized such projects as planting wood lots on denuded communal cattle-grazing grounds to make villages self-sufficient in fuelwood, to supply timber needed for the construction of village houses, and to provide the wood needed for the repair of farm implements. Both individual farmers and tribal communities were also encouraged to grow trees for profit. For example, in Gujarat, one of the more aggressive states in developing programs of socioeconomic importance, the forestry department distributed 200 million tree seedlings in 1983. The fast-growing eucalyptus is the main species being planted nationwide, followed by pine and poplar.

The role of forests in the national economy and in ecology was further emphasized in the 1988 National Forest Policy, which focused on ensuring environmental stability, restoring the ecological balance, and preserving the remaining forests. Other objectives of the policy were meeting the need for fuelwood, fodder, and small timber for rural and tribal people while recognizing the need to actively involve local people in the management of forest resources. Also in 1988, the Forest Conservation Act of 1980 was amended to facilitate stricter conservation measures. A new target was to increase the forest cover to 33 percent of India's land area from the then-official estimate of 23 percent. In June 1990, the central government adopted resolutions that combined forest science with social forestry, that is, taking the sociocultural traditions of the local people into consideration.

Since the early 1970s, as they realized that deforestation threatened not only the ecology but their livelihood in a variety of ways, people have become more interested and involved in conservation. The best known popular activist movement is the Chipko Movement, in which local women decided to fight the government and the vested interests to save trees. The women of Chamoli District, Uttar Pradesh, declared that they would embrace—literally "to stick to" (*chipkna* in Hindi)—trees if a sporting goods manufacturer attempted to cut down ash trees in their district. Since initial activism in 1973, the movement has spread and become an ecological movement leading to similar actions in other forest areas. The movement has slowed down the process of deforestation, exposed vested interests, increased ecological awareness, and demonstrated the viability of people power.

CHAPTER-7

REAL GROWTH DURING FIVE YEAR PLAN PERIODS

Apart from the growth in quantitative terms, there have been significant changes in India's economic structure since 1947. The structural changes indicate that the process of development which began in the early 1950s is still continuing. However the speed of change is slow and in certain areas one cannot say confidently whether change has really occurred.

The economy of India is based in part on planning through its five-year plans, which are developed, executed and monitored by the Planning Commission. At the time of independence, India was left with crippling economy by British, which needed attention and well planned strategies to boom again in the global market. The pioneers of the Indian government at then times formulated 5 years plan to develop the Indian economy.

The five years plan in India is framed, executed and monitored by the Planning Commission of India. Jawahar Lal Nehru was the chairman of the first Planning Commission of India. The duty of the chairman of the planning commission in India is served by the Prime Minister of the country. It was started from 1951, The tenth plan finished its term in March 2007 and the eleventh plan is currently underway.

Planning in a market economy which is becoming increasingly integrated with the world is bound to be different from what it used to be in earlier years. Much of what used to be done by governments, including especially the establishment of production units producing manufactured goods and commercial services, is now being done by the private sector. India is blessed in having a long tradition of private entrepreneurship and the private sector has responded magnificently to the new opportunities opened up by economic reforms. However, this does not mean that the role of the government must shrink. On the contrary, the government must play a much larger role in some areas even while shifting out of others.

Objectives of Five Year Plan

These five year plan aimed mainly:

- Towards the improvement in the fields of agriculture, irrigation and power.
- Towards the agriculture programs and to meet the raw material needs of industry, besides covering the food needs of the increasing population.
- To increase national income and agriculture production and to promote economic developments in backward areas; unfeasible manufacturing units were augmented with subsidies and agriculture production.
- To encourage education and create employment opportunities for the marginalized section of the society as improvement in their standard of living would only make the country economically self- reliant.
- Check inflation and various non-economic variables like nutritional requirements, health, family planning etc.
- Focused on infrastructure and agriculture.
- Focused at improving various sectors like welfare, education, health, family planning and also encouraged employment opportunities.
- Towards modernization of industries, poverty reduction, encouraging employment, strengthening the infrastructure.
- To increase agricultural and rural income and to improve the conditions of the marginal farmer and landless laborers.
- Towards making India's economy as the fastest growing economy on the global level, with an aim to raise the growth rate and to reduce the poverty rate and increase the literacy rate in the country.
- To increase GDP growth, to reduce educated unemployment, aims to reduce infant mortality and maternal mortality.

- To ensure electricity connection and clean drinking water to all villages and increase forest and tree

Development in Agriculture and Irrigation

Five year plan towards the improvement in the fields of agriculture, irrigation and power and the plan projected to decrease the countries reliance on food grain imports, resolve the food crisis and ease the raw material problem especially in jute and cotton.

The plan addressed, mainly, the agrarian sector, including investments in dams and irrigation. The agricultural sector was hit hardest by the partition of India and needed urgent attention. The total planned budget of ₹206.8 billion (US$23.6 billion in the 1950 exchange rate) was allocated to seven broad areas: irrigation and energy (27.2 percent), agriculture and community development (17.4 percent), transport and communications (24 percent), industry (8.4 percent), social services (16.64 percent), land rehabilitation (4.1 percent), and for other sectors and services (2.5 percent). The most important feature of this phase was active role of state in all economic sectors. Such a role was justified at that time because immediately after independence, India was facing basic problems—deficiency of capital and low capacity to save.

The target growth rate was 2.1% annual gross domestic product (GDP) growth; the achieved growth rate was 3.6% The net domestic product went up by 15%. The monsoon was good and there were relatively high crop yields, boosting exchange reserves and the per capita income, which increased by 8%. National income increased more than the per capita income due to rapid population growth. Many irrigation projects were initiated during this period, including the Bhakra Dam and Hirakud Dam. TheWorld Health Organization, with the Indian government, addressed children's health and reduced infant mortality, indirectly contributing to population growth.

Nearly 45% of the resources were designated for agriculture, while industry got a modest 4.9%.The focus was to maximize the output from agriculture, which would then provide the momentum for industrial growth.

Development in Industries

The second five-year plan focused on industry, especially heavy industry. Unlike the First plan, which focused mainly on agriculture, domestic production of industrial products was encouraged in the Second plan, particularly in the development of the public sector. The plan followed the Mahalanobis model, an economic development model developed by the Indian statistician Prasanta Chandra Mahalanobis in 1953. The plan attempted to determine the optimal allocation of investment between productive sectors in order to maximise long-run economic growth . It used the prevalent state of art techniques of operations research and optimization as well as the novel applications of statistical models developed at the Indian Statiatical Institute. The plan assumed a closed economy in which the main trading activity would be centered on importing capital goods. The Industrial Policy of 1956 was socialistic in nature. The plan aimed at 25% increase in national income. The plan attempted to determine the optimal allocation of investment between productive sectors in order to maximise long-run economic growth . It used the prevalent state of art techniques of operations research and optimization as well as the novel applications of statistical models developed at the Indian Statiatical Institute. The plan assumed a closed economy in which the main trading activity would be centered on importing capital goods.

Hydroelectric power projects and five steel mills at Bhilai, Durgapur, and Rourkela were established.Coal production was increased. More railway lines were added in the north east.

The Atomic Energy Commission was formed in 1948 with Homi J. Bhabha as the first chairman. TheTata Institute of Fundamental Research was established as a research institute. In 1957 a talent search and scholarship program was begun to find talented young students to train for work in nuclear power.

The total amount allocated under the second five year plan in India was Rs. 4,800 crore. This amount was allocated among various sectors:

- Community and agriculture development
- Power and irrigation
- Social services
- Communications and transport
- Miscellaneous

Target Growth: 4.5% Actual Growth: 4.0%

Development in National Income and Agriculture Production

Plan's main motive was to make the country self reliant in agriculture and industry and for this allotment for power sector was increased to 14.6% of the total disbursement.

The plan aimed to increase national income by 30% and agriculture production by 30% and to promote economic developments in backward areas; unfeasible manufacturing units were augmented with subsidies and agriculture production by 30%. Many primary schools were started in rural areas. In an effort to bring democracy to the grass root level, Panchayat elections were started and the states were given more development responsibilities.

State electricity boards and state secondary education boards were formed. States were made responsible for secondary and higher education. State road transportation corporations were formed and local road building became a state responsibility. The target growth rate of GDP(gross domestic product)was 5.6 percent. The achieved growth rate was 2.2 percent.

Development in Education and Employment

Five year plan emphasized on encouraging education and creating employment opportunities for the marginalized section of the society as improvement in their standard of living would only make the country economically self- reliant.

Another aim of the plan was to create awareness about the Family planning program among Indians. The achievements of the fourth plan were not as per the expectations as agriculture and industrial growth was just at 2.8% and 3.9% respectively.

Stress was by laid on employment, poverty alleviation, and justice. The plan also focused on self-reliance in agricultural production and defence. In 1978 the newly elected Morarji Desai government rejected the plan. Electricity Supply Act was enacted in 1975, which enabled the Central Government to enter into power generation and transmission.

The Indian national highway system was introduced for the first time and many roads were widened to accommodate the increasing traffic. Tourism also expanded.

Target Growth: 4.4% Actual Growth: 5.0

Development in Economic Liberalization

In the beginning of economic liberalization, Price controls were eliminated and ration shops were closed. This led to an increase in food prices and an increase in the cost of living. This was the end of Nehruvian Plan and Rajiv Gandhi was prime minister during this period.

Family planning was also expanded in order to prevent overpopulation. In contrast to China's strict and binding one-child policy,

Indian policy did not rely on the threat of force . More prosperous areas of India adopted family planning more rapidly than less prosperous areas, which continued to have a high birth rate.

Target Growth: 5.2% Actual Growth: 5.4%

Development in Economic Productivity

To establish growth in areas of increasing economic productivity, production of food grains, and generating employment opportunities.

The Seventh Plan marked the comeback of the Congress Party to power. The plan laid stress on improving the productivity level of industries by upgrading of technology.

The main objectives of the 7th five year plans were to establish growth in areas of increasing economic productivity, production of food grains, and generating employment .

As an outcome of the sixth five year plan, there had been steady growth in agriculture, control on rate of Inflation, and favourable balance of payments which had provided a strong base for the seventh five Year plan to build on the need for further economic growth. The 7th Plan had strived towards socialism and energy production at large.

There had been steady growth in agriculture, control on rate of Inflation, and favourable balance of payments which had provided a strong base for the seventh five Year plan to build on the need for further economic growth. This Plan had strived towards socialism and energy production at large. The thrust areas of this plan have been enlisted below:

- Social Justice
- Removal of oppression of the weak
- Using modern technology
- Agricultural development
- Anti-poverty programs
- Full supply of food, clothing, and shelter
- Increasing productivity of small and large scale farmers
- Making India an Independent Economy

Based on a 15-year period of striving towards steady growth, the 7th Plan was focused on achieving the pre-requisites of self-sustaining growth by the year 2000. The Plan expected a growth in labour force of 39 million people and employment was expected to grow at the rate of 4 percent per year.

Some of the expected outcomes of the Seventh Five Year Plan India are given below:

- Balance of Payments (estimates): Export - 33,000 crore (US$6.3 billion), Imports - (-)54,000 crore (US$10.3 billion), Trade Balance - (-)21,000 crore (US$4 billion)
- Merchandise exports (estimates): 60,653 crore (US$11.5 billion)
- Merchandise imports (estimates): 95,437 crore (US$18.1 billion)
- Projections for Balance of Payments: Export-60,700 crore (US$11.5 billion), Imports - (-) 95,400 crore (US$18.1 billion), Trade Balance- (-) 34,700 crore (US$6.6 billion)

Seventh Five Year Plan India strove to bring about a self-sustained economy in the country with valuable contributions from voluntary agencies and the general populace.

Target Growth: 5.0% Actual Growth: 5.7%

Modernization of Industries

1989-91 was a period of economic instability in India and hence no five year plan was implemented. Between 1990 and 1992, there were only Annual Plans. In 1991, India faced a crisis in Foreign Exchange (Forex) reserves, left with reserves of only about US$1 billion. Thus, under pressure, the country took the risk of reforming the socialist economy. P.V. Narasimha Rao was the twelfth Prime Minister of the Republic of India and head of Congress Party, and led one of the most important administrations in India's modern history overseeing a major economic transformation and several incidents affecting national security. At that time Dr. Manmohan Singh (currently, Prime Minister of India) launched India's free market reforms that brought the nearly bankrupt nation back from the edge. It was the beginning of privatisation and liberalisation in India.

Modernization of industries was a major highlight of the Eighth Plan. Under this plan, the gradual opening of the Indian economy was undertaken to correct the burgeoning deficit and foreign debt. Meanwhile India became a member of the World Trade Organization on 1 January 1995.This plan can be termed as Rao and Manmohan model of Economic development. The major objectives included, controlling population growth, poverty reduction, employment generation, strengthening the infrastructure, Institutional building,tourism management, Human Resource development, Involvement of Panchayat raj, Nagar Palikas, N.GO'S and Decentralisation and people's participation. Energy was given priority with 26.6% of the outlay. An average annual growth rate of 6.78% against the target 5.6% was achieved.

To achieve the target of an average of 5.6% per annum, investment of 23.2% of the gross domestic product was required. The incremental capital ratio is 4.1.The saving for invetsment was to come from domestic sources and foreign sources,with the rate of domestic saving at 21.6% of gross domestic production and of foreign saving at 1.6% of gross domestic production.

Under this plan, the gradual opening of the Indian economy was undertaken to correct the burgeoning deficit and foreign debt. Meanwhile India became a member of the World Trade Organization on 1 January 1995.This plan can be termed as Rao and Manmohan model of Economic development. The major objectives included, controlling population growth, poverty reduction, employment generation, strengthening the infrastructure, Institutional building,tourism management, Human Resource development, Involvement of Panchayat raj, Nagar Palikas, N.G.O'S and Decentralisation and people's participation. Energy was given priority with 26.6% of the outlay. An average annual growth rate of 6.78% against the target 5.6% was achieved.

To achieve the target of an average of 5.6% per annum, investment of 23.2% of the gross domestic product was required. The incremental capital ratio is 4.1.The saving for invetsment was to come from domestic sources and foreign sources,with the rate of domestic saving at 21.6% of gross domestic production and of foreign saving at 1.6% of gross domestic production. The plan helped to achieve an annual growth rate of 5.6% in GDP and also controlled inflation.

In the field of Human Development

Ninth Five Year Plan India runs through the period from 1997 to 2002 with the main aim of attaining objectives like speedy industrialization, human development, full-scale employment, poverty reduction, and self-reliance on domestic resources.

Background of Ninth Five Year Plan India: Ninth Five Year Plan was formulated amidst the backdrop of India's Golden jubilee of Independence.

The main objectives of this Plan of Human development are:

- to prioritize agricultural sector and emphasize on the rural development
- to generate adequate employment opportunities and promote poverty reduction
- to stabilize the prices in order to accelerate the growth rate of the economy
- to ensure food and nutritional security

- to provide for the basic infrastructural facilities like education for all, safe drinking water, primary health care, transport, energy
- to check the growing population increase
- to encourage social issues like women empowerment, conservation of certain benefits for the Special Groups of the society
- to create a liberal market for increase in private investments

During this plan, the growth rate was 5.35 per cent, a percentage point lower than the target GDP growth of 6.5 per cent.

In the field of reducing Growth Rate

This plan towards making India's economy as the fastest growing economy on the global level, with an aim to raise the growth rate to 10% and to reduce the poverty rate and increase the literacy rate in the country.

The plan showed success in reducing poverty ratio by 5%, increasing forest cover to 25%, increasing literacy rates to 75 % and taking the economic growth of the country over 8%.

- Attain 8% GDP growth per year.
- Reduction of poverty ratio by 5 percentage points by 2007.
- Providing gainful and high-quality employment at least to the addition to the labour force;*All children in India in school by 2003; all children to complete 5 years of schooling by 2007.
- Reduction in gender gaps in literacy and wage rates by at least 50% by 2007;*Reduction in the decadal rate of population growth between 2001 and 2011 to 16.2%;*Increase in Literacy Rates to 75 per cent within the Tenth Plan period (2002 - 2007)

Development In the field of Income & Poverty

- Accelerate GDP growth from 8% to 10% and then maintain at 10% in the 12th Plan in order to double per capita income by 2016-17
- Increase agricultural GDP growth rate to 4% per year to ensure a broader spread of benefits
- Create 70 million new work opportunities.
- Reduce educated unemployment to below 5%.
- Raise real wage rate of unskilled workers by 20 percent.
- Reduce the headcount ratio of consumption poverty by 10 percentage points.

Development In the field of Education

- Reduce dropout rates of children from elementary school from 52.2% in 2003-04 to 20% by 2011-12
- Develop minimum standards of educational attainment in elementary school, and by regular testing monitor effectiveness of education to ensure quality
- Increase literacy rate for persons of age 7 years or above to 85%
- Lower gender gap in literacy to 10 percentage point
- Increase the percentage of each cohort going to higher education from the present 10% to 15% by the end of the plan

Development In the field of Health

- Reduce infant mortality rate to 28 and maternal mortality ratio to 1 per 1000 live births
- Reduce Total Fertility Rate to 2.1
- Provide clean drinking water for all by 2009 and ensure that there are no slip-backs
- Reduce malnutrition among children of age group 0-3 to half its present level
- Reduce anaemia among women and girls by 50% by the end of the plan

Development In the field of Women and Children

- Raise the sex ratio for age group 0-6 to 935 by 2011-12 and to 950 by 2016-17
- Ensure that at least 33 percent of the direct and indirect beneficiaries of all government schemes are women and girl children
- Ensure that all children enjoy a safe childhood, without any compulsion to work

Development In the field of Infrastructure

- Ensure electricity connection to all villages and BPL households by 2009 and round-the-clock power.
- Ensure all-weather road connection to all habitation with population 1000 and above (500 in hilly and tribal areas) by 2009, and ensure coverage of all significant habitation by 2015
- Connect every village by telephone by November 2007 and provide broadband connectivity to all villages by 2012

- Provide homestead sites to all by 2012 and step up the pace of house construction for rural poor to cover all the poor by 2016-17

Development In the field of Environment

- Increase forest and tree cover by 5 percentage points.
- Attain WHO standards of air quality in all major cities by 2011-12.
- Treat all urban waste water by 2011-12 to clean river waters.
- Increase energy efficiency by 20 percentage points by 2016-17.

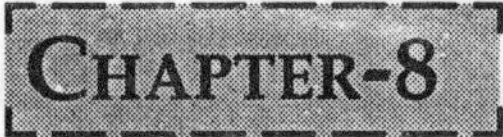

APPROACH TO ECONOMIC DEVELOPMENT

Economic development has historically been associated with structural changes in the national economies. It has, in fact, most often, been defined as a process combining economic growth with changing share of different sectors in the national product and labour force. The most common structural changes that have been observed historically have followed a sequence of shift from agriculture to industry and then to services. Thus, an underdeveloped economy is characterised by a predominant share of agriculture; with development the share of industry increases and that of agriculture declines, and subsequently after reaching a reasonably high level of development, the services sector increases in importance, becoming a major component of the economy. This pattern has not only been observed historically, but also holds across the countries with different levels of development. Structural shifts and changing sectoral shares are found to hold both for the national product and the work-force.

What exactly Economic development means?

The period of the two world wars and the decade following it, not only witnessed decolonisation and the birth of nation-states in Asia and Latin America, but enormous social upheavals within Europe. Accompanied with much soul searching on the mighty hand of technology (the Atomic bomb), the most cruelly and systematically organized genocide drives in history (concentration camps to exterminate Jews), the division of Europe between East and West, etc. the reconstruction was also accompanied by an incredible gender transformation of the labour market.

Women, who had to enter the educational institutions, the government offices and the factories to run the economies during war time, were there to stay, at least in some measure, in the labour markets. Thus, it is not surprising that the notion of economic development also changed radically during this period.

During the initial discussions on what constituted development and how development should be supported, there were broadly two schools of thought. The first school, usually referred to as the neo-classical school, focussed on 'revenue generation', either as gross national income or per capita income. It was noticed that developed countries usually had relatively higher total national income and per capita income and that the structure of their economy and trade exhibited certain common characteristics. For example, developed countries usually had a strong manufacturing sector and the manufacturing sector along with the service sector employed more than 60 per cent of the work force, whereas over 60 per cent of the workforce was engaged in agriculture and in the rural areas in developing countries. Developed countries, for the most part, exported and imported a variety of goods, while developing countries mainly exported primary goods, i.e. agricultural products or natural resources and imported finished goods. The central hypothesis put forward by this school was that any policy that increased national income and even more importantly per capita national income, would automatically initiate in its wake the accompanying processes that pushed the country into a trajectory of growth and development.

The second school, loosely referred to as the structuralist school, considered the 'capacity to generate revenue' as the prime indicator of development. In any economy, the capacity to generate revenue is determined by socio-economic parameters such as the literacy rate, life expectations and mortality rate and this meant that the focus was on a larger set of variables. The advantage of the first approach is its focus on a small set of variables on which there are well established macroeconomics theories, each theory supported by a particular ideological stance on the role of the State and the market. The advantage of the second approach is that it seems more rational and more humane to think the 'human dimension' rather than simply focus on national income. However, there can be no clear theories on how to increase the literacy rate or bring down the mortality rate, other than by direct investment in the education and health sectors.

Where is economic policy then supposed to focus: literacy, health, any other variable? What constitutes an optimal allocation of resources?

Indicators of Economic Development

Initially the providers of data on the economy were public agencies. Additional national and international agencies were set up during the post-second world war for comprehensive data collection on developing countries. Currently, the most widely used indicators at the international level are those provided by the World Bank and the United Nations Development Programme (UNDP). At the national level in India, we have the Economic Survey published annually by the Government of India and the surveys undertaken by the Central Statistical Organisation of India (CSO). Various other public and private organizations also exist for the collection of data at a sectoral level.

A recent phenomenon of the internet age is the booming market for information. Now there are innumerous private organization that conduct surveys of all sorts and sell the information as a tool for strategy formulation to firms, NGOs, academics and public agencies through the internet. There are also journals and reports by NGOs of all kinds flooding the internet on technological and economic problems that is absolutely free. A major problem with such information is that there is no standardization or peer review and therefore the credibility of such sources is not evident.

To conclude, the market for information is now supplied by both public and private organizations for a variety of prices depending on the type of market involved. Let us now come to the information products, namely the indicators. Indicators of development evolved along with the evolution of the economic philosophy on development. The first indicators focused only on economic and demographic variables such as income, population, per capita income, value generated by different industrial sectors, employment in different industrial sectors etc. and tried to relate structural features to income growth.

Economic Development in India

The economic development of India was dominated by socialist-influenced policies, state-owned sectors, and red tape & extensive regulations, collectively known as "License Raj". It led the country and its economy isolated from the world economy. However the scenario started changing from the mid-1980s, when India began opening up its market slowly through economic liberalization. The policy played a huge impact on the economic development of India. The Indian economic development got a boost through its economic reform in 1991 and again through its renewal in the 2000s. Since then, the face of economic development of India has changed completely.

The economic reform of 1991 played a pivotal role in the economic development of India. Reaping its benefit, the growth of the country reached around 7.5% in the late 2000s. It is also expected to double the average income within a decade. According to the analysts, if India can push more fundamental market reforms, it will be able to sustain the rate and can even achieve the government's target of 10% by 2011.

The economic development in India followed a socialist-inspired policies for most of its independent history, including state-ownership of many sectors; extensive regulation and red tape known as "Licence Raj"; and isolation from the world economy. India's per capita income increased at only around 1% annualized rate in the three decades after Independence. Since the mid-1980s, India has slowly opened up its markets through economic liberalization. After more fundamental reforms since 1991 and their renewal in the 2000s, India has progressed towards a free market economy.

In the late 2000s, India's growth has reached 7.5%, which will double the average income in a decade. Analysts say that if India pushed more fundamental market reforms, it could sustain the rate and even reach the government's 2011 target of 10%. States have large responsibilities over their economies. The annualized 1999–2008 growth rates for Gujarat (9.6%), Haryana (9.1%), or Delhi(8.9%) were significantly higher than for Bihar (5.1%), Uttar Pradesh (4.4%), or Madhya Pradesh(6.5%). India is the ninth-largest economy in the world and the fourth largest by purchasing power parity adjusted exchange rates (PPP). On per capita basis, it ranks 128th in the world or 118th by PPP.

The economic growth has been driven by the expansion of services that have been growing consistently faster than other sectors. It is argued that the pattern of Indian development has been a specific one and that the country may be able to skip the intermediate industrialization-led phase in the transformation of its economic structure. Serious concerns have been raised about the jobless nature of the economic growth.

Favourable macroeconomic performance has been a necessary but not sufficient condition for the significant reduction of poverty among the Indian population. The rate of poverty decline has not been higher in the post-reform period (since 1991). The improvements in some other non-economic dimensions of social development have been even less favourable. The most pronounced example is an exceptionally high and persistent level of child malnutrition (46% in 2005–6).

The progress of economic reforms in India is followed closely. The World Bank suggests that the most important priorities are public sector reform, infrastructure, agricultural and rural development, removal of labor regulations, reforms in lagging states, and HIV/AIDS. For 2010, India ranked 133rd in Ease of Doing Business Index, which is setback as compared with China 89th and Brazil 129th. According to Index of Economic Freedom World Ranking an annual survey on economic freedom of the nations, India ranks 124th as compared with China and Russia which ranks 140th and 143rd respectively in 2010.

India's Economic Development: Role of States

India is world's 12th largest economy and also the 4th largest in terms of purchasing power parity adjusted exchange rates (PPP). It is the 128th largest in the world on per capita basis and 118th by PPP. However, states have a major role to play in the economic development of India. There are few states which have higher annualized 1999-2008 growth rates comparing to others. The growth rates for the states like Gujarat (8.8%), Haryana (8.7%) and Delhi (7.4%) are considerably higher than other states like Bihar (5.1%), Uttar Pradesh (4.4%) and Madhya Pradesh (3.5%).

Economic Development – the Decisive Factors

The economic development of India largely depends upon a few factors, which prove to be decisive. According to the World Bank, for a better economic development, India needs to give due priorities in various issues like infrastructure, public sector reform, agricultural and rural development, reforms in lagging states, removal of labor regulations and HIV/AIDS.

In Agriculture

India ranks second worldwide in farm output. Agriculture and allied sectors like forestry, logging and fishing accounted for 18.6% of the GDP in 2005, employed 60% of the total workforce and despite a steady decline of its share in the GDP, is still the largest economic sector and plays a significant role in the overall socio-economic development of India. Yields per unit area of all crops have grown since 1950, due to the special emphasis placed on agriculture in the five-year plans and steady improvements inirrigation, technology, application of modern agricultural practices and provision of agricultural credit and subsidies since the green revolution.

India is the largest producer in the world of milk, cashew nuts, coconuts, tea, ginger, turmeric and black pepper. It also has the world's largest cattle population (193 million). It is the second largest producer of wheat, rice, sugar, groundnut and inland fish. It is the third largest producer of tobacco. India accounts for 10% of the world fruit production with first rank in the production of banana and sapota.

Agriculture, along with other allied sectors like fishing, forestry, and logging play a major role in the economic development in India. In 2005, these sectors accounted for almost 18.6% of the GDP. India holds the second position worldwide in terms of farm output. It also generated works for 60% of the total workforce. Though, currently seeing a steady decline of its share in the GDP, it is still the largest economic sector of the country.

In India, a steady growth has been observed in the yields per unit area of all the crops since 1950. And the reason behind this is the fact that, special emphasis was given on agriculture in the five-year plans. In 1965, the country saw green revolution. Improvements came in the various areas like irrigation, technology, provision of agricultural credit, application of modern agricultural practices and subsidies.

India has done considerably well in agriculture and allied sectors. The country is the world's largest producer of tea, coconut, cashew nuts, black pepper, turmeric, ginger and milk. India also has the largest cattle population in the world. It is world's second largest producer of sugar, rice, wheat and inland fish. It is in the third position in the list of tobacco producers in the world. India also produces 10% of the overall fruit production in the world, holding the first position in banana and sapota production. Main problems in the agricultural sector, as listed by the World Bank, are:

- India's large agricultural subsidies are hampering productivity-enhancing investment.
- Overregulation of agriculture has increased costs, price risks and uncertainty.
- Government interventions in labour, land, and credit markets.
- Inadequate infrastructure and services.

Research and development

The Indian Agricultural Research Institute (IARI), established in 1905, was responsible for the research leading to the "Indian Green Revolution" of the 1970s. The Indian Council of Agricultural

Research(ICAR) is the apex body in kundiure and related allied fields, including research and education. The Union Minister of Agriculture is the President of the ICAR. The Indian Agricultural Statistics Research Institute develops new techniques for the design of agricultural experiments, analyses data in agriculture, and specializes in statistical techniques for animal and plant breeding. Prof. M.S. Swaminathan is known as "Father of the Green Revolution" and heads the MS Swaminathan Research Foundation. He is known for his advocacy of environmentally sustainable agriculture and sustainable food security.

In Industrial Output

India is fourteenth in the world in factory output. Manufacturing sector in addition to mining, quarrying, electricity and gas together account for 27.6% of the GDP and employ 17% of the total workforce. Economic reforms introduced after 1991 brought foreign competition, led to privatisation of certain public sector industries, opened up sectors hitherto reserved for the public sector and led to an expansion in the production of fast-moving consumer goods. In recent years, Indian cities have continued to liberalize, but excessive and burdensome business regulations remain a problem in some cities, like Kochi and Kolkata. India occupies 14th position in the world in industrial output. The manufacturing sector along with gas, electricity, quarrying and mining account for 27.5% of the country's GDP. It also employs 17% of total workers. The economic reforms of 1991 brought a number of foreign companies to the Indian market. As a result, it saw the privatization of several pubic sector industries. Expansion in the production of FMCG (Fast-moving Consumer Goods) started taking place. Indian companies started facing foreign competitions, including the cheap Chinese imports. However, they managed to handle it by cutting down costs, refurbishing management, banking on technology and low labor costs and concentrating on new products designing. Post-liberalisation, the Indian private sector, which was usually run by oligopolies of old family firms and required political connections to prosper was faced with foreign competition, including the threat of cheaper Chinese imports. It has since handled the change by squeezing costs, revamping management, focusing on designing new products and relying on low labour costs and technology.

In Services

India is fifteenth in services output. Service industry employ English-speaking workers on the supply side and on the demand side, has increased demand from foreign consumers interested in India's service exports or those looking to outsource their operations. India's IT industry, despite contributing significantly to its balance of payments, accounts for only about 1% of the total GDP or 1/50th of the total services.

In services output, India occupies 15th spot in the world. Around 23% of the total workforce in India works in service industry. This is also the sector which provides quick growth with a growth rate of 7.5% during 1991-2000 from 4.5% in 1951-80. With a substantial growth in IT sector, a number of foreign consumers showing interests in India's service exports as India has got low cost, educated, highly skilled workers in abundance. Besides this, ITES-BPO sector has also become a big source of employment for a number of youths.

The ITES-BPO sector has become a big employment generator especially amongst young college graduates. The number of professionals employed by IT and ITES sectors is estimated at around 1.3 million as on March 2006. Also, Indian IT-ITES is estimated to have helped create an additional 3 million job opportunities through indirect and induced employment.

Banking and Finance

Since liberalization, India has seen substantial banking reforms. On one hand, one could see the mergers of banks, competitiveness and reducing government interference, on the other hand one can also see the presence of several private and foreign players in the banking and insurance sectors. Currently the banking sector in India has got maturity in terms of supply, reach-even and product range. The Indian banks are also said to have clean, transparent and strong balance sheets comparing to their Asian counterparts.

India's Resource Consumption

Oil

India had about 5.6 billion barrels (890,000,000 m^3) of proven oil reserves as of January 2007, which is the second-largest amount in the Asia-Pacific region behind China. Most of India's crude oil reserves are located in the western coast (Mumbai High) and in the northeastern parts of the country, although considerable undeveloped reserves are also located in the offshore Bay of Bengal and in the state of Rajasthan.

The combination of rising oil consumption and fairly unwavering production levels leaves India highly dependent on imports to meet the consumption needs. In 2006, India produced an average of about 846,000 barrels (134,500 m^3) per day (bbl/d) of total oil liquids, of which 77%, or 648,000 bbl/d (103,000 m^3/d), was crude oil. During 2006, India consumed an estimated 2.63 Mbbl/d (418,000 m^3/d) of oil. The Energy Information Administration (EIA) estimates that India registered oil demand growth of 100,000 bbl/d (16,000 m^3/d) during 2006. EIA forecasts suggest that country is likely to experience similar gains during 2007 and 2008.

Sector Organisation

India's oil sector is dominated by state-owned enterprises, although the government has taken steps in past recent years to deregulate the hydrocarbons industry and support greater foreign involvement. India's state-owned Oil and Natural Gas Corporation (**ONGC**) is the largest oil company, and also the country's largest company overall by market capitalization. ONGC is the leading player in India's upstream sector, accounting for roughly 75% of the country's oil output during 2006, as per Indian government estimates.

As a net importer of oil, the Government of India has introduced policies aimed at growing domestic oil production and oil exploration activities. As part of the effort, the Ministry of Petroleum and Natural Gas crafted the New Exploration License Policy (NELP) in 2000, which permits foreign companies to hold 100% equity possession in oil and natural gas projects. However, to date, only a handful of oil fields are controlled by foreign firms. India's downstream sector is also dominated by state-owned entities, though private companies have enlarged their market share in past recent years.

Natural gas

As per the Oil and Gas Journal, India had 38 trillion cubic feet (1.1×10^{12} m^3) of confirmed natural gas reserves as of January 2007. A huge mass of India's natural gas production comes from the western offshore regions, particularly the Mumbai High complex. The onshore fields in Assam, Andhra Pradesh, and Gujarat states are also major producers of natural gas. As per EIA data, India produced 996 billion cubic feet (2.82×10^{10} m^3) of natural gas in 2004.

India imports small amounts of natural gas. In 2004, India consumed about $1{,}089 \times 10^9$ cu ft (3.08×10^{10} m^3) of natural gas, the first year in which the country showed net natural gas imports. During 2004, India imported 93×10^9 cu ft (2.6×10^9 m^3) of liquefied natural gas (LNG) from Qatar.

Sector Organization

As in the oil sector, India's state-owned companies account for the bulk of natural gas production. ONGC and Oil India Ltd. (OIL) are the leading companies with respect to production volume, while some foreign companies take part in upstream developments in joint-ventures and production sharing contracts (PSCs). Reliance Industries, a privately-owned Indian company, will also have a bigger role in the natural gas sector as a result of a large natural gas find in 2002 in the Krishna Godavari basin.

The Gas Authority of India Ltd. (GAIL) holds an effective control on natural gas transmission and allocation activities. In December 2006, the Minister of Petroleum and Natural Gas issued a new policy that allows foreign investors, private domestic companies, and national oil companies to hold up to 100% equity stakes in pipeline projects. While GAIL's domination in natural gas transmission and allocation is not ensured by statute, it will continue to be the leading player in the sector because of its existing natural gas infrastructure.

Dialectics of Economic Development in India

A broad consensus has emerged among experts in India that the government's focus should be on the larger concept of economic development rather than on the narrow, quantitative concept of growth. This is also a vindication of the fact that "trickle down" and social responsibility cannot be taken as a natural process within the ambit of free market and the political system in the country should execute a well-designed programme for the redistribution of resources. The mammoth loan-waiver scheme, the seemingly successful MGNREGS and the huge spending on other social sector programmes are classic examples of the government actively involving itself in a planned process of redistribution.

The impetus has come from the democratic forces acting in the country. The first decade and a half of economic reforms had led to a situation of jobless growth and increasing disparities. The public at large reacted sharply to this lopsided, exclusive model of development and the government was forced to introduce various policies to ensure social justice. People gave the green signal to this renewed interest in social spending and the incumbent government was voted back to power in 2009.

It is to be noted that this new "inclusive model" of development does not reject the objective of achieving high economic growth. In fact, it considers economic growth as one of the most important parameters without compromising the wider goals of social justice and environmental protection. The sustainable development paradigm that is emerging in India is a result of a long drawn out process of dialectics. Analysing at the macro level, the Nehruvian concept of planned, centralised economic development changed into a developmental model based on economic growth during the post-1991 reform period and, finally, it has synthesised into a model that takes into account both growth and redistribution. The active participation of civil society, the media, NGOs and environmental activists in the developmental process has forced the government to take care of the environment as well.

At the micro level, the dialectical process of development in India is now heading towards another direction. It has been widely agreed among all sections of society that industrialisation is necessary, at least to a limited extent, in ushering in economic development. The larger question that is emerging now is whether it is necessary to deprive the resources of a small group of people in order to bring in development, which may be beneficial to the public at large in the long run. Is development a zero-sum game, at least in the short run? Singur and Nandigram are living examples of this debate.

The people have rejected the zero-sum thesis and the focus has suddenly shifted to rehabilitation. The Central government came up with a comprehensive Rehabilitation and Resettlement (R&R) Policy. But the success of industrialisation of rural India lies in the efficacy of implementing and operationalising this policy. Whether the emotional value an Indian attaches to his land can be compensated materially or not is altogether another debate by itself.

The industrialisation experience in the state of West Bengal can be a valuable case study model, especially in the context of the series of electoral defeats to the ruling party. It is said that the worst time for a government is when it has initiated some reforms and has gone half-way.

When eco-development starts to pick up, the aspirations of people go up and the process of relative deprivation operates strongly in the minds of the people. They feel that their situation could have been better, although their "real" situation has already improved. It is this feeling of relative deprivation that projects itself as protests and movements and finally would opt for a change in government, especially when a substitute is available. It is to be remembered that a static society that lives in sustained chronic poverty would never witness any protest because the people cannot visualise any alternative and hence there is no relative deprivation. It is apt to remember George Orwell's line, "people never had a housing problem until they were told about it." Thus it takes real courage for an incumbent government to embark on a hitherto non-existing policy of industrialisation.

The macro-dynamics of the dialectics of development is at a stage today where a new anti-thesis is emerging to counter the huge social spending of the government. The corporate sector has demanded a drastic reduction in fiscal deficit and the recent budget aims at fiscal consolidation. At the micro-level, the focus should be on evolving innovative ways of rehabilitation, prompt compensation and timely implementation.

Approaches to Economic Development

LED Approach

Local Economic Development is a strategy for employment promotion through micro and small enterprise development, support of social dialogue and development planning. At the center of the approach is the creation of public-private partnerships that bring together stakeholders in the local economy, including representatives of regional and local government, employers' and workers' organizations, Chambers of Commerce, cooperatives, producers' associations, women organizations and other NGOs.

Based on the rational use of local capacities and resources, the stakeholders will define common priorities for the development of their region taking into account the social and environmental contexts. The partnership can be developed in a forum or institutionalized in a Local Economic Development Agency (LEDA). This will reinforce the capacities to raise public awareness on the development needs of the region and to establish linkages at the national and international level. Especially in countries disrupted by conflict or in social and economic transition, experience has shown that the LED approach has a potential to contribute to the ongoing reconciliation, decentralization and democratization processes.

Factors supporting the local economic development process in these districts by:

-Improving the support services for productive activities

This includes among other things: -installation of grinding mills and rehabilitation of shops, small markets and small workshops; -improving the physical working conditions of the different public support services in the districts; -installation of a Business Service Centre in Matutuine district which provides technical assistance to business starters as well as financial services through a Credit Cooperative that has opened a branch in the Centre; -support to and improvement of the agricultural production and marketing of the agricultural products; an analysis of local investment opportunities, incorporating the local population.

- Strengthening of the available local capacities (potential), or creating new ones

This is mainly focussed on the organization and training of the local population; -promoting associative forms of labour; -developing financial mechanisms and instruments based on the local requirements and conditions; -training courses especially aimed at developing basic entrepreneurial skills, also aimed at technical staff of the public support structure in the field, mainly Ministry of Agriculture.

- Promotion and creation of provincial Local Economic Development Agencies

In Manica and Sofala province two LEDAs are being set up at the moment. These LEDAs are incorporating most of the relevant institutions and organizations that deal with the economic development at provincial level. They are currently drawing up their first operational plan.

The Regional Approach

Empowerment Zone Program as a Model for Success Regional Councils are modeled after the federal Empowerment Zone program that began under President Bill Clinton in 1994. The Empowerment Zone program encouraged comprehensive, public-private planning and targeted investment to foster sustainable economic, physical and social development in the neediest urban and rural areas in the United States. The Empowerment Zones were the center piece of the Clinton Administration's community revitalization strategy – a bold, hands-on approach that empowered residents to have a stake in the future prosperity of their own communities.

The Empowerment Zone program promoted a bottom-up, community driven planning process through which regions identified their own redevelopment goals and designed plans for achieving those goals. The federal government then helped regions implement their plans by providing direct programmatic funds, technical expertise and regulatory assistance.

At the U.S. Department of Housing and Urban Development (HUD), Governor Cuomo led the implementation of the Empowerment Zone program in conjunction with the U.S. Department of Agriculture. As Secretary of

HUD, he witnessed first-hand the power of the regional approach to affect change and produce tangible results in the nation's most distressed communities. By the end of his tenure, HUD's economic development programs had created or maintained hundreds of thousands of private-sector jobs across the country and provided an effective framework for future community-based planning efforts.

The Empowerment Zone program proved that the regional approach works. The federal government continues to implement regional economic development strategies to help spur innovation, create jobs, and empower communities.

Two Approaches to Economic Development

Since the advent of technical assistance programs to economic development, an approach that dates only to the mid-1970s, two different approaches to economic development have existed side by side. The practitioners of these approaches often talk past one another because their professional expertness, their training, and their beliefs as so opposite.

The traditional approach to economic development has been a "broker" approach. Practitioners of this approach are employed by chambers of commerce, economic development districts that are partly supported by the Economic Development Administration, and state and local government agencies promoting economic development. These practitioners hope to influence the decisions of businesses as they expand or relocate.

To influence those decisions, brokers use tools that are usually cost or funding based. They promote low tax rates, low utility rates, a skilled workforce, transportation and location factors, and other factors that are components of the community they are promoting. They also offer special deals in return for a company's decision to relocate to, expand to or even stay in a particular location. There are a variety of these but they include special tax breaks that a company qualifies for by creating jobs or investing in a location, grants that fund all or a portion of training costs for new employees or required equipment, and subsidies for buildings and construction of roads to buildings.

The technical assistance approach to economic development has been a "consulting" approach. This approach is mostly targeted to small businesses although it is also applied to some larger businesses. It is almost always, however, applied to indigenous businesses – those that already exist in the community or are being started by persons within the community. Practitioners of this approach are employed by small business development centers, small business incubators, manufacturing extension programs and procurement technical assistance centers.

The consulting approach is designed to help business owners and managers become more successful in the hope that the more successful their business is, the more jobs will be created. Where this consulting approach helps businesses obtain more resources, it is generally through assisting the business owner in securing loans through loan packaging, securing venture capital and other forms of equity, increasing sales through better marketing, and decreasing costs through better management.

The broker takes the approach that the business owners always knows the best way to proceed. So, his function is to provide incentives to change the equation being dealt with by the business owners. The consultant takes the approach that the business owners do not always know the best way to proceed. So, his function is to teach or to provide information that enables the business owners to make better decisions.

Both are targeted toward job creation. However, the broker views the consultant's approach as a waste of money because he presumes the business owners already know the right way to do things so he figures consultants are taking credit for jobs that would have been created anyway. The consultant views the broker approach as a waste of money because it foregoes tax revenue and because jobs created by the broker approach are much more expensive per job than jobs created by the consultant approach.

This is not to suggest that the practitioners of these approaches are engaged in open war or even that the practitioners of one approach can't appreciate the value of the other. After all, many state economic development agencies and other economic development organizations simultaneously support both approaches. It is to say that the practitioners of each approach take entirely different views of the value of one approach relative to another and that those views are constant subtexts to discussions about how to allocate funds. It is also to say that those engaged in public policy, especially elected officials, are often making decisions without knowing the subtext through which the proposals they review are developed.

The Big Push Approach

This theory is an investment theory which stresses the conditions of take-off. The argumentation is quite similar to the balanced growth theory but emphasis is put on the need for a big push. The investments should be of a relatively high minimum in order to reap the benefits of external economies. Only investments in big complexes will result in social benefits exceeding social costs. High priority is given to infrastructural development and industry, and this emphasis will lead to governmental development planning and influence.

The big push model is a concept in development economics orwelfare economics that emphasizes the fact that a firm's decision whether to industrialize or not depends on its expectation of what other firms will do.

The originator of this theory was Paul Rosenstein-Rodan in 1943. Further contributions were made later on by Murphy, Shleifer andRobert W. Vishny in 1989. Analysis of this economic model usually involves using game theory.

The theory of the model emphasizes that underdeveloped countries require large amounts of investments to embark on the path of economic development from their present state of backwardness. This theory proposes that a 'bit by bit' investment programme will not impact the process of growth as much as is required for developing countries. In fact, injections of small quantities of investments will merely lead to a wastage ofresources. Paul Rosenstein-Rodan, approvingly quotes a Massachusetts Institute of Technology study in this regard, "There is a minimum level of resources that must be devoted to... a development programme if it is to have any chance of success. Launching a country into self-sustaining growth is a little like getting an airplane off the ground. There is a critical ground speed which must be passed before the craft can become airborne...."

Rosenstein-Rodan argued that the entire industry which is intended to be created should be treated and planned as a massive entity (a firm or trust). He supports this argument by stating that the social marginal product of an investment is always different from its private marginal product, so when a group of industries are planned together according to their social marginal products, the rate of growth of the economy is greater than it would have otherwise been.

The Three Indivisibilities

According to Rosenstein-Rodan, there exist three indivisibilities in underdeveloped countries. These indivisibilities are responsible for external economies and thus justify the need for a big push. The externalities are as follows-

1. Indivisibility in production function
2. Indivisibility of demand

3. Indivisibility in the supply of savings

Indivisibility in production function

Indivisibilities in the production function may be with respect to any of the following:

- Inputs
- Processes
- Outputs

These lead to increasing returns (i.e., economies of scale), and may require a high optimum size of a firm. This can be achieved even in developing countries since at least one optimum scale firm can be established in many industries. But investment in social overhead capital comprises investment in all basic industries (like power, transport or communications) which must necessarily come before directly productive investment activities. Investment in social overhead capital is 'lumpy' in nature. Such capital requirements cannot be imported from other nations. Therefore, heavy initial investment necessarily needs to be made in social overhead capital (this is approximated to be about 30 to 40 percent of the total investment undertaken by underdeveloped countries). Social overhead capital is further characterized by four indivisibilities:

1. Irreversibility in time: It must precede other directly productive investments
2. Minimum durability of equipment:. Any lesser level of durability is either impossible due to technical reasons or much less efficient
3. Long gestation periods: The investment in social overhead capital takes time to generate returns and its impact in the economy is not immediately or directly visible
4. Irreducible minimum social overhead capital–industry mix: Investment needs to be of a certain minimum magnitude and spread across a mix of industries, without which it will not significantly impact the process of growth.

Indivisibility (or complementarity) of demand

Developing countries are characterized by low per-capita income and purchasing power. Markets in these countries are therefore small . In a closed economy, modernization and increased efficiency in a single industry has no impact on the economy as a whole since the output of that industry will fail to find a market. A large number of industries need to be set up simultaneously so that people employed in one industry consume the output of other industries and thus create complementary demand.

To illustrate this, Rosenstein Rodan gives the example of a shoe industry. If a country makes large investments in the shoe industry, all the disguisedly employed labor from the other industries find work and a source of income, leading to a rise in production of shoes and their own incomes. This increased income will not be expended only on buying shoes. It is conceivable that the increased incomes will lead to increased spending on other products too. However, there is no corresponding supply of these products to satisfy this increased demand for the other goods. Following the basicmarket forces of demand and supply, the prices of these commodities will rise. To avoid such a situation, investment must be spread out amongst different industries.

The situation may be different in an open economy as the output of the new industry may replace former imports or possibly find its market by way of exports. But even if the world market acts as asubstitute for domestic demand, a big push is still needed (though its required size may now be reduced due to the presence of international trade).

Indivisibility in the supply of savings

High levels of investment require a corresponding high level of savings. We cannot always rely on foreign aid as the huge levels of investments in the different sectors need to be made not only once, but multiple number of times. Hence domestic savings are a must. But in an underdeveloped economy,this is a challenge due to the low income levels.Marginal rate of savings needs to be increased following the rise in incomes due to higher investment.

How the big push works

Consider a country whose economy is characterized by a large number of sectors which are so small that any increase in the productivity of one sector has no impact on the economy as a whole. Each sector can either rely on traditional methods or switch to modern methods of production which would increase its efficiency. Let us assume that there are l workers in the economy and n sectors. Each sector therefore has l / nworkers.

Using traditional technology, a sector would produce l / n amount of output, with each worker producing one unit of the commodity.

Using modern technology a sector would produce more as the productivity would be greater than one unit per worker. However, a modern sector would require some of the workers (say h) to perform administrative tasks.

In figure 1, the x-axis represents the labor employed and the y-axis represents the level of production. The production in the traditional sector is given by the curve T and the production in the modern sector is given by M. The curve M has a positive intercept on the x-axis, implying that even with zero production, there is a minimum level of h workers who still remain employed for carrying out administrative activities. With our assumption of l / n workers in the economy, the modern sector will have a higher level of productivity than the traditional sector. The production function of the modern sector is steeper than that of the traditional sector because of the higher productivity of workers in the former. The slope of both production functions is $1 / m$, where m is the marginal labor required to produce an additional unit of output. This level of m is lower for the modern sector than it is for the traditional sector.

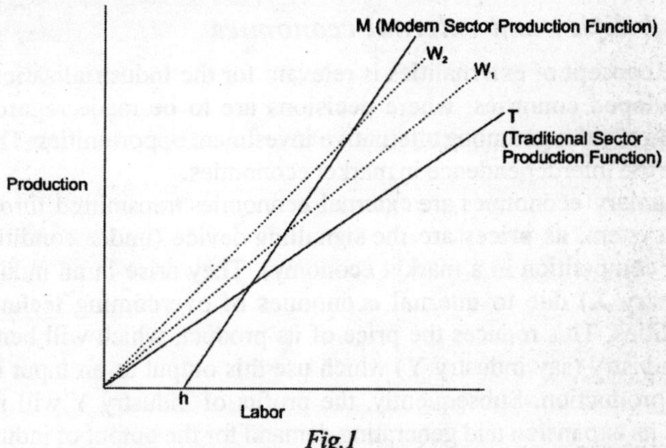

Fig.1

Assume that the traditional sector pays workers one unit of output which is subsequently spent equally by them in all sectors. The modern sector pays higher wages to workers. If all the workers are employed by the traditional sector, then the demand generated for the output of each sector is $D_1 = 1 / n$. We have two possible cases:

Wages are low – When low wages are prevalent in the economy, say w_1, a firm which faces demand D_1 will need to employ l^* workers if it wants to modernize. This will cost the firm $w_1 l^*$.

Now, wages are low. Therefore

$w_1 l^* < D_1$.

This implies that costs (given by $w_1 l^*$) are lower than the earnings (given by D_1). So the firm makes a profit and will choose to modernize (even if other firms do not).

Wages are high – When high wages are prevalent in the economy, say w_2, a firm which faces demand D_1 will make losses if no other firms choose to modernize.

This is because

$w_2 l^* > D_1$.

This implies that costs (given by $w_2 l^*$) are higher than the earnings (given by D_1).

However, if all the other firms have modernized, the firm faces a higher demand D_2, arising out of higher income levels of workers of these modernized firms. The firm will hence choose to modernize as well so that it makes profits:

$w_2 l^* < D_2$.

Indivisibilities and external economies

The concept of externalities is relevant for the Industrialization of underdeveloped countries, where decisions are to be made regarding distribution of savings among alternative investment opportunities. These arise from the interdependence in market economies.

Pecuniary economies are external economies transmitted through the price system, as prices are the signalling device (under conditions of perfect competition in a market economy). They arise in an industry (say industry X) due to internal economies of overcoming technical indivisibilities. This reduces the price of its product, which will benefit another industry (say industry Y) which use this output as an input or a factor of production. Subsequently, the profits of industry Y will rise, leading to its expansion and generating demand for the output of industry X. As a result, industry X's production and profits also expand.

However in underdeveloped countries, conditions of perfect competition are not present due to thedecentralized and differentiated nature of the market. Prices fail to act as a signalling system in the following ways:

- Prices express the situation as it is and do not predict future economic situations
- Prices can decide present productive activities but cannot determine investments which would be appropriate for developing countries
- The response of the private sector to price signals is inadequate and imperfect due to the differentiation and decentralisation in developing countries

This justifies the need for centralized pan-industry planning of investment in Developing countries, as the private sector cannot undertake such planning.

Enlargement of the market size is another important externality which arises from the complementarity of industries. There exists an incentive to expand the scale of operations because the employees of one industry become the customers of another industry. In terms of products too (as in the above example of industries X and Y), one industry generates demand for the output of the other when the scale of operations increase.

Marshallian economies also accrue to a firm within a growing industry, resulting from agglomerationof industrial districts or clusters in a particular area. These occur due to the following advantages of agglomeration identified by Alfred Marshall:

1. Spillover of information
2. Specialization and division of labor
3. Development of a market for skilled labor.

Availability of skilled labour is an externality which arises when industrialization occurs, as workers acquire better training and skills. This is not achievable by mere establishment of a few industries, but requires a large program of industrial growth. It is one of the most important external economies because absence of skilled labor is a strong impediment to industrialization.

Role of the State

The large-scale programme of industrializationz advocated by this model requires huge investments which are beyond the means of the private sector. The investment in infrastructure and basic industries (like power, transport and communications) is 'lumpy' and has long gestation periods. The role of the state in this theory is therefore critical for investment in social overhead capital. Even if the private sector had the requisite resources to invest in such a programme, it would not do so since it is driven by profit motives. Many investments are profitable in terms of social marginal net product but not in terms of private marginal net product. Due to this there is no incentive for individual entrepreneurs to invest and take advantage of external economies.

Criticisms of Big Push Model

The theory has been criticized by Hla Myint and Celso Furtado, among others, primarily on the grounds of the massive effort required to be taken by underdeveloped countries to move along the path of industrialization. Some of the major criticisms are as follows.

- *Difficulties in execution and implementation*: The execution of related projects during the course ofindustrialization may involve unexpected or unavoidable changes due to revisions of plans, delays and deviations from the planned process. Hla Myint notes that the various departments and agencies involved in the process of development need to coordinate closely and evaluate and revise plans continuously. This is a challenging task for the governments of developing countries.
- *Lack of absorptive capacity*: The implementation of industrialization programmes may be constrained by ineffective disbursement,short-term bottlenecks, macroeconomic problems and volatility, loss of competitiveness and weakening of institutions. Credit is often utilized at low rates or after long time lags. There is often a loss of competitiveness due to the Dutch disease effect.
- *Historical inaccuracy*: When viewed in light of historical experience of countries over the last two centuries, no country displayed any evidence of development due to massive industrializationprogrammes. Stationary economies do not develop simply by making large-scale investment in social overhead capital.
- *Problems in mixed economies*: In a mixed economy, where the private and public sectors co-exist, the environment for growt] may not be a conducive one. Unless there is a complementaritybetween the sectors, there is bound to arise competition between them, with the government departments keeping their plans confidential out of fear of speculative activities by the private sector. The private sector's activities are simultaneously inhibited due to lack of information of government policies and the general economic situation
- *Neglect of methods of production*: Rather than capital formation, it is productive techniques which determine the success of a country in economic development. The big push model ignores productive techniques in its support for capital formation and industrialisation.
- *Shortage of resources in underdeveloped countries*: Eugenio Gudin criticizes the theory of the big push on the grounds that underdeveloped countries lack the capital required to

provide the big push required for rapid development. If an underdeveloped nation had ample capital supply and scarcefactors, it would not be classified as *underdeveloped* at all. Limited resource availability is the first impediment to such countries. Though this problem may be overcome by foreign aids,industrialization may not take off as expected if the aid flows are volatil.e

Ignores the agricultural sector: With its heavy emphasis on industry, the model finds no place foragriculture. This is a gaping flaw in the theory, as in most underdeveloped countries it is this sector which is large and has labor surplus. Investments in agriculture need to go hand-in-hand with those in industry so as to stimulate the industrial sector by providing a market for industrial goods. If neglected, it would be difficult to meet the food requirements of the nation in the short run and to significantly expand the size of the market in the long run.

- *Inflationary pressures*: It follows from the neglect of the agricultural sector that food shortages are likely to occur with industrialization. Though it would take time for investments in social overheadcapital to yield returns, the demand would increase immediately, thus imposing inflationary pressures on the economy. Cost escalations may even cause projects to be postponed and thedevelopment process in general to slow down.
- *Dependence on indivisibilities*: The emphasis of this theory on indivisibility of processes is too much, as investments need not necessarily be on such a large scale to be economic. Social reforms are ignored, which are vital if a country is to grow on the basis of its own resources and initiatives. Development is bound to intensify if social reform is a part of the industrializationprocess.

Classical growth theory

- The modern conception of economic growth began with the critique of Mercantilism, especially by thephysiocrats and with the Scottish Enlightenment thinkers such as David Hume and Adam Smith, and the foundation of the discipline of modern political economy. The theory of the physiocrats was that productive capacity, itself, allowed for growth, and the improving and increasing capital to allow that capacity was "the wealth of nations". Whereas they stressed the importance of agriculture and saw urban industry as "sterile", Smith extended the notion that manufacturing was central to the entire economy.

- David Ricardo argued that trade was a benefit to a country, because if one could buy a good more cheaply from abroad, it meant that there was more profitable work to be done here. This theory of "comparative advantage" would be the central basis for arguments in favor of free trade as an essential component of growth.

The neoclassical Growth Model

- The notion of growth as increased stocks of capital goods (means of production) was codified as theSolow-Swan Growth Model, which involved a series of equations which showed the relationship between labor-time, capital goods, output, and investment. According to this view, the role oftechnological change became crucial, even more important than the accumulation of capital. This model, developed by Robert Solow and Trevor Swan in the 1950s, was the first attempt to model long-run growth analytically. This model assumes that countries use their resources efficiently and that there are diminishing returns to capital and labor increases. From these two premises, the neoclassical model makes three important predictions. First, increasing capital relative to labor creates economic growth, since people can be more productive given more capital. Second, poor countries with less capital per person will grow faster because each investment in capital will produce a higher return than rich countries with ample capital. Third, because of diminishing returns to capital, economies will eventually reach a point at which any increase in capital will no longer create economic growth. This point is called a "steady state".
- The model also notes that countries can overcome this steady state and continue growing by inventing new technology. In the long run, output per capital depends on the rate of saving, but the rate of output growth should be equal for any saving rate. In this model, the process by which countries continue growing despite the diminishing returns is "exogenous" and represents the creation of new technology that allows

production with fewer resources. Technology improves, the steady state level of capital increases, and the country invests and grows. The data does not support some of this model's predictions, in particular, that all countries grow at the same rate in the long run, or that poorer countries should grow faster until they reach their steady state. Also, the data suggests the world has slowly increased its rate of growth.

- However, modern economic research shows that the baseline version of the neoclassical model of economic growth is not supported by the evidence.

Theory of cognitive wealth (cognitive capitalism)

- The theory of "Cognitive capitalism" asserts that cognitive ability is the crucial factor which creates wealth in modern economies, and that the geographical factors which have been necessary in ancient societies are no longer so important. The average cognitive ability of a nation determines its wealth, each IQ point increase boosting a country's average GDP by $229. Of even more significance, the IQ of the brightest 5% of people in the nation (the cognitive elite) boosts GDP by $468 per IQ point. The cognitive elite support general efficiency, technological innovation, efficient administration, independent institutions, and economic freedom. Via these factors intelligence and knowledge stimulate growth leading to national wealth, which in turn may boost cognitive ability in a virtuous circle. The theory was developed by the two psychologists Heiner Rindermann and James Thompson. The theory is related to human capital theory.

Unified growth theory

- Unified growth theory was developed by Oded Galor and his co-authors to address the inability of endogenous growth theory to explain key empirical regularities in the growth processes of individual economies and the world economy as a whole. Endogenous growth theory was satisfied with accounting for empirical regularities in the growth process of developed economies over the last hundred years. As a consequence, it was not able to explain the qualitatively different empirical regularities that characterized the growth process over longer time horizons in both developed and less developed economies. Unified growth theories are endogenous growth theories that are consistent with the entire process of development, and in particular the transition from the epoch of Malthusian stagnation that had characterized most of the process of development to the contemporary era of sustained economic growth.

The effect of Inequality on Economic Growth

The Classical Theory

- Inequality has a positive effect on economic development. The marginal propensity to save increases with wealth and inequality increases savings, capital accumulation, and economic growth.

The neoclassical theory

- The neoclassical theory ignores the relevance of income distribution for macroeconomic analysis. It interprets the observed relationship between inequality and economic growth as a reflection of the growth process on the distribution of income.

The modern theory

- The modern theory suggests that income distribution, plays an important role in the determination of aggregate economic activity and economic growth.
- The credit market imperfection approach, developed by Galor and Zeira (1993), demonstrates that inequality in the presence of credit market imperfections has a long lasting detrimental effect on human capital formation and economic development.
- The political economy approach, developed by Alesina and Rodrik 1994) and Persson and Tabellini (1994), suggests that inequality is harmful for economic development because inequality generates a pressure to adopt redistributive policies that have an adverse effect on investment and economic growth.

Evidence

- Perotti (1996) examines of the channels through which inequality may affect economic growth. He shows that in accordance with the credit market imperfection approach, inequality is associated with lower level of human capital formation and higher level of fertility, while lower level of human capital is associated with lower growth and lower levels of economic growth. In contrast, his examination of the political economy channel refutes the political economy mechanism. He demonstrates that inequality is associated with lower levels of taxation, while lower levels of taxation, contrary to the theories, are associated with lower level of economic growth

CHAPTER-9

ECONOMIC LIBERALIZATION IN INDIA

Economic liberalization is a very broad term that usually refers to fewer government regulations and restrictions in the economy in exchange for greater participation of private entities; the doctrine is associated with classical liberalism. The arguments for economic liberalization include greater efficiency and effectiveness that would translate to a "bigger pie" for everybody.Thus,liberalisation in short refers to "the removal of controls", to encourage economic development. .

Most first world countries, in order to remain globally competitive, have pursued the path of economic liberalization: partial or full privatisation of government institutions and assets, greater labour-market flexibility, lower tax rates for businesses, less restriction on both domestic and foreign capital, open markets, etc.

The launching of the economic liberalization programme in India in 1991 was a landmark development in the post-independent economic history of India. It marked a paradigm shift in the future direction of the Indian economy which had until then operated within a narrow framework predominantly governed by a state oriented socialist philosophy. The new policy had placed India on the road to free and market economy. That such a momentous decision was initiated by a government which did not enjoy the majority strength in the Indian parliament clearly underlined the urgency for the sweeping reforms that followed. Political parties belonging to both leftist and rightist hues, despite their initial misgivings, gradually tended to support the reforms. Major economic partners of India like the US, EU, Japan, and so on, looked upon the liberalization programme with great expectation. This paper focuses particular attention on Japan's response.

The case of Japan is important because it has been a major contributor to India's economic development for over forty years. Indo-Japanese relations, which have witnessed their Golden Jubilee this year, have predominantly been economic in nature. A major trading partner, Japan's official development assistance (ODA) has been substantial since 1958 and the ODA inflows have made a significant contribution to India's economy in a number of sectors. Given its long history of interactions with India, it was expected that Japan's support for the liberalization programme would be translated into its enhanced presence in India's investment and trade scenario. But so far, the growth of Japan's investment and trade with India has been only nominal. The present article, which seeks to examine the reasons for Japan's wavering response, has three sections. First , it tries to briefly explain the circumstances leading to the introduction of economic reforms in India. Second, it briefly discusses the nature of the reforms. Third, it examines Japan's response.

In developing countries, economic liberalization refers more to liberalization or further "opening up" of their respective economies to foreign capital and investments. Three of the fastest growing developing economies today; Brazil, China and India, have achieved rapid economic growth in the past several years or decades after they have "liberalized" their economies to foreign capital.

The economic liberalization in India refers to ongoing economic reforms in India that started on 24 July 1991. After Independence in 1947, India adhered to socialist policies. In the 1980s, Prime MinisterP. V. Narasimha Rao initiated some reforms. In 1991, after India faced a balance of payments crisis, it had to pledge 20 tons of gold to Union Bank of Switzerland and 47 tons to Bank of England as part of a bailout deal with the International Monetary Fund (IMF). In addition, IMF required India to undertake a series of structural economic reforms . As a result of this requirement, the government of P. V. Narasimha Rao and his finance minister Manmohan Singh (the present Prime Minister of India) started breakthrough reforms, although they did not implement many of the reforms IMF wanted. The newneo-liberal policies included opening for international trade and investment, deregulation, initiation ofprivatization, tax reforms, and inflation-controlling measures. The overall direction of liberalisation has since remained the same, irrespective of the ruling party, although no party has yet tried to take on powerful lobbies such as the trade unions and farmers, or contentious issues such as reforming labour laws and reducing agricultural subsidies. The main objective of the government was to transform theeconomic system from socialism to capitalism so as to achieve high economic growth andindustrialize the nation for the well-being of Indian citizens. Today India is mainly characterized as a market economy.

As of 2009, about 300 million people—equivalent to the entire population of the United States—haveescaped extreme poverty. The fruits of liberalisation reached their peak in 2007, when India recorded its highest GDP growth rate of 9%. With this, India became the second fastest growing major economy in the world, next only to China. An Organisation for Economic Co-operation and Development (OECD) report states that the average growth rate 7.5% will double the average income in a decade, and more reforms would speed up the pace.

Indian government coalitions have been advised to continue liberalisation. India grows at slower pace than China, which has been liberalising its economy since 1978. McKinsey states that removing main obstacles "would free India's economy to grow as fast as China's, at 10 percent a year".

For 2010, India was ranked 124th among 179 countries in Index of Economic Freedom World Rankings, which is an improvement from the preceding year.

Liberalization Measures

In July 1991, a New Industrial Policy was announced and it clearly indicated the new path that the Indian economy was to traverse from then on. In particular, a major policy to deregulate and promote foreign direct investment has been in effect since then . Under the previous industrial policy regime, India discouraged foreign investment very strongly. It also put too many restrictions on domestic competition by means of licensing schemes and barriers to the entry of new companies. Under the new 1991 policy, doors were opened for easier flow of foreign investment. Thirty six fields have now been earmarked for the automatic approval for direct investment. Vital fields, which were once closed for foreign investors like mining, oil exploration, transport, telecommunication, etc, are now open to them. The private sector can now operate in all areas except some strategic ones like defence, atomic energy, etc. Licensing has almost been done away with except in a very few cases. The incentives the foreign investors now enjoy are truly impressive. Foreign equity is now granted to the extent of one hundred per cent. For instance, keeping in mind the acute shortage of power in the country, the government wants to attract foreign companies to power generation sector by offering one hundred per cent equity. Automatic approval is given within two weeks to proposals involving foreign equity up to 51per cent in thirty six high priority areas. These proposals need not be accompanied by technology transfer agreements. In order to speed up the process of clearing FDI proposals, the government also set up Foreign Investment Promotion Board. The government revised the Foreign Exchange Regulation Act (FERA) in order to remove unnecessary restrictions on foreign investors and bring more benefits to them like setting up branch offices, purchase of real estate, fund-raising, using their brand names, etc, on par with domestic investors. The earlier insistence on the inclusion of a high local content on foreign firms has also been scrapped. India also signed the Convention of the Multilateral Investment Guarantee Agency in order to provide protection to foreign investors. The government also liberalized imports by abolishing the import approval system. Tariff rates since 1991 have been appreciably lowered.

One direct result of the reforms can be seen in the sustained growth of the economy in the following years. Since 1992 the GDP has maintained an annual average growth of about 6 per cent. Only in 2002-03, the GDP fell to 4.3 per cent, but in 2003-04, it is expected to be above 6 per cent. Industrial growth following the reforms has contributed to major strides in capital formation. The contribution of the manufacturing industries under the private enterprise has been significant and this is undoubtedly due to the new buoyancy that the private sector has received thanks to the reforms. Exports have also witnessed quantum jump as a result of the growth of the manufacturing industries. Further there has been a steady and unprecedented growth in the accumulation of foreign exchange reserves of the country. In December 2003, the reserves constituted a whopping $96 billion.

Pre-liberalisation policies

Indian economic policy after independence was influenced by the colonial experience (which was seen by Indian leaders as exploitative in nature) and by those leaders' exposure to Fabian socialism. Policy tended towards protectionism, with a strong emphasis on import substitution, industrialization under state monitoring, state intervention at the micro level in all businesses especially in labour and financial markets, a large public sector, business regulation, and central planning. Five-Year Plans of India resembled central planning in the Soviet Union. Steel, mining, machine tools, water, telecommunications, insurance, and electrical plants, among other industries, were effectively nationalized in the mid-1950s. Elaborate licences, regulations and the accompanying red tape, commonly referred to as Licence Raj, were required to set up business in India between 1947 and 1990. In the 80s, the government led by P. V. Narasimha Rao started light reforms. The government slightly reduced Licence Raj and also promoted the growth of the telecommunications and software industries.

The Vishwanath Pratap Singh (1989–1990) and Chandra Shekhar Singh government (1990–1991) did not add any significant reforms.

Impact

- The low annual growth rate of the economy of India before 1980, which stagnated around 3.5% from 1950s to 1980s, while per capita income averaged 1.3%. At the same time, Pakistan grew by 5%, Indonesia by 9%, Thailand by 9%, South Korea by 10% and in Taiwan by 12%.
- Only four or five licences would be given for steel, electrical power and communications. License owners built up huge powerful empires.
- A huge public sector emerged. State-owned enterprises made large losses.
- Infrastructure investment was poor because of the public sector monopoly.
- Licence Raj established the "irresponsible, self-perpetuating bureaucracy that still exists throughout much of the country" and corruption flourished under this system.

Narasimha Rao government (1991–1996)

Crisis

The assassination of prime minister Indira Gandhi in 1984, and later of her son Rajiv Gandhi in 1991, crushed international investor confidence on the economy that was eventually pushed to the brink by the early 1990s.

As of 1991, India still had a fixed exchange rate system, where the rupee was pegged to the value of a basket of currencies of major trading partners. India started havingbalance of payments problems since 1985, and by the end of 1990, it was in a serious economic crisis. The government was close to default, its central bank had refused new credit and foreign exchange reserves had reduced to the point that India could barely finance three weeks' worth of imports. Most of the economic reforms were forced upon India as a part of the IMF bailout.

1991 India economic crisis

By 1985, India had started having balance of payments problems. By the end of 1990, it was in a serious economic crisis. The government was close to default, its central bank had refused new credit and foreign exchange reserves had reduced to such a point that India could barely finance three weeks' worth of imports. India had to airlift its gold reserves to pledge it with International Monetary Fund (IMF) for a loan.

The crisis was caused by currency overvaluation; the current account deficit and investor confidence played significant role in the sharp exchange rate depreciation.

The economic crisis was primarily due to the large and growing fiscal imbalances over the 1980s. During mid eighties, India started having balance of payments problems. Precipitated by the Gulf War, India's oil import bill swelled, exports slumped, credit dried up and investors took their money out. Large fiscal deficits, over time, had a spill over effect on the trade deficit culminating in an external payments crisis. By the end of 1990, India was in serious economic trouble.

The gross fiscal deficit of the government (center and states) rose from 9.0 percent of GDP in 1980-81 to 10.4 percent in 1985-86 and to 12.7 percent in 1990-91. For the center alone, the gross fiscal deficit rose from 6.1 percent of GDP in 1980-81 to 8.3 percent in 1985-86 and to 8.4 percent in 1990-91. Since these deficits had to be met by borrowings, the internal debt of the government accumulated rapidly, rising from 35 percent of GDP at the end of 1980-81 to 53 percent of GDP at the end of 1990-91. The foreign exchange reserves had dried up to the point that India could barely finance three weeks worth of imports.

In mid-1991, India's exchange rate was subjected to a severe adjustment. This event began with a slide in the value of the Indian rupee leading up to mid-1991. The authorities at the Reserve Bank of India took partial action, defending the currency by expending international reserves and slowing the decline in value.However, in mid-1991 ,with foreign reserves nearly depleted, the Indian government permitted a sharp depreciation that took place in two steps within three days (July 1 and July 3, 1991) against major currencies.

Later reforms

- The Bharatiya Janata Party (BJP)-Atal Bihari Vajpayee administration surprised many by continuing reforms, when it was at the helm of affairs of India for five years.
- The BJP-led National Democratic Alliance Coalition began privatizing under-performing government owned business including hotels, VSNL, Maruti Suzuki, Airports and began reduction of taxes, a sound fiscal policy aimed at reducing deficits and debts and increased initiatives for public works.
- The United Front government attempted a progressive budget that encouraged reforms, but the 1997 Asian financial crisis and political instability created economic stagnation.
- Economic and technology-related sanctions have repeatedly not proved to be very effective in compelling nations to change their sovereign decisions made in enlightened self-interest. India faced severe sanctions after Pokhran-I (five nuclear tests on 11 and 13 May 1998 at the Pokhran range in Rajasthan Desert), and sanctions that were more comprehensive were imposed following Pokhran-II. There were dire predictions of the collapse of the economy, double-digit inflation etc.
- After five years, most of the sanctions have been lifted and the Indian economy is continuing to grow at an acceptably satisfactory rate. The growth rate for 2003–04 was 6.0%. Though India's Gross National Income is only $477.4 billion by conventional calculations, it translates into $2,913 billion purchasing power parity (PPP), according to the latest world development indicators. In PPP terms, it is the world's fourth largest economy, behind only the US, China and Japan.

The impact of these reforms may be gauged from the fact that total foreign investment (including foreign direct investment, portfolio investment, and investment raised oninternational capital markets) in India grew from a minuscule US$132 million in 1991–92 to $5.3 billion in 1995–96.

Cities like NOIDA, Gurgaon, Gaziabad, Bangalore, Hyderabad, Pune, Chennai, Jaipur, Indore and Ahmedabadhave risen in prominence and economic importance, become centres of rising industries and destination for foreign investment and firms.

Election of AB Vajpayee as Prime Minister of India in 1998 and his agenda was a welcome change. His prescription to speed up economic progress included solution of all outstanding problems with the West

(Cold War related) and then opening gates for FDI investment. In three years, the West was developing a bit of a fascination to India's brainpower, powered by IT and BPO. By 2004, the West would consider investment in India, should the conditions permit. By the end of Vajpayee's term as Prime Minister, a framework for the foreign investment had been established. The new incoming government of Professor Manmohan Singh in 2004 is further strengthening the required infrastructure to welcome the FDI.

Today, fascination with India is translating into active consideration of India as a destination for FDI. The A T Kearney study is putting India second most likely destination for FDI in 2005 behind China. It has displaced US to the third position. This is a great leap forward. India was at the 15th position, only a few years back. To quote the A T Kearney Study "India's strong performance among manufacturing and telecom & utility firms was driven largely by their desire to make productivity-enhancing investments in IT, business process outsourcing, research and development, and knowledge management activities".

Liberalisation of services in the developing world

Potential benefits of trade liberalisation

The service sector is probably the most liberalised of the sectors. Liberalisation offers the opportunity for the sector to compete internationally, contributing to GDP growth and generating foreign exchange. As such, service exports are an important part of many developing countries' growth strategies. India's IT services have become globally competitive as many companies have outsourced certain administrative functions to countries where costs are lower. Furthermore, if service providers in some developing economies are not competitive enough to succeed on world markets, overseas companies will be attracted to invest, bringing with them international best practices and better skills and technologies. The entry of foreign service providers is not necessarily a negative development and can lead to better services for domestic consumers, improve the performance and competitiveness of domestic service providers, as well as simply attract FDI/foreign capital into the country. In fact, some research suggest a 50% cut in service trade barriers over a five- to 10-year period would create global gains in economic welfare of around $250 billion per annum.

Potential risks of trade liberalisation

Yet, trade liberalisation also carries substantial risks that necessitate careful economic management through appropriate regulation by governments. Some argue foreign providers crowd out domestic providers and instead of leading to investment and the transfer of skills, it allow foreign providers and shareholders to capture the profits for themselves, taking the money out of the country. Thus, it is often argued that protection is needed to allow domestic companies the chance to develop before they are exposed to international competition. Other potential risks resulting from liberalisation, include :

- Risks of financial sector instability resulting from global contagion
- Risk of brain drain
- Risk of environmental degradation

However, researchers at thinks tanks such as the Overseas Development Institute argue the risks are outweighed by the benefits and that what is needed is careful regulation. For instance, there is a risk that private providers will 'skim off' the most profitable clients and cease to serve certain unprofitable groups of consumers or geographical areas. Yet such concerns could be addressed through regulation and by a universal service obligations in contracts, or in the licensing, to prevent such a situation from occurring. Of course, this bears the risk that this barrier to entry will dissuade international competitors from entering the market. Examples of such an approach include South Africa's Financial Sector Charter or Indian nurses who promoted the nursing profession within India itself, which has resulted in a rapid growth in demand for nursing education and a related supply response.

Liberalization: where it has lead us and where it is headed

Since 1991, the Indian economy has been running under the mantra of "liberalization". While there has been almost unanimous approval amongst the more affluent sections of the population for liberating the consumer goods sector from the "License Raj" of the previous decades, external liberalization has been subject to far more scrutiny, and has generated considerable controversy and debate. The extent to which the economy should be decontrolled with respect to the international sector is not only of economic relevance but goes to the whole issue of national sovereignty and security.

External Liberalization

Whereas domestic industrialists and investors come under the purview of national laws - and are therefore subject to a modicum of democratic control - that can rarely be said of foriegn investors. Numerous case studies from the experience of other developing countries show that the dependance on foriegn capital has invariably led to sacrificing national policy goals in favor of the demands and conditions of international lending agencies and other powerful agents of international finance coporations like credit rating companies, analysts for banks and mutual funds, and representatives of insurance companies. The examples from Mexico, and now from South East Asia all show that even before rapid economic growth can begin to trickle down to the poorest sections of the economy - the economies end up in debt traps, and then even those sections of the population that had benefitted from the process of external liberalization go through increasing hardship.

External "Conditionalities", Cutting Import Tarriffs

As already mentioned, international lenders rarely lend without conditions. Pivotal to the issue of external liberalization has been the demand to lower import duties and this was one of the veiled "conditions" that the Congress Government of Mr Narasimha Rao accepted in 1991 when the IMF negotiated it's loan package for India. Although this step was taken under "duress", it was rationalized by the wealthiest sections of the Indian population as being necessary to introduce "competition" and "improve quality". The spurt in the range and availability of consumer goods that followed seemed to justify this measure.

But the masses whose incomes were being squeezed by limited employment opportunities and inflation were unimpressed by the new cars and refrigerators that were now available for purchase. And the increasing trade deficit also had it's detractors. Responding to this pressure in 1996, sections of the UF campaigned vigorously against the negative effects of such unbridled external liberalization.

But contrary to the UF's pre-election pledges, the UF Finance Minister, Mr Chidambaram showed no compunctions in accelerating the process of external liberalization by drastically lowering import barriers. Whereas Mr Manmohan Singh of the Congress had pleaded that he was lowering customs duties as he was bound by WTO conditions - Mr Chidambaram made no such apologies and went far beyond even what was required under the WTO regimen.

What had changed in a matter of five years is that a whole new class of businesses had emerged who had a vested interest in keeping import duties low. From international lobbyists for the big multi-nationals to their domestic partners and agents - there was a chorus of voices in favor of cheap imports. Once the import of capital goods and raw materials had been eased in 1991, several Indian manufacturers slowly became dependant on either imported parts or machinery. Others were importing kits and assembling them for domestic sale. And some were importing finished goods for resale in the domestic market. Paying high salaries to financial officers and managerial staff, and to advertising and marketing specialists - they could count on the support of Indian professionals fluent in English looking for upward mobility. This made up the new "Import Lobby".

For several years, local manufacturers had been complaining that the inverted duty structure favored imports over domestic value-addition because duties on finished goods were often less than duties on raw materials and components. Mr Chidambaram made things worse by lowering customs duties to the point where domestic excise duties and sales taxes exceeded corresponding import tarriffs. Thrilled by this unexpected windfall, the "Import Lobby" described the Chidambaram budget as a "dream budget". Unsurprisingly, this lead to a surge in imports that squeezed domestic producers and led to an industrial recession. Unmatched by a proportionate increase in exports, India's trade balance has steadily worsened. Unlike Mr Chidambaram's generosity towards foreign manufacturers - the richest trading nations have offered no such one-sided concessions to India's manufacturers, and Indian exporters continue to face all manner of tarriff and non-tarriff barriers that prevent even high quality exports from India recording any significant gains.

Squeezing the Public Sector, Reducing Social Spending

Another condition that international lenders often impose on developing nations is that they must stop supporting their public sector enterprises and allow private and external participation in key sectors of the economy. They also call for a reduction in social spending. These conditions are usually disguised as a matter of improved "efficiency" and controlling "unnecessary budget deficits". This means that budgetary support for investment in key areas such as mining, power generation, railways and telecommunication has to be drastically curtailed. Spending on affordable housing, health and education is also reduced. The "Import Lobby" is usually unperturbed by these cuts because they view these cuts as an opportunity to increase their imports. But the consequences for the rest of the population as a whole can be quite disastrous.

With the government refusing to invest in these critical areas, crippling shortages develop in vital aspects of the infrastructure. In India, even as sections of the upper middle class have relished the rapid growth in the consumer goods industry, all sections of the population have been highly frustrated with the state of the infrastructure in the country. Unaware of the naunces surounding the situation, many think that it is a problem of public sector inefficiency and join in the demands for delicensing and private participation in key sectors of the economy. And so the international dictum of "letting the private sector step in" is accepted at face value. But belying expectations, very little private investment actually materializes in these areas, and when it does, it comes at a heavy price.

International companies insist on all manner of tax breaks like extended tax holidays, subsidized land, and "counter-guarantees" before they invest. Even though such concessions go against the spirit of "free market economics" that the international lending agencies trumpet, these concessions are treated as inevitable. Costs escalate in spite of all these hidden concessions. For instance, all the power projects that are demanding counter guarantees will generate electricity at almost double the cost of a BHEL built plant in spite of various concessions that should have reduced the cost-basis of these projects.

Another borrowing condition is "open" and "transparent" bidding for infrastructure projects. On the surface, these terms do not seem at all objectionable. But in the implementation, it can turn out that these are just more code words favoring the MNCs. For instance, in the name of "openness" and "transparency", India's telecom sector was opened to international bidding. But the tender requirements were framed in a manner that no domestic company could ever win a contract without tying up with an international telecom giant. With the public clamoring for faster telephone connections - this crafty move drew little attention. But even after winning the licenses to provide new phone connections - most international companies stayed away. So the vast majority of the public's telephone requirements continue to be met by the Public Sector companies that are under-funded on the assumption that private industry will be picking up the slack.

In 1996, it appeared as if the UF was becoming aware of this situation, and some critics of the Congress rallied around it, hoping for change. In their 1996 election campaigns, sections of the UF argued vigorously for the re-invigoration of the public sector and pointed to how internationally successful public sector enterprises like BHEL and ONGC had been deliberately prevented from making new investments and bidding on new contracts. They exposed how public sector companies were being privatized at a fraction of their market value - and that the auctions were being deliberately rigged.

But, after taking office - the UF, rather than correct these policies, further aggravated the situation by cutting plan expenditures and squeezing social spending to the bone.

Liberalization, the BJP, and the Swadeshi Factor

The betrayal of the UF - the complicity of the UF with the Imports Lobby and powerful foreign commercial interests, set the ground for the emergence of the BJP as the leading party in the new Lok Sabha. One of the BJP's popular slogans was "Swadeshi". While some may argue that the BJP's popularity is solely based on it's Hindutva support base, in actual practice this also reflects the hope many Indians have placed in the Swadeshi Jagran Manch. This is especially true in the South where Hindutva does not cut much ice. Yet, the BJP has also promised to continue and accelerate the "liberalization" process.

Those who have watched the BJP's performance in Maharashtra and believe that "liberalization" and "Swadeshi" are inherently incompatible are naturally skeptical about the Swadeshi component of BJP's policies. As an example of their thinking, they point to the Enron case, where the Shiv-Sena/BJP government did a complete about-face by approving the project even after the Swadeshi Jagran Manch had strenuosly campaigned against it. Could the BJP be any different at the centre?

Since taking office, the BJP-led coalition has sent several mixed messages suggesting that there are different factions within the BJP who represent different interests. On the one hand, there are liberalizers who wish to continue the process set in motion by the previous governments, and on the other, there are those who either wish to give liberalization a nationalist face, or reverse it altogether.

Criticized by the Swadeshi Jagran Manch, one of the earlist decisions taken on behalf of the BJP-led coalition was a decision to further liberalize imports. Although, Commerce Minister Mr Hegde had been making brave noises about negotiating a better deal for India at WTO, his first step was to move 340 items (covering a whole range of consumer goods) from the restricted list to the open general licence (OGL) category. Previously, only capital and intermediate goods were in the OGL category, and the import of consumer goods required aditional licenses. Mr Hegde has argued that the effect of this change will be minimal since these items are already being produced in India at very competitive prices. But there remains a serious problem with such a decision. Contrary to Mr Hegde's clearly stated goal, such unilateral concessions on the external front cannot strengthen the bargaining position of India with respect to the WTO, and the rich trading nations have not reciprocated with any concessions of their own. Clearly, this step cannot be viewed as enhancing "Swadeshi".

Another aspect of the BJP programme is to continue with the process of privatization, delicensing and counter-guarantees for power projects. Privatization of "non-strategic" public enterprises has been presented as a pragmatic revenue-raising step that will preserve "Swadeshi" interests. But it should be noted that there is a limit to this process. Once all the viable public enterprises are hived off to private interests, this mode of raising revenues will come to an end. Moreover, once a public enterprise is privatized it is much harder to control it's ownership. As long as Foreign Institutional Investors are welcomed in the country - it will be very difficult to prevent private shareholders from selling their shares in public enterprises to foreigners.

Similiarly - as oil exploration and mining leases are granted to multi-national interests, the profits that would have normally accumulated to the public enterprises, and would have been re-invested in the local economy by the public enterprises may now be taken out of the country to meet the obligations of foreign share-holders.

A public deeply frustrated with the power situation may at present tolerate counter-guarantees to the fast track multi-national power projects. But when they have to pay the high tarriffs that these projects entail - they may feel very angry and betrayed. What may not appear to be a "Swadeshi" issue today could become one 5 years down the road.

Regionalism and Anarchism vs. Swadeshi

While liberalizers try to argue the case for private enterprise on the basis of efficiency and productivity - they often fail to cite the benefits of well-run public enterprises. Unlike private industry, which due to share-holder pressure needs to generate quick profits - public enterprises can take on vital projects that have long gestation periods where several years may go by without the company registering a profit. Public Sector enterprises can also take on projects with low profit potential that have highly redeeeming social benefits. And most importantly, public enterprises can invest in rural areas and spread their investments throughout the country in a fair and balanced way. This is crucial in a diverse country like India where lack of development can easily translate into demands for separation and disunity.

Private industry, particularly MNCs tend to focus on the major metropolitan areas, concentrating growth in some areas and completely ignoring others. Take the boom in car manufacturing - (something encouraged by all the political parties): it is concentrated in just a few major metropolitan areas. The demand is also restricted to a very narrow elite. (And so far, it has also caused a huge drain in the nation's foreign exchange reserves.) Consider also how the Software Industry is booming in a few towns, while the overwhelming majority of Indians have never seen a computer, let alone learnt to programme one!

Uneven development seems to be an uncontrollable side effect of liberalization. One of the consequences of this is that employment opportunities become concentrated in the few booming regions. This attracts migrants from under-developed regions. However, none of the booming regions are really capable of handling the housing, water and electricity needs of this migrant population. The result is unplanned urbanization and sprawling slums.

For these and other reasons, a planned economy and the public sector can be important tools for correcting regional imbalances and addressing problems of uneven development, but the path of "liberalization" makes it difficult to utilize such tools.

And when this connection is not well understood, uneven development can have unexpected political consequences that do little to mitigate the problem. When the benefits of industrialization and development are not experienced throughout the nation, regionalism becomes a powerful motive force uniting underdeveloped areas of the country. To some extent - the fragmented nature of India's parliament is already a reflection of these contrary pulls and pressures. The demand for new states and new districts is also a symptom of growing regionalism.

Regionalism can thus counterpose "Swadeshi", since "Swadeshi" will naturally seem like a hollow slogan to those who lose out in the race for investment in their regions. Regionalism when expressed as a desire for greater equity and local democratic control is not necessarily a hindrance to social progress and may in fact hasten social progress. The danger comes from regional movements who turn to foreign agents for support - (who may in turn advocate even greater liberalization and concessions to trans-national interests).

Conversely, in the urban areas where migration overpowers the city's infrastructure - there can develop a hatred for all development, and cynicism about the entire political process. Mushrooming NGOs and anarchist "peoples movements" that argue against all development become pitted against any "Swadeshi" agenda - since they view all attempts at national unity as "statist" and "oppressive".

The Railway Budget

An area almost incidental to the "Swadeshi" agenda has been the modernization and expansion of the railways. In the wake of liberalization, like previous railway ministers, Mr Nitish Kumar found himself in a situation where there was inadequate support for all the projects that the railways has wished to implement.

All over India - manual rail crossings and manual signalling slow down trains and cause accidents during inclement weather. Even though there has been considerable progress in the areas of telecommunications and electronics - the railways network is still dependant on archaic methods of signalling and security. Not only does this lead to unnecesssary delays and accidents - it also means that trains and train tracks cannot be used as efficiently as they could.

All over India, the railways has failed to press enough local and short/medium distance day trains into service. This means that commuters must rely on unreliable private minibus operators to meet their travel needs. What is particularly ironic is that many of these buses operate from one train station to another. For hours in the day - the tracks between these stations remain idle because they cater almost exclusively to long distance trains that connect the major metros. So local passengers must endure endless waiting while the private bus operators hussle more fares - and then travel cramped like sardines. They must subject themselves to endless traffic jams and noxious pollution, even when paying higher fares to compensate the bus owners for their increased petrol expenses.

A truly effective and "Swadeshi" solution to this problem, and to the growing oil import bill would be to ply more inter-city trains so that the already laid tracks are used more frequently during the day and buses are freed up to operate feeder routes from local towns and villages and develop alternative routes that complement the nation's rail network.

But the railways continues to be treated like a step-child in any discussion of transportation alternatives. While the inadequacy of the nation's road network has begun to draw attention, so far, no party has mounted an effective campaign around expanding the railways. In a densely populated nation like India, it will be impossible to procure enough land to build a network of highways that criss-cross nations like the US and Canada. It is therefore imperative that this difference is well understood and rail transportation is given the importance it deserves.

Any genuinely "Swadeshi" program must budget adequately for the continued development of our railways, addressing the concerns of not only well-heeled travellers but also budget travellers.

"Swadeshi" elements in the General Budget

In spite of these weaknesses in the BJP's Swadeshi platform, there are some aspects of "Swadeshi" that are discernible in the BJP's budget. First, there is a perceptible shift in allocations for social spending. Unlike his predecessors who kept cutting allocations for the social sector - Mr Yashwant Sinha has increased budgetary support for Education, Rural Development, Roads, Power, Science and Technology and Food Subsidies.

Second, there is an increase in of 6-7% in effective customs duties for most parts and raw materials. This has been welcomed by the National Manufacturers Association and other Indian industrialists whose dependance on such imports are minimal.

But since this additional duty does not apply to finished goods, Mr Yashwant Sinha has disappointed those manufacturers who import parts or raw materials and face unfair competition in their finished goods from foreign manufacturers whose costs may be lower due to subsidies or improved economies of scale arising from their monopoly control of the international market. As mentioned earlier, this has been a lingering problem. Ideally, import duties should be carefully graduated to encourage the highest levels of local manufacturing.

Pressures from the Import Lobby

But to some extent - some of these manufacturers have only themselves to blame since they have chosen to ally with the Import Lobby who wants import duties to be cut to bare minimal levels and even kept below excise duties - something that is completely unfair to other local manufacturers who have no choice but to pay the local excise duties. It would therefore behoove those manufacturers who are partial importers to ally with all other local manufacturers and call for calibrated duties on imports - with finished goods attracting the highest rates. But this would require standing up to the Imp›rt Lobby, something that not enough manufacturers have chosen to d› as yet.

Even the Import Lobby must understand that driving Indian manufacturers to bankcruptcy is not in their long-term interest. When domestic manufacturing is unable to expand - employment stagnates or shrinks, and purchasing power also stagnates and shrinks in proportion. This means that in the end, the market for all goods shrinks - even imported goods - and then, even importers begin to feel the crunch. This is evident from the recent experience of South East Asia. Those who suggest that the South East Asian crisis occurred only due to fiscal mismanagement and not due to demand saturation are missing a valuable lesson that is there for all to see. In a demand recession, even the best fiscal and technical management of the economy have little impact. Those who argue that India could somehow circumvent the S.E.Asian plight by prudent fiscal and technical management alone are engaging in an element of economic fantasy.

Even those familiar with only the rudiments of macro-economic theory must know that in the end - demand must drive supply. And demand cannot grow in a situation of weak purchasing power. Demand growth requires employment and wage growth to exceed the cost of essentials like food and medicine. Only then can there be a sustained demand for consumer goods and related goods . Expanding the nation's purchasing power must be a concern not only of domestic producers but importers as well. Unless liberalization causes an across-the-board sustained rise in purchasing power, the process of unfettered liberalization will not be without it's serious critics.

Ultimately, policy decisions must be evaluated not from the point of view of the theorizers and partisan proponents, but from the perspective of whether such decisions improve the quality of life of the vast majority of the Indian people. To the extent that several pressing problems remain to be solved inspite of a decade of liberalization, it would only be wise not to consider "liberalization" as a magic wand that will bring only good, or as an inevitable and only solution to socio-economic growth and development. Political forces that have treated "liberalization" in that way have been strongly rejected at the polls and that should be a lesson for all to ponder.

Globalisation in India

India had the distinction of being the world's largest economy in the beginning of the Christian era, as it accounted for about 32.9% share of world GDP and about 32.5% of the world population. The goods produced in India had long been exported to far off destinations across the world. Therefore, the concept of globalization is hardly new to India.

Investment

Foreign direct investment in India has reached 2% of GDP, compared with 0.1% in 1990, and Indian investment in other countries rose sharply in 2006.

As the fourth-largest economy in the world in PPP terms, India is a preferred destination forforeign direct investments (FDI); India has strengths in information technology and other significant areas such as auto components, chemicals, apparels, pharmaceuticals, and jewelry. Despite a surge in foreign investments, rigid FDI policies resulted in a significant hindrance. However, due to some positive economic reforms aimed at deregulating the economy and stimulating foreign investment, India has positioned itself as one of the front-runners of the rapidly growing Asia Pacific Region. India has a large pool of skilled managerial and technical expertise. The size of the middle-class population stands at 50 million and represents a growing consumer market.

India's recently liberalized FDI policy (2005) allows up to a 100% FDI stake in ventures. Industrial policy reforms have substantially reduced industrial licensing requirements, removed restrictions on expansion and facilitated easy access to foreign technology and foreign direct investment FDI. The upward moving growth curve of the real-estate sector owes some credit to a booming economy and liberalized FDI regime. In March 2005, the government amended the rules to allow 100 per cent FDI in the construction business. This automatic route has been permitted in townships, housing, built-up infrastructure and construction development projects including housing, commercial premises, hotels, resorts, hospitals, educational institutions, recreational facilities, and city- and regional-level infrastructure.

A number of changes were approved on the FDI policy to remove the caps in most sectors. Fields which require relaxation in FDI restrictions include civil aviation, construction development, industrial parks, petroleum and natural gas, commodity exchanges, credit-information services and mining. But this still leaves an unfinished agenda of permitting greater foreign investment in politically sensitive areas such as insurance and retailing. FDI inflows into India reached a record US$19.5bn in fiscal year 2006/07 (April-March), according to the government's Secretariat for Industrial Assistance. This was more than double the total of US$7.8bn in the previous fiscal year. The FDI inflow for 2007-08 has been reported as

$24bn and for 2008-09, it is expected to be above $35 billion. A critical factor in determining India's continued economic growth and realizing the potential to be an economic superpower is going to depend on how the government can create incentives for FDI flow across a large number of sectors in India.

Remittances

Remittances to India are money transfers from Indian workers employed outside the country to friends or relatives in India. India is the world's leading receiver of remittances, claiming more than 12% of the world's remittances in 2007. Remittances to India account for approximately 3% of the country'sGDP.

Since 1991, India has experienced sharp remittance growth. In 1991 Indian remittances totaled 2.1 billion USD; in 2006, they were estimated at between $22 billion and $25.7 billion. In 2006, remittances from Indian migrants overseas made up $27 billion or about 3% of India's GDP.

Money is sent to India either electronically – for example, by SWIFT – or by demand draft. In the recent years many banks are offering Money transfers and this business has grown in to huge business

The following table illustrates the Remittances to India as Percent of GDP, 1990–1991 to 2005–2010.

Year	Remittances (US$ billions)	Percent GDP
1990–1991	2.1	0.7
1995–1996	8.5	3.22
1999–2000	12.07	2.72
2000–2001	12.85	2.84
2001–2002	15.4	3.29
2002–2003	16.39	3.39
2003–2004	21.61	3.69
2004–2005	20.25	3.03
2005–2006	24.55 (projected)	3.08
2006–2007	29.10	
2007–2008	37.2	
2008–2009	51.6	
2009–2010	55.06	

1 United States dollar = 52 Indian rupees

Payments

Since independence, India's balance of payments on its current account has been negative. Since liberalisation in the 1990s (precipitated by a balance of payment crisis), India's exports have been consistently rising, covering 80.3% of its imports in 2002–03, up from 66.2% in 1990–91. Although India is still a net importer, since 1996–97, its overall balance of payments (i.e., including the capital account balance), has been positive, largely on account of increased foreign direct investment and deposits from non-resident Indians; until this time, the overall balance was only occasionally positive on account of external assistance and commercial borrowings. As a result, India's foreign currency reserves stood at $285 billion in 2008, which could be used in infrastructural development of the country if used effectively.

India's reliance on external assistance and commercial borrowings has decreased since 1991–92, and since 2002–03, it has gradually been repaying these debts. Declining interest rates and reduced borrowings decreased India's debt service ratio to 4.5% in 2007. In India, External Commercial Borrowings (ECBs) are being permitted by the Government for providing an additional source of funds to Indian corporates. The Ministry of Finance monitors and regulates these borrowings (ECBs) through ECB policy guidelines.

Trade

International trade as a proportion of GDP reached 24% by 2006, up from 6% in 1985 and still relatively moderate.

India currently accounts for 1.2% of World trade as of 2006 according to the World Trade Organization (WTO). Until the liberalisation of 1991, India was largely and intentionally isolated from the world markets, to protect its fledgling economy and to achieve self-reliance. Foreign trade was subject to import tariffs, export taxes and quantitative restrictions, while foreign direct investment was restricted by upper-limit equity participation, restrictions on technology transfer, export obligations and government approvals; these approvals were needed for nearly 60% of new FDI in the industrial sector. The restrictions ensured that FDI averaged only around $200M annually between 1985 and 1991; a large percentage of the capital flows consisted of foreign aid, commercial borrowing and deposits of non-resident Indians.

India's exports were stagnant for the first 15 years after independence, due to the predominance of tea, jute and cotton manufactures, demand for which was generally inelastic. Imports in the same period consisted predominantly of machinery, equipment and raw materials, due to nascent industrialisation. Since liberalisation, the value of India's international trade has become more broad-based and has risen to ₹63,080,109 crores in 2003–04 from 1,250 crores in 1950–51. India's major trading partners are China, the US, the UAE, the UK, Japan and the EU. The exports during April 2007 were $12.31 billion up by 16% and import were $17.68 billion with an increase of 18.06% over the previous year.

India is a founding-member of General Agreement on Tariffs and Trade (GATT) since 1947 and its successor, the World Trade Organization. While participating actively in its general council meetings, India has been crucial in voicing the concerns of the developing world. For instance, India has continued its opposition to the inclusion of such matters as labour and environment issues and other*non-tariff barriers* into the WTO policies.

Despite reducing import restrictions several times in the 2000s, India was evaluated by the World Trade Organization in 2008 as more restrictive than similar developing economies, such as Brazil, China, and Russia. The WTO also identified electricity shortages and inadequate transportation infrastructure as significant constraints on trade. Its restrictiveness has been cited as a factor which has isolated it from the global financial crisis of 2008–2009 more than other countries, even though it has reduced ongoing economic growth.

Economic liberalism is the ideological belief in giving all peopleeconomic freedom, and as such granting people with more basis to control their own lives and make their own mistakes. It is an economic philosophy that supports and promotes individualliberty and choice in economic matters and private property in the means of production. Although economic liberalism can be supportive of government regulation to a certain degree, it tends to oppose government intervention in the free market when it inhibits free trade and open competition, however it can also lead to the support of government intervention in order to remove private monopoly, as this limits the liberty of the poor. Economic liberalism emphasises that people should make their own choices with their money, so long as it doesn't infringe on the liberty of others.

Economic liberalism opposes economic planning as an alternative to the market mechanism. Economic liberalism contrasts with mercantilism, state capitalism, socialism, market socialism, and fascist economics (Corporatism).

Economic liberalism opposes government intervention on the grounds that the state often serves dominant business interests, distorting the market to their favor and thus leading to inefficient outcomes. Ordoliberalism and various schools of social liberalism based on classical liberalism include a broader role for the state, but do not seek to replace private enterprise and the free-market with public enterprise and economic planning. For example, a social market economy is a largely free-market economy based on a free price system and private property, and includes government regulation to promote competitive markets and social welfare programs to address social inequalities that result from free-market outcomes. Economic liberalism also includes support for equality of opportunity (also known as social mobility), due to the belief that a lack of equality of opportunity will lead to an increase in private monopoly and therefore infringed liberty of individuals.

Theories in support of economic liberalism were developed in the Enlightenment, and believed to be first fully formulated by Adam Smith, which advocates minimal interference of government in a market economy, though it does not necessarily oppose the state's provision of a few basic public goods with what constitutes public goods originally being seen as very limited in scope. Smith claimed that if everyone is left to their own economic devices instead of being controlled by the state, then the result would be a harmonious and more equal society of ever-increasing prosperity. This underpinned the move towards a capitalist economic system in the late 18th century, and the subsequent demise of the mercantilist system.

Private property and individual contracts form the basis of classical economic liberalism. The early theory was based on the assumption that the economic actions of individuals are largely based on self-interest (invisible hand), and that allowing them to act without any restrictions will produce the best results (spontaneous order), provided that at least minimum standards of public information and justice exist, e.g., no-one should be allowed to coerce or steal.

While economic liberalism favors markets unfettered by the government, it maintains that the state has a legitimate role in providing public goods. For instance, Adam Smith argued that the state has a role in providing roads, canals, schools and bridges that cannot be efficiently implemented by private entities. However, he preferred that these goods should be paid proportionally to their consumption (e.g. putting a toll). In addition, he advocated retaliatory tariffs to bring about free trade, and copyrightsand patents to encourage innovation. Robert Cox's further research highlighted the importance of innovation and its deeper implications on the free market.

Initially, the economic liberalism had to contend with the supporters of feudal privileges for the wealthy,aristocratic traditions and the rights of kings to run national economies in their own personal interests. By the end of the 19th century and the beginning of the 20th, these were largely defeated.

Today, economic liberalism is associated with social liberalism, social democracy, classical liberalism, "neoliberalism", "propertarian" libertarianism, and some schools of conservatism.

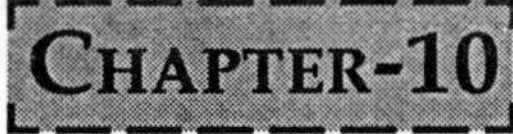

EFFECT OF RECESSION ON INDIAN ECONOMY

Recession are the result of reduction in the demand of products in the Global market. Recession can also be associated with falling prices known as deflection due to lack of demand of products. Again it could be the result of inflation or a combination of increasing prices & segment economic growth in the west.

Almost everybody today seems to be discussing about the US Recessionary trend and its impact on emerging countries, more particularly Indian Economists, Industrialists and the common man on the streets seem to have been horrified by the very thought of recession in India and that too due to US. Decreasing industrial production, inflation, decreasing job opportunities, cost cutting, reducing purchasing power parity, etc. all are the aspects discussed among them through every possible mode like articles, talks & walks and places like washrooms, canteens, etc

Recession is defined as a drastic slowing of the economy. Where gross national or domestic product has fallen in two consecutive quarters. A recession would be indicated by a slowing of a nation's production, rising unemployment and falling interest rates, usually following a decline in the demand for money. A popular distinction between recession and depression is:

'Recession is when your neighbors lose his job; depression is when you lose yours.

Causes of Recession

An economy which grows over a period of time tends to slow down the growth as a part of the normal economic cycle. A recession normally takes place when consumers lose confidence in the growth of the economy and spend less. This leads to a decreased demand for goods and services, which in turn leads to a decrease in production, lay-offs and a sharp rise in unemployment.

Impact on Indian Economy

The main Inflow and Outflow can be categorized as follows:

Main USD Inflow:

1. Export earnings
2. IT Sector Earnings
3. NRI Remittances
4. Foreign Direct Investments (FDI)
5. Portfolio Investment
6. Loans from other governments, IMF, World Bank, etc
7. External Commercial Borrowings (ECB)

India is facing the position of recession as globalization showing its negative scenario. As it was started in US and now it's touching the boundary of India also. Recession is a phase in which rupee depreciate, cash crunches, money market slowdown, inflation comes. All in all it's become difficult to bring money from the pocket of an individual.

As we know price of the steel, iron goes up, we would like to postpone our purchasing but if we won't spend, how producer could makes his bread. If the producer starts reducing the price of the commodity with such belief that customer buy the product in all case. This will bring only when he starts cutting its cost of production. Cost cutting means reduction in variable cost. As price of steel, iron, equipments, machinery, are touching sky, only way to reduce the cost is the reduction in employees. Hence people fear of their job security.

In fear of the job security, people are generally shifting their purchasing. All of them either producer, investor, customer, employee posing each other to create recession

Negative Aspect of Recession on Indian Economy

As recession have various negative effects on Indian economy. The capital market was facing the downfall, liquidity is dropping down, an individual don't have money to spend, producers are increasing their price, but to cope with market they are creating deployment.

Stock Markets & Recession

The economy and the stock market are closely related. The stock markets reflect the buoyancy of the economy. In the US, a recession is yet to be declared by the Bureau of Economic Analysis, but investors are a worried lot. The Indian stock markets also crashed due to a slowdown in the US economy.

The Sensex crashed by nearly 13 per cent in just two trading sessions in January. The markets bounced back after the US Fed cut interest rates. However, stock prices are now at a low ebb in India with little cheer coming to investors.

Current crisis in the US

The defaults on sub-prime mortgages (homeloan defaults) have led to a major crisis in the US. Sub-prime is a high risk debt offered to people with poor credit worthiness or unstable incomes. Major banks have landed in trouble after people could not pay back loans.

The housing market soared on the back of easy availability of loans. The realty sector boomed but could not sustain the momentum for long, and it collapsed under the gargantuan weight of crippling loan defaults. Foreclosures spread like wildfire putting the US economy on shaky ground. This, coupled with rising oil prices at $100 a barrel, slowed down the growth of the economy.

Effects of Recession in US, on Indian Economy

This is an oft quoted saying when it comes to the dominance of the US. This saying is also justified when it comes to the world economy and other economic matters. The US existed as a sole economic power throughout the 80's and the 90's. The US is also the biggest consumer in the whole world. It is also the largest economy in the world. As such, US influence on all economic matters around the world is substantial.

The US economy boasts of being the largest and the most technologically advanced economy in the world, with a per capita GDP of 46,000 $. The US GDP is 13.86 million$ with a growth rate of2%. The USalso has an unemployment rate of 4.7% and only 12% of the population lives below the poverty line. All of these statistics point to a large though sluggishly-growing economy.

The future however is uncertain and the danger of an economic recession looms over the largest economy of the world. Indications are already there and analysts are falling over each other to decide whether, there is a possibility of a recession now and whether it can be averted, if it can & what and how far reaching will be its impact. This is the million dollar question which doesn't have any conclusive defined answers as yet.

To find out the impact of a US recession on India and the consequences of such a recession. India all around the world is seen as a global economic superpower. The Indian Economy is one of the top six fastest growing economies all around the world. The Indian economy is also very well known for its extensive resources of trained, skilled and efficient human capital. India is also gifted with large quantities of natural resources which helps make India, a very powerful economy. According to the latest analysis, the Indian economy is growing at a healthy rate of more than 9% p.a. which is another big positive for the Indian economy.

India and US share a rich and flourishing nexus of trade and commerce. Indian exports to the USexceed the Indian imports by a large margin. So in such a scenario what happens if the US economy goes down? Will the Indian economy suffer a similar downslide? What will be the affect of a weak dollar on world trade and especially the Indian economy? Will the Indian economy be able to come out unscathed? These are some of the pertinent questions plaguing the economists today which we seek to answer in the course of the paper.

The Reasons and Causes of a US recession

With the advent of the 21 century, one thing has become extremely clear- The US is no longer the sole economic power in the world. The European Union is exerting and building its economic power and the value and the significance of the dollar is already showing signs of faltering in front of the might of the Euro. Further Asia on the basis of the combined economic strength of the two fastest growing economies has also become a giant economic power. The OPEC countries have already showed inclination towards trading in Euros which seriously undermines the monopoly which dollar exerted over international trade.

There are also serious indications that the US economy will be facing a situation of a recession in the near future, probably in the current year itself. There are certain reason which have led to this economic downturn, of which some of the most important and the most damaging are.-

- The biggest factor leading to this recession is the decrease in the consumer expenditure on goods inAmerica which has resulted because of the sharp fall in the consumer disposable income. The rise in fuel prices and the already present inflation has reduced, rather almost nullified the effect of any gains in income which have occurred. Adding to this mix, the problem of rising interest rates and lack of credit, it is safe to say that the consumers will now face the pinch. The rise in prices being more than the rise in income, the consumers are forced to reduce their expense on goods which lead to lesser income movement in the economy and leads to a negative multiplier effect which cripples the economy and its allied structures as well.
- The American Economy is plagued by a problem which is known in economic circles as the problem of sub-prime mortgage fiasco. In the US, there had been an increase in credit consumption since 2000, as there was an increase in the consumer expense on autos and housing purchases by the consumer. With the rapidly decreasing consumer disposable income, as has been stated above, houses became more and more unaffordable which led to increasing number of houses becoming unsold which led to a dip in the housing prices and thus the bubble burst and suddenly with the burden of loans mounting and consumer spending decreasing, people are trying to sell of their properties before they lose their equity or the bank repossess it. This has led to an unprecedented increase in the supply of housing, which has dropped the prices further. This has a primary effect on the loaned, but its ramifications and secondary effects have other far reaching consequences too. Basically if there is an over-supply of houses, then the construction of new houses will be adversely affected, which will lead to lowering of the level of economic activity in the economy and also increased unemployment which will lead to further credit and will lead to a vicious cycle which will drag the economy down unless attended to at the earliest.
- Another factor effecting negatively not only the American economy but economies all around the world is the rising prices of crude oil. On 2nd January 2008, the price of crude oil per barrel for the first time crossed $100 a barrel. This has lead to an increase in the cost of energy, an essential pre-requisite when it comes to production and has thus eaten into the

producers profits, thus forcing them to either cut the wages or reduce employment which again leads to increase in unemployment rate of the country. This again leads to a downward cycle which ends only in a state of depression.

Impact of a strong rupee on the Indian Economy

Indian economy is among the fastest growing economies of the world. The appreciation of the rupees against the dollar would be another giant sign towards its economic prosperity. The Dollar in comparison to the rupee has fallen from a rate of 48 Re. for 1$ to a rate which is expected by the RBI to range from 39.15 Re - 39.50 Re. There has been almost a 20% increase in the Indian rupee. The appreciation of the rupees will help the economy in many ways. The dollar has been the popular medium of foreign exchange for a long time. Most of the payment for the export or import is made through dollar.

This development has a significant bearing on the Indian Economy. This is because, the dollar though comparatively weak is still strong and is still used as, an in demand currency for all forms of foreign trade and commerce. Moreover most of the countries have accumulated their reserves in the form of dollars, which further adds to its strength. There are 3 major and significant variables which will suffer the impact of a stronger rupee first. They are-

- In respect of **Exporters-** The exporters in India, in a case of depreciating dollar will have a lesser income than before. The price of an export goods cannot be said to be unit elastic to the exchange rate because as the dollar depreciates, if the exporters increase their prices so as to receive the same income in rupees as they did before, the demand of their commodities will fall and lead to greater losses. As such in the case of a depreciating dollar, exporters will have to bear the loss as a cut in margins which in some cases will also lead to loss. This will lead to an adverse effect on India's economy and lead to a long term loss to India's growth.
- In respect to **Importers-** India imports generally Petroleum products, capital goods, fertilizers, chemicals, pulp and uncut stones. The importers in the case of a stronger rupee will now have to pay less for the same commodity. As such the imports to India will increase in quantity and importers will gain increased profits which will lead to economic growth in the country.

- In respect of **FDI-** FDI or Federal Direct Investment, is the investment by foreign nationals in a country's industries. In case of weakening of US$, there will be lesser funds in terms of rupees, invested by the US citizens and thus the FDI from US as such will be effected adversely. However with the USindustries in turmoil, India will become a very attractive destination for all investment, within the US and without. Therefore the impact of a weak US dollar on FDI as such will be suitably compensated by the increase in FDI from other sources.

The following figures and statistics help elucidate the impact of a US recession on the economy.-

INDO-US TRADF US trade with India (2007)
(In US$ million)

Month	Exports	Imports	Balance
January	1031.6	1999.0	-967.4
February	898.1	1700.6	-802.5
March	958.5	2131.6	-1173.1
April	773.1	1980.2	-1207.1
May	1522.2	1995.0	-472.7
June	1,091.8	1,901.5	-809.7
July	2,356.2	1,782.3	573.9
August	1,816.1	2,172.1	-356.0
September	1,624.9	1,910.4	-285.4
October			
November			
December			
Total	12,072.6	17,572.6	-5,500.0

Source: Us Census Bureau

It can be clearly seen in the table above, that the exports to the US exceed the imports by a substantial amount. As such, in a purely economic sense, exports to the US are much more essential for the economy and for the livelihood of all involved. Thus it can be said that the loss which Indian economy will face through the loss in exports will far out-weight the gain for the importers.

The Impact of a Possible US recession on the Indian Economy

It has been already said in the Introduction to this paper that the US is a powerful economy. The US is the largest economy of the world and it is also the biggest consumer in the world. As such many countries in the world export their products to the US and their economies are as such centered on theUS economy.

A US recession if it occurs will thus completely offset such economies. The effect of a US recession will devastate their economies and as such render them economically backward. There are many countries such as which depend upon the US for such trade.

Examining such an affect on the continent of Asia, some noteworthy points can be deduced. India and China are the main force behind economic development in Asia. However the impact of a US recession on both of these will be very different. China is an economy which thrives on exporting low-cost, high-quality goods to the US market. A recession in the US and a weakening dollar will adversely and substantially affect the Chinese economy.

However the impact on India will be lesser in comparison to other smaller countries. This is because India unlike other Asian Countries possesses a strong and well established domestic market. The Indian factors such as those of a strong internal demand, a richer population, an exploding middle class, increased employment along with the increasing basket of services which India has to offer will cushion the impact of the shockwaves which will spread, once a recession occurs in the US economy.

However, India's neighbours and the other small Asian States will be badly affected by such a recession. Even China, which is another growing economy, will suffer the impact, assuming that they do not devalue the yuan again. As such the trade ratio of India with other countries will also be affected, courtesy a US recession. Thus a US recession will have a sizable impact, directly and indirectly on the Indian Economy. However the adverse impact on India will not be as much as that on other countries. Some of the industries which will be worse affected in the light of such a recession will be the BPO industry for one and also the export industry.

Another practical ramification of a US recession, will be the forex reserves of all countries around the world. Most of the countries all around the world maintain their reserves in dollars. Due to a US recession, there will be widespread devaluation of dollar as a currency and it will lead to the meltdown of US dollar. This will thus lead to an evaporation of a country's forex reserves leading to huge and substantial losses. The countries at present are waiting with bated breath as even if one of the countries shifts its reserves to any other currency, there will be a huge drop in the dollars prices which will lead to a selling spree leading to a fall in dollar prices and loss to all countries around the world.

To identify and examine the effect of a US recession on the Indian Economy. For this purpose the factors responsible and the indicators of US recession were analyzed. There are mainly 3 main factors which are mainly responsible for the recession in the US. They are-

- Decrease in Consumer Expenditure.
- Sub-prime mortgage fiasco.
- Increase in energy prices.

The depreciation in the value of dollar is a natural consequence of recession. Such a recession will adversely affect the exporters and favor the importers. However as has been analyzed, the quantum of Indian exports to the US far exceeds the imports. Thus for the greater gain and good of the India businesses, it is safe to say that a US recession will be unfavorable to the Indian trade.

Further, it can also be said that, a US recession though not having any major direct impact on the Indian economy, will adversely affect the economy in many other ways. The Indian economy is shielded in part from an impending recession as India has a well established and growing domestic market and a booming economy to offset any direct impact of recession. However, a US recession will hamper the economic development of other countries and thus adversely affect India's trade over a long period.

Another important point is that, the Indian forex reserves which presently stand at a figure of 276,250 million dollars will be instantly evaporated in case of a US recession and a depreciating dollar.

It can be thus concluded that the impact of a US recession on the Indian economy though comparatively minimal will have a substantial affect on India's future prospects and growth opportunities and thus reduce the rate of growth.

Impact of a Possible US Recession in India

Though no one likes or wants a recession, almost everyone appears (looking at WEF, Davos) reconciled to one in the United States. Meanwhile, politicians continue to downplay any fears of global repercussions, citing decoupling of the United States and other economies as a buffering factor. But what is the reality for countries like India?

It would be naïve to imagine that a recession in the United States would have no impact on India. The United States accounts for one-fourth of the world GDP and any significant slowdown is bound to have reverberations elsewhere. On the other hand, interdependencies between the US economy and emerging economies like India and China has reduced considerably over the last two decades. Thus, the effect may not be as drastic as would have been the case in the 1980s.

Even so, fears of a US recession led to panic in the Indian stock market. January 21 and 22 saw a meltdown with a mind-boggling US$450 billion in market capitalization being vaporized. An unprecedented interest cut by the Fed led to a bounce-back on January 23 and at the time of this writing, the benchmark index (BSE) has gained 2.5%, almost in line with Hang-Seng, Nikkei, and Kospi.

History might hold a clue here. The last time the bubble burst (2001-2002), the DJIA went down by 23%, while the Indian Index fell by 15%.

Much has happened between then and now. The Indian economy has shown a robust and consistent growth trajectory and the projection for 2008 is 9%. Indian exports to the United States account for just over 3% of GDP. India has a healthy trade surplus with the United States.

In other words, the effects of this recession on India may be quite distinct from those of the past. Here are some areas worth following:

1. A credit crisis in the United States might lead to a restructuring of asset allocation at pension funds. It has been suggested that CalPERS is likely to shift an additional US$24 billion to its international portfolio. A large portion of this is likely to flow into India and China. If other funds follow suit, a cascading effect can be expected. Along with the already significant dollar funds available, the additional funds could be deployed to create infrastructure—roads, airports, and seaports—and be ready for a rapid takeoff when normalcy is restored.
2. In terms of specific sectors, the IT Enabled Services sector may be hit since a majority of Indian IT firms derive 75% or more of their revenues from the United States—a classic case of having put all eggs in one basket. If Fortune 500 companies slash their IT budgets, Indian firms could be adversely affected. Instead of looking at the scenario as a threat, the sector would do well to focus on product innovation (as opposed to merely providing services). If this is done, India can emerge as a major player in the IT products category as well.

3. The manufacturing sector has to ramp up scale economies, and improve productivity and operational efficiency, thus lowering prices, if it wishes to offset the loss of revenue from a possible US recession. The demand for appliances, consumer electronics, apparel, and a host of products is huge and can be exploited to advantage by adopting appropriate pricing strategies. Although unlikely, a prolonged recession might see the emergence of new regional groupings—India, China, and Korea?
4. The tourism sector could be affected. Now is the time to aggressively promote health tourism.Given the availability of talented professionals, and with a distinct cost advantage, India can be the destination of choice for health tourism.
5. A recession in the United States may see the loss of some jobs in India. The concept of Social Security, that has been absent until now, may gain momentum.
6. The Indian Rupee has appreciated in relation to the US dollar. Exporters are pushing for government intervention and rate cuts. What is conveniently forgotten in this debate is that a stronger Rupee would reduce the import bill, and narrow the overall trade deficit. The Indian central bank (Reserve Bank of India) can intervene anytime and cut interest rates, increasing liquidity in the economy, and catalyzing domestic demand. A strong domestic demand would also help in competing globally when the recession is over.

In summary, at the macro-level, a recession in the US may bring down GDP growth, but not by much. At the micro-level, specific sectors could be affected. Innovation now may prove to be the engine for growth when the next boom occurs.

For US firms, who have long looked at China as a better investment destination, this may be a good time to look at India as well. After all, 350 million people with purchasing power cannot be ignored. This is not a sales pitch for India, but only a gentle suggestion to US corporations.

Global Economic Recession: It's Impact on Indian Economy

The world is presently facing economic crisis due to which economics world over are considered to be entering into prolonged slowdown in economic activities. The intensity of present economic crisis is so high that is being compared with the global economic recession in 1873, great depression of 1930s and East Asian crisis of 1990s. The current economic slowdown is considered to be sub prime mortgage crisis in the financial sector of United States. Global economics recession and its impact on Indian economy, in this paper we tries to explain the impact of three distinct channels, that is, the capital flows, sect oral growth and financial sector.The global economic recession has taken its toll on the Indian economy that has led to multi-crore loss in business and export orders, tens of thousands of job losses, especially in key sectors like the IT, automobiles, industry and export-oriented firms.

Indian economy also passed through these stages during the year 2008. The economic growth rate, which was above 8% for consecutive period of three years since 2006, suddenly plunged to an average of 5.5%. Developed world is under the fear that recession may not turn out to be continuous process resulting into great depression. Generally recessions are for two quarters, but depression is a severe economic downturn that lasts several years. Earlier India was affected less by external world depressions as it relied more on internal consumption, saving and import substitutions.

However, after 1991 India opened up its economy to global players, share of exports, both goods and services, in GDP grew significantly.

The effects of the global financial crisis have been more severe than initially forecast. By virtue of globalization, the moment of financial crisis hit the real economy and became a global economic crisis; it was rapidly transmitted to many developing countries. India too is weathering the negative impact of the crisis. There is, however, an important difference between the crisis in the advanced countries and the developments in India. While in the advanced countries the contagion traversed from the financial to the real sector, in India the slowdown in the real sector is affecting the financial sector, which in turn, has a second-order impact on the real sector. The paper is an attempt to analyze the variables responsible for India's recent growth, impact of world recession on these variables and their significance. It needs to validate whether India's economy has shifted away from consumption and saving to external sector dependence.

Introduction: Every day the main headline of all newspapers is about our falling share markets, decreasing industrial growth and the overall negative mood of the economy. For many people an economic recession has already arrived whereas for some it is just round the corner. In our opinion the recession has already arrived and it has started showing its.

Evaluating the impact of domestic and external shocks on the growth of developing. Economies is of utmost importance, as the consequences of these shocks push millions of People into abject poverty and deprivation. Broadly, there are five distinct types of shocks that have affected the performance of the Indian economy, sometimes working in tandem. The first two types are domestic shocks:

1. Drought, i.e., below normal rainfall. Since the agricultural sector is still significant part of the economy and has strong demand and supply interlinks ages with the rest of the economy, this is perhaps the shock that causes maximum damage to the Indian economy.
2. Fiscal profligacy of the government, which is a non-developmental expenditure undertaken due to political economic compulsion or to mitigate the effect of other shocks, leading to a fiscal burden. The next three types are external shocks
   - Hike in the international price of oil (petroleum). This is a major import item and is highly price inelastic as a result of which it has a strong impact on the economy.
   - Stagnation or fall in world trade. World trade is a strong determinant of Indian exports and hence any fluctuation in this also affects the economy adversely.
   - Sudden capital outflow induced foreign exchange market shock. This is phenomenon that has precipitated a crisis in many developing economies and India is no exception to that.

Bibliography

- Arora Ashok Kumar, Financing of small Scale Industries, Deep & Deep Publishers, New Delhi 2002.
- Bala Sashi, Management of small Scale Industries, Deep & Deep Publications, New Delhi.
- Balkrishnan G, Financing of small Scale Industry India, Asia Publishing House, New Delhi 1999.
- Batra G.S & Dangwal R.C, Entrepreneurship and small Scale Industries (New Publishers) By Deep & Deep Publishing Pvt. Ltd., New Delhi.
- Bhattacharya S.N, Development of small-scale industries, New Delhi.
- Datt, Ruddar; Sundharam, K.P.M. (2009). Indian Economy. New Delhi: S. Chand Group. p. 976. ISBN 978-81-219-0298-4.
- Desai S.M, Industrial Economy of India, Himalaya Publishing House, 1998.
- Desai Vasant, Management of small Scale Industries, Himalaya Publishing House, 1998 & 1999 Revised Edition.
- Desai Vasant, Small Scale Industries and Entrepreneurship, Himalaya House 2001, Sixth Revised Edition & 4thEdition.
- Dhingra Ishwar C, The Indian Economy Published by S, Chand & Sons, 10thEdition, 2005
- Drèze, John; Sen, Amartya (1996). India: Economic Development and Social Opportunity. Oxford University Press. p. 292. ISBN 978-0-19-564082-3.

- Dutt Ruddar & Sundaram K.P.M, Indian Economy published by S. Chand & Company Ltd. Ram Nagar, New Delhi, 1993.
- Gupta C.B & Srinivasan N.P, Entrepreneurial Development, Published by S. Chand & Sons 2000.
- Khan M.Y, Indian Financial System Theory & Practice, Vikash Publishing, New Delhi 2003.
- Kulkarni P.V, Business Finance, principles and Problems, Himalaya Publishing House 2002.
- Kumar, Dharma (2005). The Cambridge Economic History of India, Volume II : c. 1757 - 2003. New Delhi: Orient Longman. p. 1115. ISBN 978-81-250-2710-2.
- Matiw T.P, Institutional Finance India, Agra Sahitya Bhawan - 1998.
- Mohanty T, Orissa Roundup, Pustak Mahal, Bhubaneswar 1987
- Nehru, Jawaharlal (1946). The Discovery of India. Penguin Books. ISBN 0-14-303103-1.
- Panagariya, Arvind (2008). India: The Emerging Giant. Oxford University Press. p. 514. ISBN 978-0-19-531503-5.
- Pattanaik K.M, Rural Industrialization by Kitab Mahal, Orissa.
- Pattanaik K.M., Economic profile of Orisaa, Subi Printers Cuttack, Orissa.
- Pattnaik S.M, Development Strategy for small Scale Industries Bombay, Himalayan, Publishing House 2001
- Rajendran. S, Institutional Support to SSI, Published by the Hindu Survey of Indian Industry2002.
- Ramakrishnna K.T, Finance for small Scale industry in India, Asia Publishing House, Bombay - 1998.
- Raychaudhuri, Tapan; Habib, Irfan (2004). The Cambridge Economic History of India, Volume I : c. 1200 - c. 1750. New Delhi: Orient Longman. p. 543. ISBN 978-81-250-2709-6.
- Roy, Tirthankar (2006). The Economic History of India 1857-1947. Oxford University Press. p. 385. ISBN 978-0-19-568430-8.

INDEX